1007509084

Alexander von Humboldt's Translantic Personae

Who was Alexander von Humboldt? Was he really a lone genius? Was he another European apologist for colonialism in the Americas or the father of Latin American independence? Was he a roving Romanticist, or did his sensibilities belong to the Enlightenment?

Naturalist, philosopher, historian, and proto-sociologist – to name just some of the fields to which he contributed – Humboldt is impossible to contain in a single identity or definition. His voluminous writings range across so many different fields of knowledge that his scholarly-scientific personae multiplied even during his lifetime, and they have continued to proliferate since his death in 1859. A household word throughout the nineteenth century, Humboldt was eventually eclipsed by Charles Darwin (whose own travels had been motivated by Humboldt's) and disappeared from view for much of the twentieth century, notably in the United States.

The essays in this collection testify to the renewed interest that Alexander von Humboldt's multi-faceted work is inspiring in the twenty-first century, especially among cultural and literary historians from both sides of the Atlantic.

The articles in this book were originally published in *Atlantic Studies*.

Vera M. Kutzinski is the Martha Rivers Ingram Professor of English, Professor of Comparative Literature, and Director of the *Alexander von Humboldt in English* (HiE) project at Vanderbilt University, USA. For this project, she is editing (with Ottmar Ette) a series of new English translations of Humboldt writings for Chicago University Press. Kutzinski has written widely on the literatures of the Americas. Her forthcoming book is entitled *The Worlds of Langston Hughes: Modernism and Translation in the Americas.*

Alexander von Humboldt's Translantic Personae

Edited by
Vera M. Kutzinski

Routledge
Taylor & Francis Group

LONDON AND NEW YORK

First published 2012
by Routledge
2 Park Square, Milton Park, Abingdon, Oxon, OX14 4RN

Simultaneously published in the USA and Canada
by Routledge
711 Third Avenue, New York, NY 10017

Routledge is an imprint of the Taylor & Francis Group, an informa business

© 2012 Taylor & Francis

This book is a reproduction of *Atlantic Studies*, volume 7, issue 2, with two articles from *Atlantic Studies*, volume 6, issue 3. The Publisher requests to those authors who may be citing this book to state, also, the bibliographical details of the special issue on which the book was based.

British Library Cataloguing in Publication Data
A catalogue record for this book is available from the British Library

ISBN13: 978-0-415-69787-3

Typeset in Times New Roman
by Taylor & Francis Books

Publisher's Note
The publisher would like to make readers aware that the chapters in this book may be referred to as articles as they are identical to the articles published in the special issue. The publisher accepts responsibility for any inconsistencies that may have arisen in the course of preparing this volume for print.

Contents

Notes on Contributors

Ottmar Ette is Professor of Romance Literatures at the University of Potsdam, Germany. He is the author of award-winning books on Alexander von Humboldt, José Martí, and Roland Barthes, and the editor of several new editions of Humboldt's writings in German. He is the new series editor for de Gruyter's *Mimesis: Romance Literatures of the World* and has recently brought together a collection of essays for that series, entitled *Nanophilologie*. Together with Vera M. Kutzinski, he edits the *Alexander von Humboldt in English* (HiE) series for the University of Chicago Press.

Rodolfo Guzmán M. is Associate Professor of Spanish and Hispanic Studies at Earlham College in Richmond, Indiana, USA. His teaching and research interests include narratives and the history of ideas in the Iberian world with special emphasis on the colonial period. His research interests also include Afro-Hispanic poetry and indigenous narratives of the Andean region. He is currently preparing a manuscript on the idea and representation of cities in colonial texts.

Vera M. Kutzinski is the Martha Rivers Ingram Professor of English, Professor of Comparative Literature, and Director of the *Alexander von Humboldt in English* (HiE) project at Vanderbilt University, USA. For this project, she is editing (with Ottmar Ette) a series of new English translations of Humboldt writings for Chicago University Press. Kutzinski has written widely on the literatures of the Americas.

Marilyn Miller is Associate Professor and Chair in the Department of Spanish and Portuguese at Tulane University, USA. She has published previously on the works of Juan Francisco Manzano in several venues, including the *Revista Iberoamericana* and *Colonial Latin American Review*. She is currently at work on a book-length comparative study of the relationships between poetry and slavery in North America and Cuba from the colonial to the contemporary period, entitled *The Poetics of Slavery*.

Fernando Ortiz Fernández (July 16, 1881–April 10, 1969) was a Cuban essayist, ethnomusicologist and scholar of Afro-Cuban culture. Ortiz was a prolific polymath dedicated to exploring, recording, and understanding all aspects of Cuban culture. Ortiz coined the now widely used term 'transculturación', the notion of converging cultures. He helped found a number of journals and institutes. Among them, the *Revista Bimestre Cubana, Archivos del Folklore Cubano, the Sociedad de Estudios Afrocubanos* and *Estudios Afrocubanos*.

John Pizer is Professor of German and Comparative Literature at Louisiana State University, USA. His most recent books are *Toward a Theory of Radical Origin: Essays on Modern German Thought* (1995); *Ego-Alter Ego: Double and/as Other in the Age of German Poetic Realism* (1998); and *The Idea of World Literature: History and Pedagogical Practice* (2006).

Friedrich Wilhelm Heinrich Alexander Freiherr von Humboldt (September 14, 1769 – May 6, 1859) was a German naturalist and explorer. Between 1799 and 1804, Humboldt travelled extensively in the Spanish colonies in the Americas. His scientific findings and cultural analyses were published in more than 30 volumes, most of them in French.

Introduction
Alexander von Humboldt's transatlantic personae

Déjà l'Océan Atlantique se présente a nos yeux sous la forme d'un canal étroit qui n'éloigne pas plus du Nouvelle-Monde les états commerçans de l'Europe, que dans l'enfance de la navigation le bassin de la Méditerranée a éloigné les Grecs du Péloponnèse de ceux de l'Ionie, de la Sicile et de la Cyrénaïque.

[Already, the Atlantic Ocean appears to our eyes as a narrow channel that does not divide Europe's trading states from the New World any more than the Mediterranean basin separated Peloponnesian Greeks from Greeks in Ionia, Sicily, and Cyrene, when navigation was in its infancy.]

Alexander von Humboldt[1]

It is hardly a stretch to think of the Prussian explorer, scientist, and philosopher, Alexander von Humboldt (1769-1859) within an Atlantic studies framework. Between 1799 and 1804, he traveled in various parts of the Americas, from Venezuela, Colombia, Cuba, Ecuador, and Mexico to the United States. It would seem that the 30 volumes of his *Voyage aux régions équinoxiales du Nouveau Continent* (1804-29) [*Voyage to the Equinoctial Regions of the New Continent*] in which he reported his findings and impressions—including his unorthodox and unfinished travel narrative, the immensely popular *Relation historique* [*Personal Narrative*]—would more than suffice to place him squarely in an Atlanticist context.[2] But Humboldt did not stop there. He returned to the subject of the New World in almost all of his other work, even when writing about another hemisphere (as in *Asie Centrale*, 1834), and throughout *Kosmos* (1854-62). With the five volumes of his now typically neglected *Examen critique de l'histoire de la géographie du Nouveau Continent et des progrès de l'astronomie nautique aux quinzième et seizième siècles* (1834-39) [Critical examination of the history of the geography of the New Continent and the advancement of nautical astronomy during the fifteenth and sixteenth centuries], he also offered his readers what might be "a key, perhaps the privileged key for an understanding of his entire oeuvre."[3] But simply crossing the Atlantic Ocean and writing about it is not quite enough to make an Atlanticist *avant la lettre*, even for someone who tried to sail so self-consciously in Columbus's wake. Many others undertook such crossings, both before and after Humboldt, and some of their accounts are better known today than even Humboldt's were in his own time. Charles Darwin is one obvious example.

There was something very different about the direction and the quality of Alexander von Humboldt's thinking, something that set him apart from all other potential proto-Atlanticists and also his later "proxies" and "surrogates": his insistently holistic vision (of nature primarily but by no means exclusively) and his abiding interest in movement, change, and exchange, that is, in the dynamic forces behind distributions, interactions, and migrations, not just on a hemispheric but on a global scale. Ottmar Ette puts it succinctly in his afterword to the magnificent new German edition of the *Examen critique* (2009): "An die Stelle einer Raumgeschichte tritt unter Humboldts Feder eine Bewegungsgeschichte, deren Schwerpunkt nicht mehr auf dem Territorialen, sondern auf dem Relational-Dynamischen und Mobilen liegt" [Humboldt's pen replaced spatial history with a history of movement whose major concern is no longer the territorial but the relational, the dynamic and the mobile].[4] Humboldt, in brief, was after *mapping* complex spatial and temporal patterns not easily discernible to the eye, and to incorporate in them multiple points of view.[5] To arrive at such representations of the multidirectional flows of large-scale civilizational analysis, he needed data of all sorts, which he culled both from his own fieldwork and from the vast intellectual network that he built and carefully nurtured throughout his lifetime.

The point of Humboldt's extensive analyses and his complicated "tableaux"—highly compacted visual (re)presentations of knowledge[6] —was to show not only that but *how* "the European world-system cannot be explained on the basis of causes originating exclusively from within Europe." I borrow William Boelhower's words to signal a perhaps rather unexpected overlap of the conceptual project of the new Atlantic studies he outlines, and the methodological challenges implicit in it,[7] with Humboldt's own approaches and sensibilities in the early nineteenth century. Humboldt tellingly concluded his voluminous *Essai politique sur le royaume de la Nouvelle-Espagne* (1811) [*Political Essay on the Kingdom of New Spain*] by insisting, "que le bien-être des blancs est intimement lié à celui de la race cuivrée, et qu'il ne peut y avoir de bonheur durable, dans les deux Amériques, qu'autant que cette race humiliée, mais non avilié par une longue oppression, participera à tous les avantages qui résultent des progrès de la civilisation et du perfectionnement de l'ordre social" [that the wellbeing of the whites is intimately linked with that of the coppery race, and that it cannot find any durable happiness in the two Americas, unless that humiliated race, which has not been debased by being oppressed for so long, participates in all the benefits that derive from the progress of civilization and the perfecting of the social order].[8]

Unsurprisingly, this call for racial and economic equality was a rather unpopular sentiment at the time, and Carlos IV of Spain was no more pleased than he would be when Humboldt took up the cause of anti-slavery in his *Essai Politique sur l'île de Cuba* [*Political Essay on the Island of Cuba*] 15 years later. Shared political and ethical sensibilities aside, however, it is still well to ask whether the "New Atlantic Studies matrix"[9] is but the most recent ideological garb in which to clothe the Prussian savant, or if something else, something more, can be gained from reconsidering Humboldt's work in a context that may be new for us but that was assuredly not so for him. Put differently, how can we make Humboldt fruitful for Atlantic studies beyond turning him into yet another venerated ancestor figure?

At the conclusion of his 2005 *Metabiography* of Alexander von Humboldt, Nicolaas Rupke offers an appealing thought experiment pertaining to the "quest for the historical Humboldt" with which he begins his book. "Imagine," Rupke writes, "that the various Humboldts [portrayed over time by his biographers] became incarnate, embodied in flesh and blood, and were brought together, seated around a table, including Humboldt's autobiographical self. Imagine further that the question be asked, 'Will the real Humboldt please stand up?' Who would be the one to rise to his feet? The answer must be: all and none. In the biographical literature, there is no essential, no complete Humboldt. And there is no definitive Humboldt biography."[10]

Rupke is, of course, quite right. The representations (and appropriations) of Alexander von Humboldt—in biography, critical studies, literature, painting, etc.—have always been ineluctably linked to specific cultural, political, and institutional contexts, which would make the quest for the "true" Humboldt a rather foolhardy endeavor. (And, as Rupke implies above, it would make no difference at all had Humboldt been less reluctant and tight-lipped of an autobiographer.) All great (and long dead) writers have the uncanny ability to be all things to all people, and Humboldt is certainly no exception.

Since the nineteenth century, Humboldtian avatars have been constructed to shore up all sorts of discourses and, at times, have been deployed even for opposing political causes. His often daring exploits in the Americas, which included his passion for climbing active volcanoes such as Chimborazo, then believed to be the highest mountain in the world, seemed to make Humboldt a good fit for the image of the heroic scientist that La Condamine had so effectively cultivated several decades earlier.[11] When Humboldt's reputation was at its peak at mid-century, the pro-slavery journalist John Thrasher famously tried to appropriate his *Political Essay on the Island of Cuba* for the cause of U.S. annexationism (with Cuba as the desired target), an attempt that backfired badly because of Humboldt's vociferous protest.[12] This protest, in turn, made the aging Humboldt, who loathed slavery in all of its forms, the darling of US abolitionists.[13] In the twentieth century, when the fortunes of Humboldtian science had waned in the USA and elsewhere as a result of increasing academic specialization,[14] Humboldt's work was used both as an apology for Nazism and in defense of Marxism.[15] While some historians have regarded him as the father of Latin American independence (mainly because of his partly imagined association with Simón Bolívar), others deemed him an uncritical aider and abettor of European colonialism and early capitalism.[16]

More recent portrayals on both sides of the Atlantic have tended to be more thoughtful and nuanced.[17] Particularly notable is the work that has been done on restoring and making available Humboldt's actual texts.[18] During the past decade, a host of new translations and lavishly produced editions of Humboldt's writings have seen print in Germany: *Ansichten der Natur* [*Views of Nature*] (2004), *Ansichten der Kordilleren* [*Vues of the Cordilleras*] (2004), *Kosmos* (2004), *Über einen Versuch den Gipfel des Chimborazo zu ersteigen* ["About an Attempt to Climb to the Top of Chimborazo"] (2005), and the complete *Kritische Untersuchungen* [Critical examination] (2009), almost all of them edited or co-edited by Ottmar Ette. The members the Alexander-von-Humboldt-Forschungsstelle [research institute] at the Berlin-Brandenburg Academy of Sciences, notably Margot Faak, Ulrike Leitner, and Ingo Schwarz, have contributed important resources to Humboldt studies. In 2000, Leitner (together with the late Horst Fielder) published *Alexander von Humboldt's Schriften* [Alexander von Humboldt's writings], a detailed bibliography of his separately published works, which is invaluable for Humboldt scholars. Both Leitner and Faak have also edited significant portions of Humboldt's travel diaries, written in German and in French, in *Reise durch Venezuela* [Travels through Venezuela] (2000), *Alexander von Humboldts amerikanische Reisejournale: eine Übersicht* [Alexander von Humboldt's American travel journals: an overview] (2002), *Lateinamerika am Vorabend der Unabhängigkeitsrevolution* [Latin American on the eve of the independence revolution] (2003), and *Von*

Mexiko-Stadt nach Veracruz [Form Mexico City to Veracruz] (2005), while Schwarz has focused on Humboldt's correspondence. The letters in Schwarz's *Alexander von Humboldt und die Vereinigen Staaten. Briefwechsel* [Alexander von Humboldt and the United States: letters] (2004) and *Alexander von Humboldt / Samuel Heinrich Spiker Briefwechsel* (2007) are an excellent addition to earlier collections of Humboldt's letters, such as Charles Minguet's *Carta americanas* (1980) [American letters] and Ulrike Moheit's *Briefe aus Amerika* (1993) [Letters from America]. In 2001, Leitner also rediscovered Humboldt's 1804 Cuba diary, which had long been believed lost, among the papers of the Biblioteka Jagiellonska in Crakow, Poland. The diary awaits full transcription and publication.[19] Recent contributions from the Spanish-speaking world are *Diarios de viaje en la Audiencia de Quito* [Journals of the travels in the Audiencia of Quito] (2005), edited by Segundo E. Moreno Yánez in a translation by Christiana Borchart de Moreno, which may be regarded as a companion piece to Estuardo Núñez Hague and Georg Petersen's *Alexander von Humboldt en el Perú: diario de viaje y otros escritos* [Alexander von Humboldt in Peru: travel diary and other writings] (2002).[20]

For the last several years, the French National Library has been in the process of making downloadable PDF scans of Humboldt's works in French available on its website,[21] and Tobias Kraft and Katharina Einert have done the field a tremendous service by bringing together in one place links to full texts of all of Humboldt's original writings in digital form.[22] Among other notable web resources on Humboldt is the somewhat misnamed Humboldt Digital Library from the University of Kansas in collaboration with the University of Offenburg,[23] which offers only existing English translations of Humboldt's writing in searchable PDFs, along with—and this is the really valuable part of this site—a visualization of Humboldt's travels that uses Google Earth. The problem with the English versions on this site (which are transcriptions of published texts) is that these translations, some of which are almost 200 years old now, are quite unreliable.[24] They will soon be superseded by a series of new translations in annotated critical editions, produced by the Alexander von Humboldt in English (HiE) project, a collaboration between the English Department at Vanderbilt University and Romance Literatures at the University of Potsdam. The series is being published by the University of Chicago Press, with the first volume the *Political Essay on the Island of Cuba*, now in print.[25] Also available from Chicago, is a new translation of Humboldt's *Essay on the Geography of Plants* (2009).

There has been no dearth of scholarly monographs either in the decade leading up to the 150th anniversary of Humboldt's death, which provided the occasion for several conferences in Germany, the USA and England—as well as for this collection.[26] The most recent German study is Ette's *Alexander von Humboldt und die Globalisierung* [Alexander von Humboldt and globalization] (2009), a monograph that focuses on issues of transdisciplinarity and on the art of Humboldtian narrative. In his earlier essays on Humboldt—notably in *Ansichten Amerikas* [Views of America] (2001), *Alexander von Humboldt: Aufbruch in die Moderne* [Alexander von Humboldt: setting out toward modernity] (2001), and *Literatur in Bewegung* [*Literature in Motion*]—and in his first monograph on Humboldt, *Weltbewusstsein* [World-consciousness] (2002),[27] Ette had already called attention to the global dimensions of Humboldt's writings and had situated the Prussian's intellectual praxis at the center not just of modernity but of an "alternative" modernity—what the book's subtitle calls *"das unvollendete Projekt einer anderen Moderne"* [the unfinished project of an other modernity]. Ette's *Weltbewusstsein* appeared in the same year as Nigel Leask's *Curiosity and the Aesthetics of*

Travel Writing, 1770-1840 (2002), and both deserve much credit for being the first to take seriously and analyze in detail the literary dimension of Humboldt's writing, in the process addressing the at times vexed relationship between the natural sciences and Romanticism.[28]

In the English-speaking world, where there are scores of articles about Humboldt's work from a variety of disciplines in the social sciences and the humanities,[29] few book-length studies have been devoted entirely to Humboldt. The two that come closest are Anne Marie Claire Godlewska's *Geography Unbound. French Geographic Science from Cassini to Humboldt* (1999) and Laura Dassow Walls's *Passage to Cosmos. Alexander von Humboldt and the Shaping of America* (2009). In addition to focusing on the "discursive formation of geography" in France 200 years ago as a much needed context for Humboldt's scientific and philosophical thought, Godlewska is after what she calls "the hard thinking behind Humboldt's attitude to representation," examining the ways in which Humboldt "pointed the way toward a new multidiscursivity through the universal language of mathematics."[30] The book recalls to our attention not only major players, such as the Cassini family, but also more neglected figures such as Adrien Balbi, Conrad Malte-Brun, and Edme-François Jomard, whose work Humboldt frequently consulted and cited. A third example is Aaron Sachs's widely-reviewed study, *The Humboldt Current. Nineteenth-Century Exploration and the Roots of American Environmentalism* (2006). While Humboldt himself plays a major role in Sachs's very engaging book, seven out of his ten chapters deal with what he calls "Humboldtianism,"[31] that is, Humboldt's impact on later nineteenth-century explorers of regions that the Prussian himself never visited, such as Antarctica, the North Polar region, and the US's western frontier. Foremost among these explorers were J.N. Reynolds (another inveterate volcano climber), Clarence King, George Melville, and John Muir. Sachs tells a good story, and he has to be congratulated for giving us a Humboldt who is very accessible and for restoring him to some of his former prominence in US American scientific and cultural history. There was, after all, a reason why so many places not just in Latin America but also in the USA were named after Humboldt. Yet, for much of the book, mention of Humboldt is relegated to short dependent clauses, which makes the connections Sachs is after appear less solid than they might otherwise have. Sachs's Humboldt is primarily what Rupke calls the "green Humboldt,"[32] the founding father of ecology and environmentalism, a figure whose specter began to emerge in the 1990s. We reencounter that Humboldt in Laura Dassow Walls's *Passage to Cosmos*, a book that covers roughly the same period of time but traverses different cultural ground. Walls, like Ette, is concerned with Humboldt as a scientist *and* a writer, and she deftly places him in the resonant company of the group of writers who, to F.O. Mathiessen, made up the "American Renaissance"—Ralph Waldo Emerson, Henry David Thoreau, Edgar Allen Poe, and, above all, Walt Whitman, whose poetic "Cosmos" is so unmistakably Humboldtian. These writers all held Humboldt's work dear, and Walls, unlike Sachs, tells and shows us exactly how and why. In her compelling book, we never lose sight of Humboldt; he is the main act throughout. Walls's book stands as an effective appeal to recover Humboldt from the oblivion to which his work has been consigned in the US academy for entirely too long.

While the scope of both Sachs's and Walls's respective studies is the U.S., that "American" nation, and both dwell mainly in the nineteenth century, two other studies, Jorge Cañizares-Esguerra's *Nature, Empire, and Nation. Explorations of the History of Science in the Iberian World* (2006) and Neil Safier's *Measuring the New World.*

Enlightenment Science and South America (2008), offer more of an Atlanticist perspective on Humboldt and some of his illustrious predecessors. Neither book casts Humboldt in the role of protagonist; yet, the inveterate Prussian lurks in all the nooks and crannies, since he was more than just acquainted with the work of the explorers and naturalists who take center stage here. Safier invokes Humboldt briefly and then moves back in time to the South American expedition of Louis Godin, Charles-Marie de La Condamine, and Pierre Bouguer. Later chapters feature Jean-Baptiste Bourguignon d'Anville and the Spanish military officers (and cartographers) Jorge Juan and Antonio de Ulloa, all of whom were important sources for Humboldt's own work. Safier is interested in how knowledge about South America was produced during the Enlightenment, specifically through what he calls "transatlantic scientific commemoration," that is, the ways in which "empirical observations were transformed into tangible, memorable products."[33] He also hopes that closer examination of the broad (narrative) interactions that went into the production of colonial science will increasingly steer scholars away from "speaking of British, French, and Iberian 'Atlantics'" to realize that we need approaches that would "integrate local, national, and imperial perspectives rather than merely comparing across geographic lines."[34] Safier's call for such approaches, and his book itself, stand as implicit criticisms of Cañizares-Esguerra's exclusive focus on the Iberian Atlantic. Humboldt does play more of a leading part in *Nature, Empire, and Nation*, notably in the chapter entitled "How Derivative was Humboldt?" Although this chapter seeks further to deflate the image of Humboldt as the lone scientific genius, emphasizing the American contributions to his work, what it really does, by exploring his interactions with colonial naturalists such as Francisco José de Caldas, José Celestino Mutis (in Colombia), and Hipólito Unanué (in Peru) is show just how keen Humboldt was on exchanging data with his colleagues, in the Americas and elsewhere, and how intent he was on building up a functioning scientific network. Humboldt was neither a lone universal genius nor the last of the Renaissance men; nor did he share the arrogance and Eurocentrism characteristic of many other European men of science and letters who preceded and followed him. Scholars such as Antonello Gerbi and, more recently, Mary Louise Pratt would have been well advised to read Humboldt a bit more closely before making claims about his totalizing vision and his "god-like, omniscient stance."[35]

Last but not least, let me mention a few contributions from art history, notably Sigrid Achenbach's *Kunst um Humboldt* (2009) [Art around Humboldt], a beautiful catalogue for a current exhibition of works by Johann Moritz Rugendas, Ferdinand Bellermann, and Eduard Hildebrandt, painters whom Humboldt inspired and encouraged to visit the New World.[36] While Bellermann went to Venezuela, Rugendas and Hildebrant spent time in Brazil, a country Humboldt was unable to visit during his own journey. This catalogue is a useful complement to Katherine Manthorne's *Tropical Renaissance* (1989), which focuses on nineteenth-century North American visual artists, and Cañizares-Esguerra's essay on "Landscapes and Identities" in late-nineteenth century Mexico.[37]

My brief survey of select recent work on Alexander von Humboldt shows that while transatlantic perspectives on him are quite present, most scholarship still tends to be firmly attached either to "a somewhat staid and exceptionalist version of American studies" (with the USA as the seemingly inescapable center)[38] or follow, as Safier has noted, the Atlanticist version of area studies which divides the Atlantic world into Iberian, French, British (and, one might add, German and Dutch) components. Add to this the kind of linguistic balkanization that makes little sense in a world of not just hemispheric but global movement and migrations. (According to Ette, we are now in what he calls "the fourth phase of accelerated globalization,"[39] that is, if we count forward from Columbus's voyage and the conquest of the New World that began in short order.) Clearly, Humboldt's own work does not separate South America from the United States, or Mexico and Canada from the Caribbean islands, nor, for that matter, from Europe, Asia, Africa, and the rest of the world. At a time when nations were but projections, he was well aware that borders are political fictions that too often conflict with both natural and cultural realities, and that arrest, or at least impede, the flow of goods and peoples that is at the heart of today's Atlantic studies inquiries. To restore this circumatlantic, and indeed global, flow to the forefront of our scholarly consciousnesses, we might consider not only Humboldt's comparative methodologies but also his sense of the importance of large-scale intellectual networks that cross all sorts of borders, be they political or linguistic. (Just imagine what Humboldt could have done with email and the internet!) Humboldt's intellectual legacy may well help Atlanticists to question both theoretical and institutional strictures (divisions into separate departments, promotion guidelines, etc.). I am not naive about the difficulties of modifying academic structures to make them more responsive to the needs of different epistemologies and disciplines. But for the new Atlantic studies to be "seen in proper relief," it will not do simply to project the work of colleagues in related fields as "transcended and cancelled."[40] In developing new approaches, we should be concerned with the sum of the different parts and perspectives that their work offers, however 'erroneous' some of them might strike us.

Innovation, as Humboldt's own pursuits demonstrate so well, is fundamentally a function of intellectual exchange and collaboration, and, as Ette shows in the essay included here, of ferreting out errors in productive ways. Critical to any constructive use of errors and failings, including one's own, is an "awareness of *lack* of territory proper,"[41] along with a willingness both to theorize this awareness and translate it into practical scholarly and institutional applications. If what distinguishes new from old Atlanticists is precisely such an awareness, along with an alertness to "the abrupt perspectival reversals of postcolonial studies or the interpretative innovations of cultural and indigenous studies"[42] then the essays in this book deserve to be placed squarely into this category—singly and together.

What frames the views of Humboldtian personae in this collection is one of Humboldt's own most dramatic crises: his failure to reach the very top of Chimborazo, a colossal volcano that, to him, represented the quintessential sublime. What was a personal disappointment for him nonetheless added significantly to his worldwide fame, because he literally went where no human had (then) gone before. Ottmar Ette comments on this key episode in the issue's opening essay, "Everything is Interrelated, even the Errors in the System," placing it in the context of Humboldt's contemplation of Columbus's legendary mistake in *Examen critique*. The book closes with Humboldt's own reflections on the aborted trek. In 1853, fifty-one years after his visit to what was then known as the Audiencia of Quito, Humboldt tellingly titles his essay "Über einen *Versuch*, den Gipfel des Chimborazo zu ersteigen" ["About an *Attempt* to Climb to the Top of the Chimborazo"] (my emphasis). The revised 1853 piece appears here in its complete English translation for the first time, as does Ette's essay, whose original version constitutes the final chapter—or "Achse 2" [second axis] in his carefully crafted "Mobile des Wissens" [mobile of knowledge]—in *Alexander von Humboldt und die*

Globalisierung. Particularly valuable about Humboldt's belated meditations is that rather than filtering out his failed attempt at getting to the top of the world, he explores its scientific and aesthetic potential for generating future knowledge.[43] He turns a crisis of knowledge into a welcome occasion for updating and correcting the results of his earlier field work while, at the same time, creating an often sensual narrative that consists of as many layers as the high plateaus stacked up against the imposing peak.

Ette's Humboldt bears little resemblance to the Prussian's fictionalized personae in German literature, from Christoph Hein's little known short story, "Die russischen Briefe des Jägers Johann Seifert" [The Russian letters of the Hunter Johann Seifert] to Daniel Kehlmann's popular *Die Vermessung der Welt* (2005), translated as *Measuring the World* in 2007. Oddly, Kehlmann's satiric novel seems to have been mistaken for realist fiction in its English version. The Humboldt we encounter (alongside a rather senile Immanuel Kant) in the literary works that John Pizer analyzes in his essay, "Skewering the Enlightenment," is a creature of the Enlightenment; this Humboldt is rational to a fault. Even Chimborazo obliquely reappears in what Pizer regards as the comic high point in Kehlmann's novel: Humboldt's inept, wooden translation of one of the most celebrated poems in the German language. This character does not have a sensual bone in his body, and not a shred of Romantic sensibility.

The Humboldt who emerges from Rodolfo Guzmán M.'s essay, "Welcoming Alexander von Humboldt in Santa Fé de Bogotá, or, The Creoles Self-Celebration in the Colonial City," is a character alert to colonial politics and political intrigue (he was, after all, also a diplomat). Guzmán M.'s fascinating case study places Humboldt in the company of the distinguished Linnaean botanist José Celestino Mutis, who was eagerly awaiting Humboldt and Aimé Bonpland's visit, and not only because of their shared scientific interests. Guzmán M. takes his initial cue from Cañizares-Esguerra's work on Humboldt's relations with Latin American scientists but spins it in a different direction by focusing on the growing political tensions between the *criollo* elite in the Spanish colonies, in this case New Granada, and the Spanish crown. Guzmán M.'s detailed reading of Humboldt's spectacular reception in colonial Santa Fé de Bogotá by Mutis and his disciples, a group of Creole naturalists, uses performance theory to bring into clearer view subtle symbolic displays of political power that would, in fairly short order, lead to the wars of independence in Spain's American viceroyalties.

In "Reading Juan Francisco Manzano in the Wake of Alexander von Humboldt," Marilyn Miller takes us from Colombia back to Cuba (where Humboldt had been for several months before he set out for Cartagena and then Bogotá). Some may greet with initial skepticism Miller's unexpected combination of Alexander von Humboldt and Juan Francisco Manzano, poet and author of the only known slave narrative in the Hispanic Americas. But they will be quickly drawn into the intriguing parallels she delineates. Miller's arguments have little, if anything, to do with matters of influence, literary or otherwise. Instead, she shows us, in Humboldtian fashion, how different trajectories, both connected through plantation slavery and the rise of abolitionism, can intersect in very productive ways when considered as vectors within the Atlanticist traffic between Cuba and Britain. This essay brings into relief the kinds of important connections that a more limited focus on either the British or the Iberian Atlantic might miss.

The next two essays continue Miller's focus on Cuba. Humboldt saw the island of Cuba (which he visited twice during the course of his American travels) not only as the centerpiece of the Caribbean region but, indeed, as a global island par excellence, a place where many trade routes intersected, and where many different peoples and cultures had been thrown together as a result of slavery and the transatlantic slave trade. A Jacobin throughout his life, Humboldt was also an impassioned abolitionist, someone who hated slavery from the bottom of his heart. But even though he was convinced that the fate of the enslaved Africans was as closely intertwined with the fortunes of the Spanish colonists in Cuba and elsewhere in the Caribbean, as were the lives of the indigenous populations in the continental colonies. Humboldt was not a political activist. Some have regarded this as a sign of equivocation, ambivalence, and perhaps even a "lack of personal integrity."[44] Humboldt, however, frequently made his feelings about slavery very plain. He had already done so in the *Essai politique sur l'île de Cuba* [*Political Essay on the Island of Cuba*] (1825-26), and he re-emphasized his sentiments when, in the summer of 1856, he publicly rebuked the annexationist and Buchanan supporter John Thrasher for distorting his views on slavery matter in his English translation of that book. This letter, widely reprinted in the USA during an important presidential campaign, made Humboldt quite a celebrity in anti-slavery circles.[45] Fernando Ortiz's "El traductor de Humboldt en la historia de Cuba"—"Humboldt's translator in the context of Cuban history"—and my commentary on different translations of Humboldt's *Essai politique* both draw attention to the tricky business, indeed the perils, of translation. The story of the English translations of the *Essai politique* is particularly worth telling (in English) because the Humboldt whom readers of the Thrasher edition encountered was not at all the Humboldt who wrote in French. And, until recently, Thrasher's version of that text was the only one readily available to an English-speaking audience.[46] In "Translations of Cuba," I take a close look at *The Island of Cuba*, as Thrasher titled his translation, placing his attempt at twisting Humboldt's writing into pro-slavery and pro-annexationist propaganda in the context of other translations of this controversial text. I argue that Alexander von Humboldt's resistance to dogmatism finds its literary equivalent in his non-totalizing narrative structures and his richly textured voice, both of which have tended to disappear in translation. There is a need, then, for a literary (rather than social-scientific) approach to translating Humboldt's prose to remedy such defacements, be they unwitting or willful.

It is only fitting, then, that Alexander von Humboldt have the last word in this collection—in what I hope is a more felicitous act of ventriloquism. His essay on Chimborazo stands as a reminder to us to transform our epistemological crises– the errors in our own systems of thought–into opportunities for sharpening our scholarly tools and ideas. The debate around the new Atlantic studies shows quite clearly that Humboldt's open-ended, dynamic inscriptions of knowledge are not just the stuff of history. By always extending outward into the future, these inscriptions make all subsequent scholarship the on the Atlantic world part of Humboldt's projected work-in-progress.

References

Achenbach, Sigrid. *Kunst um Humboldt. Reisestudien aus Mittel- und Südamerika von Rugendas, Bellermann, und Hildebrandt im Berliner Kufterstichkabinett.* Berlin and Munich: Staat-liche Museen zu Berlin, Hirmer Verlag, 2009.

Beck, Hanno, ed. *Alexander von Humboldt. Werke.* Studienausgabe. 2nd ed. 7 vols. Darmstadt: Wissenschaftliche Buchgesellschaft, 2008.

Boelhower, William."The Rise of the New Atlantic Studies Matrix." *American Literary History* 20, no.1 (2007): 83-101.

Cannon, Susan Faye. "Humboldtian Science." In *Science and Culture: The Early Victorian Period*, 73-100. New York: Dawson and Science History Publications, 1978.

Cañizares-Esguerra, Jorge. *Nature, Empire, and Nation. Explorations of the History of Science in the Iberian World*. Stanford: Stanford University Press, 2006.

Cushman, Gregory T. "Humboldtian Science, Creole Meteorology, and the Discovery of Human-Caused Climate Change in Northern South America." In *"Revisiting Klima."* Special Issue, *Osiris* 26 (2011): in-press.

Dettelbach, Michael. "Alexander von Humboldt between Enlightenment and Romanticism." *Northeastern Naturalist* 8. no. 1 (2001): 9-20.

Dettelbach, Michael. "The Face of Nature: Precise Measurement, Mapping, and Sensibility in the Work of Alexander von Humboldt." *Studies in History and Philosophy of Biological and Biomedical Sciences* 30, no. 4 (1999): 473-504.

Esty, Jed. "Oceanic, Traumatic, Post-Paradigmatic: A Response to William Boelhower." *American Literary History* 20, no. 1 (2007): 103-7.

Ette, Ottmar. *Alexander von Humboldt und die Globalisierung. Das Mobile des Wissens*. Franfurt am Main: Insel, 2009.

Ette, Ottmar. *Literatur in Bewegung. Raum and Dynamik grenzüberschreitenden Schreibens in Europa und Amerika*. Weilerswist: Velbrück Wissenschaft, 2001.

Ette, Ottmar. "The Scientist as Weltbürger: Alexander von Humboldt and the beginning of Cosmopolitics." *Northeastern Naturalist* 8, no. 1 (2001): 157-82.

Ette, Ottmar. *Weltbewusstsein. Alexander von Humboldt und das unvollendete Projekt einer anderen Moderne*. Weilerswist: Velbrück Wissenschaft, 2002.

Ette, Ottmar, and Ute Hermanns, Bernd M. Scherer, and Christian Suckow, eds. *Alexander von Humboldt—Aufbruch in die Moderne*. Berlin: Akademie Verlag, 2001.

Fiedler, Horst, and Ulrike Leitner. *Alexander von Humboldt's Schriften. Bibliographie der selbständig erschienenen Werke*. Berlin: Akademie Verlag, 2000.

Gerbi, Antonello. *The Dispute of the New World. The History of a Polemic, 1750-1900*. Transl. and ed. Jeremy Moyle. Pittsburgh, PA: University of Pittsburgh Press, 1973. First published in 1955.

Godlewska, Anne Marie Claire. *Geography Unbound. French Geographic Science from Cassini to Humboldt*. Chicago: University of Chicago Press, 1999.

Graczyk, Annette. *Das literarische Tableau zwischen Kunst und Wissenschaft*. Munich: Wilhelm Fink Verlag, 2004.

Holl, Frank, ed. *Alejandro de Humboldt: una nueva visión del mundo. En conmemoración al bicentenario de la llegada de Humboldt a México*. Mexico City: Universidad Nacional Autónoma de México, 2003.

Holmes, Richard. *The Age of Wonder. How the Romantic Generation Discovered the Beauty and Terror of Science*. New York: Pantheon Books, 2008.

Hulme, Peter, ed. "Special Issue. Alexander von Humboldt and America." *Studies in Travel Writing* 15, no. 1 (February 2011).

Humboldt, Alexander von. *Ansichten der Kordilleren und Monumente der eingeborenen Völker Amerikas*. Ed. Ottmar Ette and Oliver Lubrich. Trans. Claudia Kalscheuer. Frankfurt am Main: Eichborn, 2004.

Humboldt, Alexander von. *Alexander von Humboldts amerikanische Reisejournale: eine Übersicht*. Ed. Margot Faak. Berlin: Akademie Verlag, 2002.

Humboldt, Alexander von. *Alexander von Humboldt en el Perú: diario de viaje y otros escritos*. Ed. Estuardo Núñez Hague and Georg Petersen. Lima: Banco Central de Reserva del Perú, 2002.

Humboldt, Alexander von. *Alexander von Humboldt/Samuel Heinrich Spiker Briefwechsel*. Ed. Ingo Schwarz. Berlin: Akademie Verlag, 2007.

Humboldt, Alexander von. *Alexander von Humboldt und die Vereinigten Staaten: Briefwechsel*. Ed. Ingo Schwarz. Berlin: Akademie Verlag, 2004.

Humboldt, Alexander von. *Ansichten der Natur*. Frankfurt am Main: Eichborn, 2004. First published 1849.

Humboldt, Alexander von. "Baron von Humboldt's Political Essay on Cuba: Letter from the Author on the Omission of a Chapter by the Translator." *New York Daily Times*, August 12, 1856, 2.

Humboldt, Alexander von. *Briefe aus Amerika*. Ed. Ulrike Moheit. Berlin: Akademie Verlag, 1993.

Humboldt, Alexander von. *Cartas americanas*. Ed. Charles Minguet. Trans. Marta Traba. Caracas: Biblioteca Ayacucho, 1980.

Humboldt, Alexander von. *Correspondance: 1805-1858. Alexander von Humboldt et Aimé Bonpland*. Ed. Nicolas Hossard. Paris: Harmattan, 2004.

Humboldt, Alexander von. *Diarios de viaje en la Audiencia de Quito*. Ed. Segundo E. Moreno Yánez. Trans. Christiana Borchart de Moreno. Quito: Occidental Exploration and Production, 2005.

Humboldt, Alexander von. *Ensayo político sobre la Isla de Cuba*. Ed. Miguel Ángel Puig-Samper, Consuelo Naranjo Orovio, and Armando García González Aranjuez. Madrid: Ediciones Doce Calles, 1998.

Humboldt, Alexander von. *Essai politique sur le royaume de la Nouvelle-Espagne*. 4 vols. Paris: F. Schoell, 1808-11. Second ed. 1825-1827.

Humboldt, Alexander von. *Essai politique sur l'île de Cuba*. 2 vols. Paris: Gide Fils, 1826.

Humboldt, Alexander von. *Essay on the Geography of Plants*. Ed. Stephen T. Jackson. Trans. Sylvie Romanowski. Chicago: University of Chicago Press, 2009.

Humboldt, Alexander von. *Examen critique de l'histoire de la géographie du Nouveau Continent et des progrès de l'astronomie nautique dans le XVe et XVIe siècles*. 5 vols. Paris: Gide, 1834-8.

Humboldt, Alexander von. *Kosmos: Entwurf einer physischen Weltbeschreibung*. Ed. Ottmar Ette and Oliver Lubrich. Frankfurt am Main: Eichborn, 2004.

Humboldt, Alexander von. *Kritische Untersuchung zur Historischen Entwicklung der Geographischen Kenntnisse von der Neuen Welt und den Fortschritten der nautischen Astronomie im 15. und 16. Jahrhundert*. Ed. Ottmar Ette. 2 vols. Frankfurt am Main: Insel, 2009.

Humboldt, Alexander von. *Lateinamerika am Vorabend der Unabhängigkeitsrevolution: eine Anthologie von Impressionen und Urteilen aus seinen Reisetagebüchern*. Corr. Ed. Margot Faak. Berlin: Akademie Verlag, 2003.

Humboldt, Alexander von. *Personal Narrative of Travels to the Equinoctial Regions of the New Continent during the Years 1799-1804 by Alexandre de Humboldt and Aimé Bonpland*. Trans. Helen Maria Williams. 7 vols. London: Longman, Rees, Brown, & Greene, 1814-29.

Humboldt, Alexander von. *Personal Narrative of Travels to the Equinoctial Regions of America, During the Years 1799-1804. Abridged*. Transl. Thomasina Ross. London: Henry G. Bohn, 1852-53.

Humboldt, Alexander von. *Political Essay on the Kingdom of New Spain, by Alexander von Humboldt*. Trans. John Black. 4 vols. London: Longman Hurst, Reed, Orme, & Brown, 1811.

Humboldt, Alexander von. *Political Essay on the Island of Cuba*. Ed. Vera M. Kutzinski and Ottmar Ette. Chicago: University of Chicago, 2011.

Humboldt, Alexander von. *Reise durch Venezuela: Auswahl aus den amerikanischen Reisetagebüchern*. Ed. Margot Faak. Berlin: Akademie Verlag, 2000.

Humboldt, Alexander von. *The Island of Cuba*. Trans. John S. Thrasher. New York: Derby & Jackson, 1856.

Humboldt, Alexander von, *The Island of Cuba. A Political Essay by Alexander von Humboldt*. Ed. by and Luis Martínez-Fernández. Princeton and Kingston: Markus Wiener and Ian Randle Publishers, 2001.

Humboldt, Alexander von. *Über einen Versuch den Gipfel des Chimborazo zu ersteigen*. Ed. Ottmar Ette and Oliver Lubrich. Frankfurt am Main: Eichborn, 2006.

Humboldt, Alexander von. *Von Mexiko-Stadt nach Veracruz: Tagebuch*. Ed. Ulrike Leitner. Berlin: Akademie Verlag, 2005.

Humboldt, Alexander von. *Voyage aux régions équinoxiales du Nouveau Continent fait en 1799, 1800, 1802, 1803, et 1804, par Al. de Humboldt et A. Bonpland*. 30 vols. Paris: F. Schoell, 1805-29.

Humboldt, Alexander von. *Vues des Cordillères et monumens des peoples indigènes de l'Amérique*. Paris: F. Schoell, 1810-13.

Lack, H. Walter. *Alexander von Humboldt and the Botanical Exploration of the Americas*. Munich, London, New York: Prestel, 2009.

Leask, Nigel. 2002. *Curiosity and the Aesthetics of Travel Writing, 1770-1840*. Oxford: Oxford University Press.

Manthorne, Katherine. *Tropical Renaissance. North American Artists exploring South America, 1839-1879*. Washington, D.C.: Smithsonian Institution Press, 1989.

Mathewson, Kent. "Alexander von Humboldt's Image and Influence in North American Geography, 1804-2004." *Geographical Review* 96, no. 3 (July 2006): 416-38.

Pratt, Mary Louise. *Imperial Eyes. Travel Writing and Transculturation*. London and New York: Routledge and Kegan Paul, 1992.

Rupke, Nicolaas. *Alexander von Humboldt. A Metabiography*. Chicago: University of Chicago Press, 2006.

Sachs, Aaron. *The Humboldt Current. Nineteenth-Century Exploration and the Roots of American Environmentalism*. New York: Viking Penguin, 2006.

Safier, Neil. *Measuring the New World. Enlightenment Science and South America*. Chicago: University of Chicago Press, 2008.

Thrasher, John Sidney. "Baron Humboldt and Mr. Thrasher." *New York Daily Times*, August 17, 1856.

Walls, Laura Dassow. *The Passage to Cosmos. Alexander von Humboldt and the Shaping of America*. Chicago: University of Chicago Press, 2009.

Villanova, Manuel. 1887. Humboldt y Thrasher, V. *La Semana* (Havana), (October 3): 6-7.

Zeuske, Michael. "Comparando al Caribe: Alexander Humboldt, Saint-Domingue y los comienzos de la comparación de la esclavitud en las Americas." *Estudios Afro-Asiáticos* 26:2 (2004): 381-416.

Notes

1 Humboldt, *Essai politique sur l'île de Cuba* II.102. All translation are my own, unless otherwise noted.
2 See Humboldt, *Voyage*; Humboldt, *Personal Narrative*, transl. Williams.
3 Ette, "Zwischen Welten," in Humboldt and Ette, *Kritische Untersuchung* II.227.
4 Ibid., 241. Ette has elsewhere called this "vectorial history." See also Godlewska, *Geography Unbound*, 245.
5 I use the term "mapping" advisedly here, and in cautious reference to William Boelhower's privileging of what he calls the cartographic text. Such a text, "representing a stratified and temporally rich skein of intersecting discursive and material trajectories across the Atlantic world–allows us to refer to Atlantic studies research practices as a new disciplinary matrix" (Boelhower, "Rise," 90).
6 On the representational synthesis of art and science, see Graczyk, *Das literarische Tableau*, 291-410.

7 Boelhower, "Rise," 85.

8 Humboldt, *Essai politique sur le royaume* IV.286.

9 Boelhower, "Rise,"83.

10 Rupke, *Metabiography*, 210-1.

11 See Safier, *Measuring the New World*.

12 See Humboldt, *Island of Cuba*, trans. Thrasher; Humboldt, "Baron von Humboldt's Political Essay"; and Thrasher, "Baron Humboldt." See also Ette, *Globalisierung*, 292; Kutzinski, 'Translations of Cuba"; Walls, *Passage to Cosmos*, 201-6; and Zeuske, "Comparando al Caribe."

13 See Walls, *Passage to Cosmos*, 206-9.

14 See Sachs, *Humboldt Current*, 339.

15 See Rupke, *Metabiography*, chap. 3 and 4.

16 See Pratt, *Imperial Eyes*.

17 I offer here a review of select scholarship on Humboldt rather than attempting a complete account. Such an account even for just the past decade would exceed the space of this introduction.

18 There are also a number of print-on-demand or reprint publishers, such as Kessinger, BiblioBazaar, and Cambridge Scholars Publishing which, in 2009, flooded the market with cheap editions of just about everything available by Humboldt, most often reprints of old translations. Even the seven volumes of Hanno Beck's incomplete and not very thorough edition of Humboldt's *Werke* from the 1990s was reissued as a set in 2008.

19 See Zeuske, "Comparando al Caribe."

20 See also Humboldt, *Ensayo político*.

21 See at http://www.gallica.bnf.fr.

22 See *Humboldt im Netz* X, 19, 2009, at http://www.uni-potsdam.de/u/romanistik/humboldt/hin.

23 See http:// www.avhumboldt.net.

24 A rare embarrassment was the 2001 prize-winning reprint of John Thrasher's mutilated translation under the title *The Island of Cuba. A Political Essay* in an edition by Luis Fernández-Martínez. See Kutzinski, "Translation of Cuba."

25 HiE also has its own website with additional materials for scholarly and pedagogical use. See http://www.press.uchicago.edu/humboldt.

26 Outside of Germany, several recent conferences were devoted to Humboldt: "Alexander von Humboldt and the Hemisphere," Center for the Americas, Vanderbilt University, in January 2009; "Humboldt's Transatlantic Personae," Louisiana State University (LSU) in May 2009; and "Alexander von Humboldt and America," at the British Academy of Sciences, London, in November 2009. For select proceedings of the London conference, see Peter Hulme's special issue of *Studies in Travel Writing*. Earlier Humboldt conferences in the USA of which there are proceedings and/or essays collections took place in Boston and at the Bildner Center for Hemispheric Studies at the CUNY Graduate Center: see *Northeastern Naturalist*, Special Issue 1: Alexander von Humboldt's Natural History Legacy and Its Relevance for Today (2001), and "Alexander von Humboldt: From the Americas to the Cosmos," 2004; papers available at http://web.gc.cuny.edu/dept/bildn/publications/humboldt.pdf. Most of the essays in this book were either presented at or inspired by the LSU Humboldt conference, which was sponsored by the Program in Caribbean and Louisiana Studies at LSU. Our collective thanks go to John Lowe and Christian Fernández Palacios for making this event possible. The editor also wishes especially to thank William Boelhower.

27 Ette writes mainly in German, French, and Spanish, and little of his work on Humboldt is available in English. One exception is Katharina Vester's translation of *Literatur in Bewegung*, entitled *Literature in Motion* (Amsterdam; Rodopi, 2003), which does Ette's prose rather a disservice. See also Ette's "The Scientist as Weltbürger."

28 Dettelbach squarely confronts the discomfort that historians of science have with the relationship between the natural sciences and Romanticisms, still regarding "the emergence of modern physical science [as] escaping from Romanticism as though from a bad dream" ("Dettelbach, "Face of Nature," 473). See also Dettelbach, "Alexander von Humboldt." For a recent account that connects nineteenth-century scientific developments mainly in Britain with the work of that country's Romantic poets, see Holmes, *Age of Wonder*.

29 For geography, see especially Mathewson, "Alexander von Humboldt's Image" and Cushman, "Humboldtian Science." For botany, see Lack, *Botanical Exploration*.
30 Godlewska, *Geography Unbound*, 241, 264.
31 See Cannon, "Humboltian Science."
32 Rupke, *Metabiography*, 185-6.
33 Safier, *Measuring*, 12.
34 Ibid., 15.
35 See Gerbi, *Dispute*; Pratt, *Imperial Eyes*, 124. Pratt's reasons for excluding both of Humboldt's "Political Essays" because they fall outside of her focus on South America strike me as spurious.
36 There are various publications that have come out of exhibitions on Humboldt organized by Frank Holl in Germany, Mexico, and Cuba.
37 See Cañizares-Esguerra, *Nature*, chapter 7. See also Holl, *Alejandro de Humboldt*.
38 Esty, "Oceanic, Traumatic, Post-Paradigmatic," 107.
39 Ette, *Globalisierung*, 13.
40 Esty, "Oceanic, Traumatic, Post-Paradigmatic," 107.
41 Boelhower, "Rise," 94 (my emphasis).
42 Ibid., 84.
43 See Ette, *Globalisierung*, 27.
44 See Villanova, "Humboldt y Thrasher."
45 See Walls, *Passage to Cosmos*, chapter 4.
46 For a new translation of the *Essai politique sur l'île de Cuba*, see Kutzinski and Ette's critical edition of Humboldt's *Political Essay on the Island of Cuba*.

Everything is interrelated, even the errors in the system: Alexander von Humboldt and globalization

Ottmar Ette
Translated by Vera M. Kutzinski

> This article is an English version of the final chapter of Ette's *Alexander von Humboldt und die Globalisierung: das Mobile des Wissen*, published by Insel in 2009.

In his *Examen critique de l'histoire de la géographie du Nouveau Continent et des progrès de l'astronomie nautique au quinzième et seizième siècles* [*Critical Examination of the Historical Development of the Geographical Knowledge of the New World and the Progress of Nautical Astronomy in the Fifteenth and Sixteen Centuries*], Alexander von Humboldt wrote in detail about the different traditions of cartographic representation in the New World. In his discussion of three-dimensional forms of representation, he not only remarked on the famous terrestrial globe of Martin Behaim, the *Erdapfel* [earth apple] from 1492 (see Figure 1), but also on the terrestrial globe of Johannes Schoner, which showed a direct sea connection between the Caribbean and the Pacific Ocean as late as 1520. Humboldt commented on Schoner's depiction of a strait, instead of a neck of land, in the region of the Central American isthmus:

> Le passage de la Mer des Antilles à l'Océan Pacifique, indiqué par Schoner, n'était donc que le produit d'un esprit systématique et de fausses idées sur l'expédition de Balboa. On peut être surpris de voir que l'erreur que nous signalons se soit conservée si long-temps.

> [The passage from the Sea of the Antilles to the Pacific Ocean, as Schoner showed it, was but the result of a systematic mindset and incorrect ideas about the explorations of Balboa. One can indeed be astonished at how the error that we pointed out could propagate for such a long time.][1]

However, Humboldt did not stop with a simple statement about the errors, mistakes, and false ideas of a "systematic mindset," but insisted on asking as much about the sources and traditions of such "misrepresentations" as he did about their productive results. He added: "Les détails de l'histoire des sciences ne sont utiles qu'autant qu'on les réunit par un lien commun" [The details of the history of the sciences maintain their usefulness only insofar as one interconnects them].[2] But if one wanted to reach a "vue générale sur les progrès de l'intelligence et la marche de la civilization" [higher perspective on the progress of intelligence and the movement

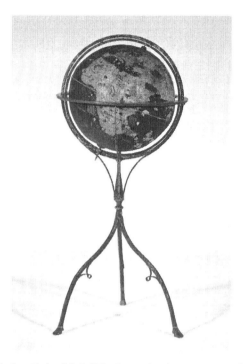

Figure 1.   Martin Behaim, Erdapfel (1492). Reproduction courtesy of Ottmar Ette from his *Alexander von Humboldt. Geographischer und Physischer Atlas der Aquinoktial-Gegenden des Neuen Kontinents – Unsichtbarer Atlas aller in der Kritischen Unterrsuchung audgeführen und analysierten Karten*. Frankfurt am Main: Insel Verlag (2009).

of civilization], one also had to include "circonstances accidentelles en apparence ... qui révèlent une nécessité dans les destinées du monde" [seemingly accidental events ... that reveal a necessity in the measurement of the world], especially along with erroneous notions and systematic errors.[3] Such a changed perspective would make possible a different, more profound understanding of the great successes and discoveries (and, of course, of spectacular failures).

> L'histoire ne conserve généralement que la tradition des entreprises heureuses, des grands succès obtenus dans la carrière des découvertes. Ce qui prépare le mouvement et le succès appartient à des combinaisons d'idées et à de petits événemens qui agissent par simultanéité. Leur importance ne se fait sentir que lorsque de grands résultats ont été obtenus, tels que nous les devons à Diaz, Colomb, Gama et Magellan.

> [History generally only passes on happy enterprises and great successes on the road to discovery. That which prepares the path for movement and for success belongs to the interlinking of ideas and the connection between minor events, which exert a simultaneous and common influence. Their importance emerges with some clarity only when great successes have been achieved, such as those for which we can thank Diaz, Columbus, Gama, and Magellan.][4]

Humboldt was opposed to all intentions to apply, as Robertson did in his *History of America*, "l'idée vague du destin, là où l'enchaînement mutual de tant de causes et d'effets n'est pas difficile à reconnaître" [the vague concept of fate in contexts where the mutual interconnection of numerous causes and effects is not difficult to perceive].[5] If one wanted to understand an event that vitally changed "les destinées de tant de peuplades éparses dans l'immensité des mers, hors du contact de la civilization européenne" [the fate of peoples scattered across the immeasurable expanse of the oceans, who were outside of the purviews of European education],[6] then one had to analyze precisely those errors in systematic thinking that determined the relations between coincidence, possibility, and necessity to such a large extent. At the center of Humboldt's epistemological metaphors – the repetition of the word in the above citations proves it – is the image of interconnection, an "allgemeine Verkettung, nicht in einfacher linearer Richtung, sondern in netzartig verschlungenem Gewebe" [general interlinking, not in a simple linear direction but in an intricate net-like fabric], which is how Humboldt defines it on the very first page of his *Kosmos*.[7] Not only does the dynamically intertwined texture of the fabric of the net(work) characterize the planned openness of his different books and writings; it also, above all, constitutes a relational epistemology at whose core is a not just superficially holistic insight. Humboldt already registers this insight, in German, in his Mexican travel diary, tellingly as an insertion into his climatological and geo-ecological thoughts: "L'évaporation, causée par la chaleur, produit le manque d'eau et de rivières, et le manque d'évaporation (source principale du froid atmosphérique) augmente la chaleur. Alles ist Wechselwirkung" [The evaporation caused by the heat produces the lack of water and of streams, and the lack of evaporation (the main source of atmospheric cold) increases the heat. Everything is interrelated].[8]

For Humboldt, the mostly damaging impact of humans on the climate and atmosphere of our planet resulted from the "general intertwining" of ordinary factors and conditions with systematic errors whose consequences, he claimed, are already visible very early on in the history of the discovery and conquest of the New World. Similarly, as Humboldt tried to work out in his history of the New World, system errors are characteristic of human beings' conscious and intentional actions. In the three volumes of *Asie Centrale* from 1843, Humboldt celebrated Christopher Columbus as that "extraordinary man"[9] who, as if he were a prototype of the modern scientist, had pointed to the negative consequences of the rapid deforestation on the water economy of the Antilles. At the end of the main part of this work, Humboldt did not leave any doubts that clear-cutting and other massive interferences with the water economy, above all "the great volume of steam and gaseous substances" that were emitted into the atmosphere primarily in the great centers of "industrial culture," would have considerable effects on the climate.[10]

Alexander von Humboldt could not possibly have judged the full impact of this process in his time; but today, we are more than familiar with the errors in the system to which the author of *Ansichten der Natur* [*Views of Nature*] pointed then. One cannot overlook the fact that Alexander von Humboldt included in his concept of world consciousness precisely the mistakes and errors that humans made systematically, in order to draw from them lessons about future developments and about possibilities for counteracting negative results as early as possible on the basis of a highly complex analysis of factors. From this perspective, what we now call, rather innocently, attempts at "estimating the consequences of technology" might be seen as an effort at systematically analyzing the errors in the system of occidental modernity, regardless of whether these are mistakes in relation to nature or in the intellectual and material engagement with other cultures. But, as the above citations already signal, Humboldt understood errors by no means simply as more or less serious "disruptions" and "work accidents," but fundamentally as productive forces of human knowledge production and insight. For mistakes and errors can also create new knowledge within the network structures of interrelations: it is a matter of making them part of (world) consciousness.

Fascinating mistakes/fascinated by mistakes

No other historical personality fascinated Alexander von Humboldt as much and for as long as Christopher Columbus did.[11] Humboldt's *Examen critique*, based as it was on decades of preparation, can be seen as a single broad attempt at comprehending the figure of this "homme extraordinaire" who had been "On le dit tour à tour noble Portugais, Bohémien de race slave, natif de l'île Fayal (dans le groupe des Açores), citoyen de Nuremberg" [made out to be a noble Portuguese at times, at others a Bohemian of the Slavic race, and at yet others a native of the island Fayal (of the Azores), not to mention a citizen of Nuremberg].[12] Yet, Humboldt's historiographical (and literary) engagement with this cosmopolitan European was far from being focused exclusively on Christopher Columbus's courage and daring, his cleverness and intelligence, his advanced nautical knowledge and quasi-scientific ability to make precise observations. Rather, what also concerned Alexander von Humboldt were the errors in the system of the Genovese seafarer's calculations and to show how these mistakes and miscalculations had the power to produce innovative knowledge.

For Humboldt, this European discoverer par excellence was thus much more than the resolute hero of an adventurous discovery story that had made (world) history. With his systematic errors, Columbus represents precisely the transitional period that he was able to accelerate so effectively – and here we have to remember that, for Humboldt, the philosopher of history, great men were first and foremost those who sped up developments that would still have occurred without them but in a "delayed" manner: "elles accelerant et vivifient le movement" [they accelerate and revive movement].[13]

In this sense, and at the level of cultural history and historical philosophy, the Genovese mariner is clearly, as Humboldt notes at the opening of his preface, a liminal being: "Placé entre deux genres de civilization, il offre comme un monde intermédiaire appurtenant à la fois au moyen-âge et aux temps modernes" [we see him in between two formative levels of civilization that were completely different from each other, as if in a liminal world (Zwischenwelt) that belongs at once to the Middle Ages and the more modern age].[14] But Columbus not only appears as a dweller in a liminal world on the threshold of two epochs of Western intellectual history, not solely as a persistent traveler first between different European countries and later between the Old and the New World, a position that predestined him; in a manner of speaking, he engaged in what I have called *ZwischenWeltenSchreiben* [writing between worlds].[15] Columbus also moves back and forth, on the level of knowledge and insight, between the quest for truth and the persistence with which he remained loyal to his errors; between "inherited" (pre)science and a dynamic knowledge of experience; between the erroneousness of systematic thought (in Humboldt's sense) and an empirically based search for insight that is aware of its own errancy. It is, therefore, for good reason that one could go so far as to call the entirety of the *Examen critique* a meditation on the productive power of errors and mistakes, of failures and delusions. Alexander von Humboldt does not tire of drawing repeated attention to the sources of Christopher Columbus's philosophical, literary, and cartographic errors – be they part of antiquity or the modern world, Western or non-European – without which the great plan would have never unfolded. It is not for nothing that the Prussian savant opens the "First Part" of this work as follows:

> D'Anville a dit avec esprit que la plus grande des erreurs dans la géographie de Ptolémée a conduit les hommes à la plus grande découverte de terres nouvelles … tout ce qui excite au mouvement, soit erreur, soit prévision vague et instinctive, soit argumentation raisonnée, conduit à étendre la sphère des idées, à ouvrir de nouvelles voies au pouvoir de l'intelligence.

> [D'Anville made the witty remark that the greatest of all errors in Ptolemy's geography had led humans to great discoveries of new areas of the world … Everything that inspires movement, whether the moving power is miscalculations, uncertain hunches, instinctive divinations, reasoned argument, all these lead to a broadening of the intellectual horizon, to the discovery of new paths for the power of intelligence.][16]

Decisive, then – and characteristic of Humboldt's thinking – is movement, the moving (and revitalizing) power of the imagination; it matters not if this power is based on facts, experiences, legends, hunches, or (what are from our perspective today) errors. Humboldt succeeds countless times in demonstrating how errors and miscalculations have an inherent power of movement that advances history. Different from stereotypical common sense, they are *movens* that anticipate Humboldt's magic word *movement*, which applies to spatial discovery as much as it does to ideas. Would Columbus ever have been willing to brave the perils of crossing the Atlantic had he not firmly believed that he would find the Asiatic mainland, the world of Marco Polo, by sailing to the west? Would the Genovese ever have set out on his voyage had he not "known" that water accounted for only seven percent of the earth's surface, and that the distance between the westernmost part of Europe and the easternmost part of Asia was quite small?

The *Examen critique* poses such questions by no means only to pursue more precise knowledge of all the details and prehistories of the so-called discovery. Rather, Humboldt is interested in the processes (and contradictory nature) of human knowledge production as such. For what is a "broadening of the intellectual horizon" or "the discovery of new paths for the power of intelligence," if all these movements and paths are based upon erroneous and mistaken motivations? No doubt, for Humboldt, errors were not just an annoyance but also, above all, this: something that fascinated him and that always challenged the power of his intellect. Did not the professors of Salamanca make colossal mistakes, when, in their dispute with Columbus, they challenged the ways of this seafarer who, in their eyes, was only semi-educated?[17] And did not Hernán Colón, who correctly proved that the Spanish chronicler Fernando González de Oviedo did not have the requisite competency in Greek, make numerous lexical and other mistakes that Humboldt, in his turn – and he himself was not above such errors – tries to prove?[18] Alexander von Humboldt's arguments show that he himself tirelessly and doggedly pursued meticulous, scientifically precise foundations for his own arguments, at the same time as being well aware that knowledge is not equivalent to an arrival in a safe haven.

One may confidently use Alexander von Humboldt's self-reflective insight below to argue against an age that believes to have finally broken the "code of nature" and to be only a few steps away from revealing a formula for the world:

Durch den Glanz neuer Entdeckungen angeregt, mit Hoffnungen genährt, deren Täuschung oft spät erst eintritt, wähnt jedes Zeitalter dem Culminationspunkte im Erkennen und Verstehen der Natur nahe gelangt zu sein. Ich bezweifle, dass bei ernstem Nachdenken ein solcher Glaube den Genuss der Gegenwart wahrhaft erhöhe. Belebender und der Idee von der grossen Bestimmung unseres Geschlechtes angemessener ist die Ueberzeugung, dass der eroberte Besitz nur ein sehr unbetrachtlicher Theil von dem ist, was bei fortschreitender Thätigkeit und gemeinsamer Ausbildung die freie Menschheit in den kommenden Jahrhunderten erringen wird. Jedes Erforschte ist nur eine Stufe zu etwas Höherem in dem verhängnissvollen Laufe der Dinge.

[Inspired by the splendor of new discoveries, nourished by hope, whose deception often comes only later, each age claims to have reached a culmination point in its knowledge and understanding of nature. I doubt that, upon serious reflection, such a belief really heightens the pleasure of the present. More revitalizing and more appropriate to the idea of the great purpose of our species is the conviction that the conquered territory is but a very inconsiderable part of what free humanity will accomplish with continued activity and collective education during the centuries to follow. Any exploration/ research is but a step toward something higher in the fateful course of things.][19]

Alexander von Humboldt, it should be clear, was not a proponent of perfectionism. Instead, he was able to show, both historically and cartographically, how errors and miscalculations served as sources, motivations, and accelerators of knowledge. The historical errors of Christopher Columbus became wrong paths that, in their turn, led to a place that had not been sought: America. In the shape of America, what is imagined is intricately linked with what is found: errors in the system led to a New World.

Humboldt's analyses, presented with great philological meticulousness, are also aimed at the imagined worlds to which his contemporaries at times ascribed little significance for the advancement of knowledge. For instance, he devoted himself in detail to the elements of the "géographie mythique" [mythic geography][20] that, in the fourteenth and fifteen centuries, were still present on many world maps in the shape of imaginary island worlds believed to change their location and shape; they fired the fancy of mariners and indeed led to many actual discoveries. Using the examples that others dismissed as mere mistakes and chimeras – the island of Sanborondón, the island of the holy Brendan, the island Antilia, or Lake Parime of El Dorado, the "golden king," which had existed on many maps of America for centuries – Humboldt showed the power of the imagination to inspire realities and endeavors of great consequence.

Here, errors and fiction overlap and make lies and truths into new realities not only of interest for historians. Humboldt knew how myopic it would have been to brush such cartographic data aside as "les fausses combinaisons de l'érudition classique" [the wrong application of classical scholarship],[21] and thus as mere errors. From his perspective, the mistakes were much more systematic than that and, for this reason, had to be analyzed systematically. Consequently, Alexander von Humboldt also tried to utilize the error in the system (which always fascinated him) for his own research, his own epistemology and argumentation. In what follows, I will examine exactly how this worked by using not the example of Columbus's voyage, but Humboldt's own travels in the equinoctial regions of the New Continent. In the end, these travels, the moving parts, are the foundation and actual *movens* of Humboldt's world of knowledge and science.

(No) light at the end of the cave

Alexander von Humboldt studies have barely paid any attention to the fact that most of the extraordinary (and at the same time most popular) episodes of his very successful American voyage stand under the sign of failure. Bonpland and Humboldt's famous Orinoco trip, for instance, is framed by two cave explorations, both of which "fail" in ways that have multiple significances.[22] The account of the first visit, to the Cave of Guacharo, on which Indian guides and Spanish nobles accompanied the two explorers, already calls attention, very consciously and poetically as in a *mise en abyme*, to the aporias of the Humboldtian concept of science and of the project of European modernity. Despite the massive intervention on the part of the Christian missionaries, the Indians vehemently refuse to go deeper into the cave, which, according to their "idées mystiques à cet antre habité par des oiseaux nocturnes" [mystical notions, back there, in the depths, was inhabited by the souls of their ancestors].[23]

The Europeans, who had come with their torches in order to bring light to the darkness of their research subject/object, had to realize that they were up against the limits of intercultural acceptance, even though they were there in the name of the progress of all humanity. Humboldt's travel narrative suggests unequivocally that the Indians would have vehemently resisted any further penetration into the cave by the Franco-German research team accompanied by a Spanish clergyman. The European scientific travelers had no other option but to turn back, which they did rather reluctantly: "Il fallut céder à la pusillanimité de nos guides, et retourner sur nos pas" [We had to give in to the cowardice of our guides and turn back].[24] Humboldt, no doubt, did not make the decision to turn back easily, since he had learned that a Catholic bishop, of all people, with "gros cierges de cire blanche de Castille" [thick candles made of Castilian wax],[25] had, a long time ago, gone much further into the cave than these representatives of European science on the threshold of the nineteenth century.

At the same time, Humboldt shaped this passage, replete with literary and historical-philosophical allusions, in such a way that it brings home the meeting of two different logics. The failure of the endeavor sparks critical (self-) reflection on the part of the researchers, even in the midst of their palpable anger. Here, the Europeans are confronted with the limits of a science that, though deemed "universal" even in our days, has clearly Western cultural features. And here is a fundamental error in the system of European science, which Humboldt marks emphatically in his *Relation historique du voyage aux régions équinoxiales du Nouveau Continent*.

In the second part of his allegory of the cave, Humboldt uses the example of the Cave of Ataruipe to show what consequences the knowing transgression of the limits of the principles of respect of the cultural other can have. In the second cave, the European explorers collect a number of skeletons that belong to a native tribe and that had been put to their final rest in this place. The scientifically justified prevalence of the self, which culminates "zum grössten Ärgerniss unserer india-nischen Führer" [to the great anger of our Indian guides][26] in the wrongful possession of the other's body, finally results in the irretrievable loss of the "research objects" when Humboldt's friend, the Franciscan Juan González, who accompanied some of the boxes Humboldt sent to Europe, is shipwrecked during his Atlantic crossing in 1801; it is as if the whole enterprise had been cursed. This is a shipwreck with an observer who intuits his mistake: "Wie im Vorgefühl dieses schmerzhaften Verlustes, in ernster Stimmung, entfernten wir uns von der Gruft eines untergegangenen Völkerstammes" [As if with a presentiment of this painful loss, in a grave mood, we departed from the sepulcher of a drowned tribe].[27]

That Alexander von Humboldt would revise this scene for decades in different texts is a testament not only to a great measure of personal empathy but also, above all, proves his intention to reflect upon a concrete scientific border situation and to use failure to illuminate the aporias of (one's own) scientific actions. In this way, the Cave of Ataruipe becomes the source of an error.

That Humboldt did not illuminate the depth of the cave and eschews the ready excuse that the stealing of the skeletons had produced important new insights into the history of the human species points to his unquestionable intellectual integrity. The author of *Views of Nature* was fully aware of the problematic nature of Western scientific practices and of fundamental system errors, which he repeatedly put on the literary stage. Perhaps it is in this way that his writings throw light on the back of the cave after all.

An ascent shy of the summit

Surely the most celebrated episode from the life of Alexander von Humboldt is his risky attempt at climbing the summit of Chimborazo on 23 June 1802. No other mountain has left a similar imprint on the image of the Prussian traveler as the giant volcano in today's Ecuador, which, at the time of the attempted ascent, was deemed the highest mountain in the world.[28] In his little-known dramatic prose sketch from 1837, which he revised for his *Kleinere Schriften* in 1853, Humboldt is fixated on the moment when the clouds of fog broke open and suddenly revealed the summit, just before a crevasse, a deep crevice in the rock, made the peak of this volcano forever unreachable for Aimé Bonpland, Carlos Montúfar, Alexander von Humboldt, and their companion:

> Die Nebelschichten, die uns hinderten, entfernte Gegenstände zu sehen, schienen plötzlich, trotz der totalen Windstille, vielleicht durch elektrische Processe, zu zerreissen. Wir erkannten einmal wieder, und zwar ganz nahe, den domformigen Gipfel des Chimborazo. Es war ein ernster, grossartiger Anblick.

> [The layers of fog that prevented us from seeing distant objects seemed suddenly, despite the complete calm, to break up, perhaps because of electrical processes. Once again, we beheld, and now very close to us, the dome-shaped summit of Chimborazo. It was a grave, magnificent view.][29]

The glimpse of the sublime, which was, quite in Kant's sense, attended by fright and awe, is inserted into the text fleetingly, only to disappear just as quickly. As in a Romantic painting, bizarre rock formations follow. However, in contrast to Caspar David Friedrich's well-known painting from around 1818, there is no "traveler standing above the sea of clouds" here. In other words, there is no dominating position here from which to behold (and master) that sea of clouds. In its splendor, the peak of Chimborazo seems temptingly close, only to recede immediately back into the realms of the ungraspable. In this carefully created scene, nature slips away from human mastery. Humboldt resorts once again to the rhetorical device of the *mise en abyme*, and this time quite literally: in his travel diary, it is precisely in the place where the yawning rock crevasse makes impossible any attempt to reach the summit that we find a gap in Humboldt's manuscript, into which he inserts other parts of the text. In the original French manuscript, the small two-syllable word *crevasse* opens a gigantic cleft at the two margins from pages 38 to 45. This chasm obstructs the continuation of the narrative and the ascent alike.

The true chasm of the *mise en abyme* made visible in Humboldt's diary is that it literally represents an *abyme* (or *abîme*, cleft, chasm, immeasurability) both in the text and in the written sign; it is an experimental method that might be compared to Laurence Sterne's *Tristam Shandy*. At the same time, however, the experimental character of Humboldt's writing spotlights an understanding of science that aims not at the art of mastery or domination, but at the emergence of an art of failure. It is only through this artful epistemology of failure that one can prevent epistemological failings.

The art of failure displayed with the flair of a great writer first refers to a literarily staged failing that always bears the stamp of the provisional. After Humboldt noted in his travel diary that the cleft was "mindestens 90 Toisen tief und vielleicht 10 Toisen breit" [at least 90 toises deep and perhaps 10 toises wide], he added: "Das waren unsere Säulen des Herkules" [These were our own Pillars of Hercules].[30] But the rocks of Gibraltar and Ceuta, whose edges mark the chasm that separates the European from the African coast of the Mediterranean and also mark the sea's westernmost border, did not, as Humboldt well anticipated in his *Examen critique* of the history of Western expansionism, form any permanent obstruction for human movement; after all, the Phoenicians had already gone well beyond that particular border.

The gap between the two rocks and their stony scaffolding represent, in a deeply ambivalent fashion, the markings of a border and, at the same time, the ability to surpass it. After all, Christopher Columbus had also once decisively transgressed the borderlines of the Old World, with which he had been so amply familiar. Much as the Genovese mariner's voyage of discovery was based not only on audacity and acuity but also on miscalculations and false assumptions, Humboldt knows his own endeavors not to be without their own errors. On the contrary: Alexander von Humboldt tried to make precisely those failings fruitful as a fuel for his scientific thinking and acting, for his epistemology as much as for his scientific practice.

The Humboldtian art of failure is an art of living.[31] It aims at the happiness that comes with not reaching the top, at arriving nowhere; for if one did reach one's goal, history would end. In this famed but rarely analyzed passage – analyzed, that is, from the perspective of its literary form – Humboldt celebrates an ascent without any arrival: the happiness of being always in motion, always on the move.

About the art and the happiness of never arriving anywhere

On page 85 of the fifth volume of *Kosmos*, which appeared posthumously in 1862, there is a passage of text that breaks off unexpectedly, followed by several lines of dashes and a note with the signature of the editor in brackets: "*Der Tod des grossen Autors* hat den Faden dieses Werkes abgeschnitten. S. die weiteren Worte am Ende der Anmerkungen S. 99" [The death of the great author severed the thread of the work. S(ee) the additional remarks at the end of the notes, p. 99].[32] Alexander von Humboldt had died on 6 May 1859, his "life work" having remained unfinished.

That the dashes at the end of the main text are followed by additional notes in Humboldt's own handwriting, which are also "completed" by dashes, may be more than typical of the author of *Views of Nature*, a book whose actual text was often outdone by 12 times the number of notes. Even at the very end of his life, Humboldt made further additions. Even if Eduard Buschmann added the purported final words to the effect that "*Der Tod hat den grossen Autor seinem Werke vor dessen Vollendung entrissen*" [Death has wrested the great author away from his work before its conclusion],[33] many of Humboldt's contemporaries, especially those familiar with his writings, must have been quite alert to the fact that the illustrious author, who died at the age of almost 90, had rarely ever really finished any of his works, that is, "concluded" them. Humboldt's work is a single open book.

It was not just Humboldt's *Kosmos* that was left unfinished after thousands of pages and thousands of notes.[34] The monumental 30-volume *Voyage* was but a fragment. Likewise, the fifth volume of the *Examen critique*, which appeared in January 1839 and proved that this endeavor had long surpassed the original dimensions of a mere "explication" of the *Atlas géographique et physique des régions équinoxiales du Nouveau Continent*, remained the last volume. The work, which was supposed to have been twice as long to encompass 10 octavo volumes, was not continued. Alexander von Humboldt's *Relation historique*, the actual travelogue of the American exploration, covered only one-third of the entire journey and broke off after the third volume, just as abruptly; the fourth volume, which Humboldt had announced several times, never appeared. The first edition of Humboldt's *Views of Nature* from 1808 featured a "Volume 1," yet a second volume was never published. *Views of Nature* saw a second edition in 1826 and another, once again expanded, multivolume edition in 1849, but these *Views* – quite in keeping with the book's title – had a consciously open structure, so that they could proliferate endlessly, in an almost rhizomatic manner, through incessant additions. Like the *Views* before them, Humboldt's *Kleinere Schriften* appeared without a second volume. It was announced that the (fragmented) first edition of *Fragmens de géologie et de climatologie asiatiques* from 1831 would soon be replaced by a new, revised edition; instead, however, there came the very different three volumes of *Asie Centrale*, which superseded and "crowded out" the *Fragmens*. The last volume of *Asie Centrale* ended just as abruptly as had the fifth volume of the *Examen critique* and the third of the *Relation historique*.

Was it that Alexander von Humboldt was unable to finish and really complete any book project? Did he perhaps not know, as claimed his friend Dominique François Arago, to whom the *Examen critique* is dedicated, what a book really was? Arago wrote to his Prussian friend quite bluntly: "Humboldt, tu ne sais pas comment se compose un livre; tu écris sans fin; mais ce n'est pas la un livre, c'est un portrait sans cadre" [Humboldt, you have no idea how to compose a book. You write interminably; but that is not a book; it is a portrait without a frame].[35] Was Alexander von Humboldt a writer who did not know anything about writing, who fell prey to endless writing because he was unable either to find or to construct frames for his portraits?

Arago obviously did not understand Humboldtian writing, but he did characterize it quite aptly as *écrire sans fin*, writing without an end, without a final goal or target, without conclusion. Today, it is time to discover the literary qualities of Alexander von Humboldt's writing. The inter- and transmedial structural openness of the two volumes of *Vues des Cordillères et Monumens des Peuples Indigènes de l'Amérique* is no less characteristic of Humboldt's experimental writing than the fundamental inconclusiveness of all the books he wrote during his lifetime.

If one considers the totality of Humboldt's prodigious scientific-literary production, one can see clearly to what extent the insight that everything is interrelated found its epistemological expression also, and particularly, at the level of his writing. More than seven decades of book production created a dense and dynamic network of mutually intertextual relations, within which each book has its own position; at the same time, each also has a distinctive, often experimental "style." This totality, which took Humboldt the equivalent of several generations of scientist-scholars to produce, is surely something of an intellectual biography; but it is also, simultaneously, a totality that is in continuous motion, held together not by a homogeneous structure but by a fractal one. The whole shines through in each "fragment."

It would, therefore, be a rather unproductive failure to follow Arago in perceiving an artistic failure in Humboldt's writing. Humboldt's errors are systematic. In the final analysis, the *movens* of and in the system of Humboldtian science results, at least in part, from the fact that the author of *Kosmos* neither dwelled inside an academic ivory tower nor represented a culture of perfection. Humboldt's self-criticisms were no less pronounced and pointed than his criticisms of others. In the different installments of his works, he was habitually (self-) critical (often even in the same work) toward the previously published results of his research and, from this later perspective, corrected earlier hypotheses and concrete analyses and results; at times, he even inserted lengthy passages from critics of his work into his own books.

Beyond the intellectual integrity of the admission of his own failings and errors, such a practice identifies Humboldt's own position and the state of his research as temporary and transitory, never as definitive. Precisely the mistakes and the gaps are what stimulate one's own thinking anew and put it in motion to reach for new perspectives and possibilities in one's thinking, which is something that a work regarded as complete no longer considers necessary. The mistakes are what give Humboldt's thinking ever new spurs. It is plain, from this perspective, that such a mode of thinking would have as its equivalent a way of writing that is fractal and employs the *mise en abyme* as a core principle. Unsurprisingly, Alexander von Humboldt quite consciously built into his writing contradictions and *mistakes in the weave*, with which he hoped to compel readers to think for themselves and to reassess their own positions.

In this way, Humboldt smuggled small errors into lists and accounts that, at first sight, appear logical; he added elements that "really" belonged neither to the space under discussion or even to the time period. Into his lists of the places that he himself had visited and of which he could report first hand, Humboldt frequently inserted references to places that he himself had never seen. His systematic lists in particular contain such errors in their weave, which one can easily miss in a superficial reading.

In the end, it is these small, seemingly unsound deviations, contradictions, and "mistakes" that help Alexander von Humboldt succeed in stripping his own ideas of the fixity and the schematism for which he rebuked the *idées systématiques* [systematic ideas], for instance, of the main proponents of the discourse on America, which he countered with his new discourse on the New World.[36] Cornelius de Pauw, Guillaume-Thomas Raynal, and William Robertson, whom Humboldt still considered the smartest of the historians of America,[37] believed that they could uphold sharp distinctions between "barbaric" and "civilized" nations, which is untenable upon closer inspection. Humboldt had already long found the error in their system.[38]

Humboldt loathed systematic thinking in the sense of empirically baseless abstractions that – as in the case of the *géographie systématique*[39] – merely tried to ward off all disagreement. He did not want scientific theory and practice to turn into rigid systematic thinking but to work systematically on his own scientific-scholarly flexibility and ability to move. His decade-long engagement with Christopher Columbus and the history of discovery, as well as his own experiential and imaginative knowledge, had shown Humboldt just how much mistakes and errors, as fundamental stimuli of research and scholarship, could accomplish in generating innovative knowledge.

Against the thinking in systems and schemas, and against a culture unable to admit errors in its own system, Alexander von Humboldt held out writing for which every endpoint is a new beginning; thinking that makes productive use of system errors and that bets on the chance that one will never arrive anywhere in particular. This epistemology, this *movens* of knowledge, is also the art of living.

Notes

1. Humboldt, *Examen critique*, II.27. All translations from Humboldt are by Vera M. Kutzinski.
2. Ibid., II.30.
3. Ibid.
4. Ibid., II.30–1.
5. Ibid., II.33.
6. Ibid., II.26.
7. Humboldt, *Kosmos*, I.33.
8. Humboldt, *Reise*, 358.
9. Humboldt, *Asie Centrale*, I.537.
10. Ibid., I.537.
11. See Ette, "Entdecker über Entdecker."
12. Humboldt, *Examen critique*, I.256–7.
13. Ibid., II.34.
14. Ibid., I.viii.
15. See Ette, *ZwischenWeltenSchreiben*.
16. Humboldt, *Examen critique*, I.11–2.
17. See Ibid., I.102–5.
18. See Ibid., I.106.
19. Humboldt, *Kosmos*, II.398–9.

20. Humboldt, *Examen critique*, II.163.
21. Ibid., II.162.
22. See Ette, *Weltbewusstsein*.
23. Humboldt, *Relation historique*, I.419.
24. Ibid., I.421.
25. Ibid.
26. Humboldt, *Ansichten der Natur*, 328.
27. Ibid.; see also Blumenberg, *Schiffbruch mit Zuschauer*.
28. See Preface in Humboldt, *Über einen Versuch*, 7–76.
29. Humboldt, *Kleinere Schriften*, 150; also Humboldt, *Über einen Versuch*, 142; see also 163.
30. Humboldt, *Über einen Versuch*, 96.
31. See Osten, *Die Kunst*.
32. Humboldt, *Kosmos*, V.85.
33. Ibid., V.99.
34. See Fiedler and Leitner, *Alexander von Humboldts Schriften*.
35. Humboldt, *Correspondance scientifique et littéraire*, xxxv.
36. Humboldt, *Vues des Cordillères*, 194.
37. Ibid.
38. See de Pauw, *Recherches*; Raynal, *Histoire*; and Robertson, *History*.
39. See Broc, *La Géographie des philosophes*.

References

Blumenberg, Hans. *Schiffbruch mit Zuschauer: Paradigma einer Daseinsmetaphor.* Frankfurt am Main: Surhkamp, 1979.

Broc, Numa. *La Géographie des philosophes: géographes et voyageurs français au XVIIIe siècle.* Paris: Éditions Ophrys, 1985.

Ette, Ottmar. "Entdecker über Entdecker: Alexander von Humboldt, Cristóbal Colón und die Wiederentdeckung Amerikas." In *Columbus zwischen zwei Welten: historische und literarische Wertungen aus fünf Jahrhunderten*, ed. Titus Hydenreich, 401–39. Vol. 1. Frankfurt am Main: Vervuert Verlag, 1992.

Ette, Ottmar. *Weltbewusstsein: Alexander von Humboldt und das unvollendete Project einer anderen Moderne.* Weilerwist: Velbrück Wissenschaft, 2002.

Ette, Ottmar. *ZwischenWeltenSchreiben: Literaturen ohne festen Wohnsitz.* Berlin: Kulturverlag Kadmos, 2005.

Fiedler, Horst, and Ulrike Leitner. *Alexander von Humboldts Schriften: Bibliographie der selbständig erschienenen Werke.* Berlin: Akademie Verlag, 2000.

Humboldt, Alexander von. *Ansichten der Natur mit wissenschaftlichen Erläuterungen.* Tübingen: Cotta, 1808.

Humboldt, Alexander von. *Asie Centrale: recherches sur les chaines de montagnes et al climatologie comparee.* 3 vols. Paris: Gide, 1843.

Humboldt, Alexander von. *Correspondance scientifique et littéraire.* Ed. Jean-Bernard-Marie-Alexandre Dezos de la Roquette. Vol. 1. Paris: E. Ducrocq, 1865.

Humboldt, Alexander von. *Examen critique de l'histoire de la géographie du Nouveau Continent et des progrès de l'astronomie nautique au quinzième et seizième siècles.* 5 vols. Paris: Gide, 1836–9.

Humboldt, Alexander von. *Fragmens de géologie et de climatologie asiatiques.* 2 vols. Paris: Gide, Pihan, Delaforet et Delaunay, 1831.

Humboldt, Alexander von. *Kleinere Schriften.* Vol. 1, *Geognostische und physikalische Erinnerungen.* Stuttgart: Cotta, 1853.

Humboldt, Alexander von. *Kosmos: Entwurf einer phyische Weltbeschreibung.* 5 vols. Stuttgart: Cotta, 1845–62.

Humboldt, Alexander von. *Reise auf dem Río Magdalena, durch die Anden und Mexico.* Ed. Margot Faak. Part 1. Berlin: Akademie Verlag, 1986.

Humboldt, Alexander von. *Relation historique du voyage aux régions équinoxiales du Nouveau Continent fait en 1799, 1800, 1801, 1802, 1803, et 1804 par Al. de Humboldt et A. Bonpland rédigé part Alexandre de Humboldt*. Ed. Hanno Beck. 3 vols. Stuttgart: Brockhaus, 1970. First published 1814–25.

Humboldt, Alexander von. *Über einen Versuch, den Gipfel des Chimborazo zu ersteigen*. Ed. Ottmar Ette and Oliver Lubrich. Frankfurt am Main: Eichborn Verlag, 2006.

Humboldt, Alexander von. *Vues des Cordillères et Monumens des Peuples Indigènes de l'Amérique*. Nanterre: Éditions Erasme, 1989. First published 1813.

Osten, Manfred. *Die Kunst, Fehler zu machen*. Frankfurt am Main: Suhrkamp, 2006.

Pauw, Cornelius de. *Recherches philosophiques sur les Américains, ou Mémoires intéressants pour servir a l'histoire de l'espèce humaine*. 2 vols. Berlin: Chez Georges Jacques Decker, Imprimeur Du Roi, 1768–9.

Raynal, Guillaume-Thomas. *Histoire philosophique et politique des établissements et du commerce des européens dans les deux Indes*. 3rd ed. 4 vols. Geneva: Chez Jean-Leonard Pellet, Imprimeur de la Ville et de l'Académie, 1781.

Robertson, William. *The History of America*. 2 vols. London: H. Strathan, 1777.

Skewering the Enlightenment: Alexander von Humboldt and Immanuel Kant as fictional characters

John Pizer

Recent German fiction has given an imaginative nuance to the general postmodern critique of the Enlightenment by parodying some of its leading adherents. This essay analyzes two of these works: Daniel Kehlmann's *Die Vermessung der Welt*, a fictional biography of the intertwined lives of the explorer Alexander von Humboldt and the mathematician Carl Friedrich Gauß, and Klaas Huizing's novel *Das Ding an sich*, a fantastic tale which takes a real-life episode from the life of the philosopher Johann Georg Hamann and gives it a grotesque twist in order to parody the man who first defined the Enlightenment in Germany, Immanuel Kant. For purposes of contrast, the author examines another work of Humboldt fiction that tends to valorize the Enlightenment and Humboldt's place in this movement: Christoph Hein's short story "Die russischen Briefe des Jägers Johann Seifert." The author stresses both Kant's influence on Humboldt and the antithetical trajectory of their lives at the conclusion.

Christian Stahl opens his review of Daniel Kehlmann's novel *Die Vermessung der Welt* [*Measuring the World*] (2005) by claiming that the author resorts to a well-known, reliable formula. One selects a figure prominent in German "intellectual history" ["Geistesgeschichte"] and creates literary capital from the intellectual's "eccentricity" ["Verschrobenheit"]. As examples of this tried-and-tested approach to the historical novel, Stahl cites three recent works from the vein tapped by Kehlmann: Bernhard Setzwein's novel on Nietzsche, *Nicht kalt genug* [*Not Cold Enough*] (2000); Gert Hofmann's *Die kleine Stechardin* [*The Little Flower Girl*] (1994), whose central character is the late eighteenth-century scientist and aphorist Georg Christoph Lichtenberg; and Klaas Huizing's fictional treatment of the relationship between Kant and his friend the philosopher Johann Georg Hamann in *Das Ding an sich* [*The Thing in Itself*] (1998). Stahl closes his brief review of Kehlmann's book on the scientific explorer Alexander von Humboldt and the mathematician-astronomer Carl Friedrich Gauß by congratulating the author for his entertaining and intelligent novel, and for being nominated for the inaugural German Book Prize.[1]

Though Kehlmann's novel did not win this particular prize, it did claim several other prestigious awards, such as the Candide Prize, the Heimito-von-Doderer Prize, and the Kleist Prize. It was also an enormous commercial success, staying on top of the German magazine *Spiegel*'s best-seller list for 35 weeks.[2] It is by far the most acclaimed work among the historical novels Stahl cites as profitably mining the eccentricities of well-known German intellectuals from the past. I will examine *Die*

Vermessung der Welt primarily in order to show how such caricature serves a purpose prominent in contemporary German letters: the skewering of the German Enlightenment. Prior to discussing Kehlmann's book, I will look at another, largely ignored work of Humboldt fiction: Christoph Hein's epistolary tale "Die russischen Briefe des Jägers Johann Seifert" [The Russian Letters of the Hunter Johann Seifert], part of the collection *Einladung zum Lever Bourgeois* [*Invitation to the Lever Bourgeois*] (1980), to show how Humboldt fiction can *uphold* Enlightenment discourse. I will also examine Huizing's book not only to show how another work of contemporary imaginative biography broadly calls Enlightenment values and methodologies into question, but also, at this essay's conclusion, briefly to contrast Kant's theoretical geography with Humboldt's applied Kantian treatment of this domain as reflected in Kehlmann's book.

In order to contextualize the contributions of Kehlmann and Huizing, I begin by looking at the contiguous treatment of Kant and Humboldt by the seminal twentieth-century philosopher Hans Blumenberg as paradigmatic representatives in the evolution of a key Enlightenment *movens*: theoretical curiosity.[3] As the trope of scientific curiosity divorced from both theological concerns and human emotions is a key issue in the works that are the centerpieces of this essay, Blumenberg's investigation will provide a useful background for their analysis. I precede my examination of *Die Vermessung der Welt* by looking at Hein's treatment of Humboldt through the deliberately distorted lens of his assistant Seifert. Hein's story provides a useful pendant to Kehlmann's creative look at the explorer because Hein's unusual technique allows his Humboldt, in contrast to that of Kehlmann, to emerge as a somewhat heroic exemplar of a *valorized* Enlightenment.

Blumenberg treats Kant and Humboldt as seminal figures in the development of scientific curiosity as a paradigm from the time of its subordination to theological concerns in the pre-Enlightenment, to its full realization as a discrete domain in the psychoanalytic/anthropological age characterizing the turn to the twentieth century. Blumenberg reveals the authoritarian political strain in Kant's later treatment of the problem of self-imposed lack of maturity and the regulative, rather than random, principle of knowledge when the Enlightenment is regarded as the self-preservation of reason. Kant's famous argument in the essay "Was ist Aufklärung?" [What Is Enlightenment?] (1784) presumed that such immaturity was based on one's inability to engage personal understanding without external guidance, an inability stemming from a lack of courage and decisiveness. In 1786, he comes to believe that state guidance – what Blumenberg terms "politische Nothilfe" [emergency political help][4] – is necessary to preserve order, implying that freedom of thought independent of the laws of reason destroys itself. The authoritarian streak of the late Kant is reflected in the personality with which Huizing imbues him. Kant, in Blumenberg's view, comes to face an irresolvable dilemma. Reason, driven by theoretical curiosity and thirst for knowledge, tries to comprehend the conditional from its own conditions and thereby arrives at the unconditional. However, reason cannot grasp something that, according to Kant, does not exist under the conditions of comprehensibility. This ungraspable, unknowable essence to which Blumenberg refers is the thing in itself, and the irresolvable aporia in Kantian philosophy to which he alludes is precisely the dilemma faced by Hamann, Kant, and Kant's servant Lampe, the three main characters in Huizing's novel, in confronting the physically manifest thing in itself alluded to by the book's title. Blumenberg finds that Humboldt exemplifies the type of curiosity evident in the first half of the nineteenth century which prizes scientific objectivity and accuracy. Humboldt, therefore, comes to deplore the twin tendencies increasingly evident by the middle of that century: popular curiosity, fanned by increasing media interest in scientific exploration, and enhanced state intervention into such pursuits. These are among the chief irritants that the fictional Humboldt of both Hein and Kehlmann face. In a passage cited by Blumenberg, Humboldt deplores the steering of science into the support of political dispositions and claims that he is anything but a friend of such tutelage.[5] Particularly in Hein's story, but in Kehlmann's novel as well, Humboldt is forced to chafe precisely under such state, and state-mediated, tutelage.

Einladung zum Lever Bourgeois encompasses an eclectic range of stories written and published when Hein was a citizen of the German Democratic Republic (GDR). Most have a contemporary East German setting, including one – "Der neuere (glücklichere) Kohlhaas: Bericht über einen *Rechtshandel* aus den Jahren 1972/73" [The New (More Successful) Kohlhaas: Report on a *Legal Dispute* from the Years 1972/73][6] – which adapts Kleist's tale to a modern setting in narrating a chair factory bookkeeper's relentless battle against the state to obtain 40 marks he felt were unjustly withheld from his annual incentive bonus. Hubert K.'s triumph, and the obvious disproportion between the miniscule gravity of his grievance and the effort he expends to redress it, turns Kleist's tragedy into a comedy. Two of the tales, including the collection's title story, are historical fictions featuring prominent intellectuals. "Einladung zum Lever Bourgeois"[7] shows the playwright Jean Racine as an aging, ill man, tormented by his failure to have reported a horrible crime he witnessed, committed by French soldiers, feeling that the absolutist state would have papered over an offense perpetrated by its troops against foreign (in this case, Dutch) victims. The other historical fiction in Hein's collection is "Die russischen Briefe des Jägers Johann Seifert."[8] Johann Seifert was Humboldt's valet and servant from 1827 until Humboldt's death in 1859. Indeed, Humboldt made Seifert his sole inheritor. Seifert was married when he began his service for Humboldt, and his wife helped supervise Humboldt's household.[9] Seifert accompanied Humboldt on the latter's Russian expedition, and Hein's tale consists of fictional letters written by the servant to his wife in Berlin, where the three of them lived together. Uniquely among all the authors covered in this book, Hein employs a completely colloquial eighteenth-century German diction in composing Seifert's letters from the Russian expedition.[10] Hein captures the period style so accurately that Günther Drommer, editor of the collection's East German edition, believed Seifert must have written the letters, only to discover later that nothing written by the servant remains to posterity.[11]

A man with a limited education, Hein's Seifert is naïve, chauvinistic, zealously religious, and profoundly bigoted. From the very first letter, he seems in constant despair, plagued by insects, surrounded by people and customs he does not comprehend, gullible, and utterly homesick – a homesickness enhanced by his wife's apparent failure to respond to his letters, thus arousing his suspicions. Given this circumstance, Hein clearly intends for the reader to sympathize with the forlorn servant but also to assume that his perspectives are dubious at best, particularly when Seifert reports on his disputes with Humboldt. Seifert describes his master as an unpatriotic cosmopolitan, revealing a clear dislike for Russia and Russians. Because an internationalist perspective and deference to the Russian-led Soviet Union were expected of GDR citizens, this circumstance alone would enhance

Humboldt's image there and underscore Seifert's unreliability among those East German citizens – perhaps even then a minority – whose attitudes adhered to those of their nation's leaders. Seifert alludes to Humboldt's reputation at the Sanssouci Palace as among the "reddest" of the Jacobins,[12] though he reveals that Humboldt prefers to remain silent on the extreme social injustices he observes in Russia when he believes that protests on his part might impede his scientific pursuits. Nevertheless, Humboldt comes across as a man of the Enlightenment in the most positive sense of that term: tolerant, cultivated, cosmopolitan, and a defender of the Other. Seifert reports on how, in the course of upbraiding him for his anti-Semitism, Humboldt argues that the hatred of Jews reflects the philosophy of mediocrity. The unsuccessful and the dilettante seek their salvation in denouncing the Other and the foreign. Rejected suitors call all women whores. Jews and homosexuals, in this Humboldt's view, are a favorite target of those who blame the Other for their own failures and shortcomings: "Und mit ganz besonderer Vorliebe stürze sich der Chorus dieser Kuemmerlinge auf die Männerliebe (sic!) und die Juden, um sich für sein banales, ungluekseliges Leben zu rächen" [And with special fondness this chorus of wretches pounces on manlove (sic!) and the Jews, in order to take revenge for their banal, unfortunate life]. Seifert finds Humboldt's perspective here eccentric and seems not to comprehend it.[13]

Humboldt's anti-nationalist cosmopolitanism becomes evident in his response to Seifert's question concerning how long they will have to travel through Siberia before their grasp of their mother tongue becomes little more than a distant memory:

> Er lachte, schüttelte den Kopf und antwortete, er sei, habe er nur eine LandesGrentze ueberschritten, unfähig, weiterhin ein Deutscher zu sein, und man würde im gesammten TransUral keinen national gesinnteren Sibirjaken finden als ihn. Er sei, wenn er sich auch nicht dazu verstehe, auf sein Vaterland zu verzichten, keinesfalls ein Vaterländer.

> [He laughed, shook his head and answered, he was incapable of remaining a German once a national border was crossed, and one would find in the entire Trans-Urals a no more nationally oriented Siberiack than he was. While he would never agree to renounce his fatherland, he was absolutely not a fatherlander.]

He goes on to note that one can forget one's own language comfortably at home; a trip is not suitable for such purposes.[14] Through the veil of Seifert's colloquial eighteenth-century German diction, Humboldt emerges as both possessed of sardonic humor and as a true citizen of the world. Particularly the former quality is completely lacking in the figure Kehlmann represents, and precisely this deficiency in *Die Vermessung der Welt* makes Humboldt seem relentlessly Prussian, mitigating the attribute of a dynamic transatlantic globalism that contemporary scholarship has discovered in his work and in his person. This explains the negative reception of Kehlmann's novel by academics such as Ottmar Ette, discussed below, though I will argue that Humboldt's cosmopolitanism is nevertheless evident in the portrayal of the explorer in *Die Vermessung der Welt*.

Humboldt has been assumed by many commentators, then and now, to have been a homosexual. Hein's Seifert alludes to these rumors in the narrative, though he categorically denies them.[15] At any rate, Humboldt is not victimized by such rumors in the tale, but rather by the sort of political interventions into his scientific expeditions and experiments which Blumenberg regarded as a hallmark of his later years, and about which he cites complaints in Humboldt's writing.[16] Hein's

Humboldt, however, is quite adroit at minimizing the impact of this state interference, and not solely by turning a blind eye to the oppression he witnesses. As Marianne Krumrey observes in analyzing the story, Humboldt makes use of the narrow-mindedness and infantilism of the Czarist bureaucrats and military officials in order to appease them, holding their mistrust in check even though the courtiers and petty state officials, motivated by jealousy, resentment, and a hatred of intellectual, creative endeavor, continuously make his life difficult.[17] Through the filter of Seifert's letters, Humboldt's contempt for such figures becomes clear; they are poisonous toads ["Kröten"] who give vent to their own spleen by hiding their malicious intent behind a veneer of sanctimonious moral and political pretence.[18] Like all GDR authors who dared veer from socialist realist orthodoxy, Hein had to deal with such state servants as well, and his identification with Humboldt in this regard is obvious.[19] But Humboldt is not merely the target of Russian jealousy in the story. The mineralogist Gustav Rose, who accompanied Humboldt on his Russian expedition, complains to Seifert that courtiers such as Humboldt, Goethe, and Schelling are anxious to sit "in the shadows of power," in contrast to "modest gardeners" such as himself who must content themselves with useful but more modest accomplishments.[20] In spite of his political expediency, Hein's Humboldt emerges through the filter of Seifert's letters as a thoroughly sympathetic Enlightenment figure, a misunderstood victim of those who resent the genius.

Kehlmann's *Die Vermessung der Welt* contains a chapter that includes an account of Humboldt's journey to Russia. Indeed, it is the novel's penultimate episode, in which both Humboldt and Gauß make their final appearance. The denouement narrates the voyage of Gauß's son Eugene to America, the result of a forced exile after he is arrested at a rally featuring an agitator in the mold of German nationalist Turnvater Jahn. Kehlmann's treatment of the Russian expedition, like Hein's story, features the mineralogist Rose and the zoologist Christian Ehrenberg (who also accompanied the historical Humboldt's trip to the Russian Far East), though Seifert himself is never mentioned. As is typical in *Die Vermessung der Welt*, and unlike in Hein's story, the narration of the Russian expedition is suffused with a comic nuance at once subtle and ribald, as when a Kalmyck Buddhist lama pats his substantial abdomen as a sign of his inner strength, then touches Humboldt's more meager chest and proclaims: "Aber da sei nichts. Wer das nicht verstehe, werde rastlos, laufe durch die Welt wie der Sturm, erschüttere alles und wirke nicht" [But there is nothing there. Whoever doesn't understand that becomes restless, runs through the world like the storm, upsetting everything and effecting nothing]. The perplexed Humboldt replies that he doesn't believe in nothing, but in the fullness and richness of nature, and assumes that there is a translation problem when the lama claims, in turn, that nature is unredeemed and breathes despair.[21] This brief exchange reveals the antithetical perspectives of Hein and Kehlmann with respect to Humboldt as an Enlightenment figure. Through the confused filter of Seifert's letters, Humboldt emerges as a shrewd, albeit calculating, champion of Enlightenment scientific progress, rationality, and tolerance, while it is Kehlmann's Humboldt who is obviously confused, displaying the limits of Enlightenment rationality in comprehending a culture radically at variance with that of contemporary Western Europe.

While Hein's epistolary tale derives entirely from Humboldt's Russian expedition, *Die Vermessung der Welt* can be described as a rather unique double *Bildungsroman*, for its initial chapters alternately narrate the non-contiguous childhood, education, and personal and career development of Humboldt and Gauß. The two men do not meet until some two-thirds of the way through the novel, when Humboldt succeeds in persuading Gauß to travel from his home in Göttingen for a court reception in Berlin, where Humboldt resides after 1827. At times, Gauß is shown to follow Humboldt's adventures as they are related by newspaper accounts. Kehlmann employs a somewhat dialectical approach in narrating the lives of the two scientists. This dialectical effect is achieved by alternating chapters until well into the novel, devoted exclusively to one or the other of the two scientists in their early lives, which show them to be virtually antithetical in their personal make-up, experiences, and proclivities. The polarities in their personas continue to be evident even after they meet. To be sure, both suffer somewhat brutal childhoods – Gauß through his alcoholic father and a grammar school teacher who treats him with the same cruelty (until he discovers Gauß's genius) he employs with the other lower-class children, and Humboldt through his older brother Wilhelm, portrayed as a sadist who tries to lure Alexander to his death on two occasions. Disappointed that he cannot become a Latin scholar, Gauß follows his mathematical calling somewhat reluctantly. He develops into a passionate, earthy man who comes close to suicide when his eventual wife spurns his first proposal of marriage and he expects the same result the second time around; he is on the verge of poisoning himself with a substance Humboldt is investigating on his South American explorations when her consent arrives by mail. He detests travel, his work as a surveyor, and his pedagogical duties as a Göttingen professor who must teach mathematics to students who cannot grasp even simple principles. Humboldt, by contrast, is entirely devoted to "measuring the world" in South America and the Caribbean. Kehlmann portrays him as so single-minded in his pursuit of scientific verity that he is virtually devoid of personal needs and seemingly asexual. Neither a young girl nor a young boy sent on different occasions to his dwelling are capable of seducing him, though he is somewhat excited by the latter and, late in the book, admits to his homosexual inclinations. While he deplores human and natural exploitation and slavery in the abstract, even affronting American President Jefferson's foreign minister James Madison by speaking of the "Alpdruck der Sklaverei" [nightmare of slavery] before Madison hints at the president's slave holdings,[22] he seems oblivious to individual suffering. To the astonishment of his assistant and traveling companion, Aimé Bonpland, whom Humboldt periodically upbraids for seeking to fulfill the appetite he shares with Gauß, Humboldt does not realize that a screaming adolescent girl they come across was the victim of rape, believing she must be lost and suffering from the heat.[23]

Kehlmann casts Humboldt as an almost blind adherent of the Enlightenment, with his zealous belief in reason and his conviction that geographical domains only become real once they have been measured and their coordinates determined.[24] Gauß, by contrast, believes that such measurements rob the natural world of its corporeal facticity and comes to perceive that his surveying activity does not merely measure tracts of land but invents them.[25] Though Humboldt's measuring mania takes him around the world, from Spain to the Americas and later to Russia, while Gauß stays at home in pursuing his mathematical, astronomic, and surveying activities, Kehlmann clearly intends us to regard Gauß as the true forerunner of scientific modernism. As Mark Anderson has observed in an essay on Kehlmann, Humboldt's belief in the universality of time and space is shown to be in error and he works with outmoded media not adapted to the terrain he explores, while Gauß, with his postulate on "curved space," is shown to establish the foundation for the contemporary scientific perception of the world.[26] Thus, when Humboldt claims that "understanding" ["der Verstand"] forms natural laws, and Gauß replies that this is old Kantian nonsense – "Der Verstand forme gar nichts und verstehe wenig. Der Raum biege und die Zeit dehne sich" [Understanding forms nothing and understands little. Space curves and time expands][27] – it is clear that Kehlmann's sympathies lie with Gauß's anti-Kantian, anti-Enlightenment perspective.

In Acapulco, Humboldt, while lying on his back and looking at the heavens through a telescope (he is clearly more comfortable with the popular press than the Humboldt of Blumenberg or Hein), tells a journalist that a precise atlas of New Spain will promote the settlement of the colony and the domination of nature.[28] The image of Humboldt lying on his back with the telescope, not ceasing to survey the heavens even as he talks to a reporter, adds a tone of levity to his advocacy of the Enlightenment's telos of dominion over nature and indigenous people. The contemporary reader is expected to recognize this utterance as portending the global ecological catastrophe humanity faces in the twenty-first century. As Heinz-Peter Preußer has argued, the phenomenal popularity of *Die Vermessung der Welt* stems from Kehlmann's ability to turn an ambience of future chiliastic decline from tragedy to comedy, creating a classical critique of civilization by selling it as a "means to pleasure" ["Genussmittel"].[29] Kehlmann's Humboldt is the Enlightenment personified, progressive with respect to issues such as slavery and individual liberty but tone deaf with respect to social and cultural nuances, as when (in an entirely fictitious episode) he buys South American slaves, gives them their freedom, and is surprised when they simply do not know what to do next.[30] Humboldt's desire to make nature productive by measuring and dominating it, setting the stage for future environmental catastrophe, is a major element in Kehlmann's humor-laced, anti-Enlightenment polemic.

Clearly, the image of Humboldt as a caricatured Enlightenment visionary, enhanced through dialectical contrast with the skeptical Gauß figure in Kehlmann's novel, does not necessarily do justice to the historical Humboldt. Tang Chenxi has argued persuasively that Humboldt was profoundly impacted by Romantic convictions concerning the landscape of mood and convinced that an immersion in landscape painting and poetry furthered the study of nature, even though his ultimate aim was objective truth and a "universally valid scientific gaze" that could be extended to any geographic region.[31] Thus, a comic high point in *Die Vermessung der Welt*, Humboldt's translation of Goethe's celebrated poem – which begins with the line "Über allen Gipfeln" [Over all the hilltops] – into a literalizing Spanish,[32] certainly would never have been conceived by the landscape-poetry-loving historical Humboldt. Of course, as a creative writer, Kehlmann had to be free to take liberty with the true nature of historical personages such as Humboldt and Gauß, as with broader historical facts themselves. Kehlmann eloquently defended the liberties he takes in *Die Vermessung der Welt* in his essay "Wo ist Carlos Montúfar?" [Where Is Carlos Montúfar?], an appropriate title since this traveling companion of Humboldt in South America is nowhere mentioned in the novel. The key point here is that Kehlmann draws on his poetic license with respect to Humboldt with the goal of creating a pointed, but humorous, Enlightenment caricature.

In a recent book, Ottmar Ette takes Kehlmann to task for distorting Humboldt by making him appear as a humorless adherent of the Enlightenment. Like Tang

Chenxi, Ette emphasizes that the explorer was deeply attuned to the literary sensibilities of his time, a circumstance Kehlmann's novel ignores. Ette argues that, in creating his image of Humboldt, Kehlmann drew on clichéd representations of the explorer, such as Friedrich Schiller's 1797 letter to Christian Gottfried Körner claiming that Humboldt's thinking was marked by pure unadorned reason, shameless in its surveying of nature. Ette indicates that Kehlmann preferred to draw on anecdotal remarks about Humboldt, such as Schiller's, rather than examining his actual oeuvre. Ette regrets that the cosmopolitan, emancipatory character of Humboldt's perspective is masked by *Die Vermessung der Welt*, and claims that it is time to discover this strain in Humboldt's world view by renewed attention to the works themselves.[33] One might argue that passages such as the explorer's dialogue with Madison actually allow his progressive, cosmopolitan thought to emerge. While Ette is fundamentally correct in his analysis of Kehlmann's sources and about the one-sided caricature the novelist draws, it is also important to remember that Humboldt is only the secondary target of his satire; through his humorous treatment of this figure and his contrast with Gauß, the Enlightenment itself becomes the primary object of the novel's ridicule.

The issue of the historical Humboldt's relationship to the Enlightenment is a rather vexed one. In his comprehensive overview of Humboldt's reception from 1848 to the present day, Nicolaas Rupke has shown that the explorer/scientist has been appropriated by various political and social groups according to their own ideological needs. For example, the National Socialists ignored the strong impact of the Berlin Enlightenment, including that of its Jewish adherents such as Moses Mendelssohn, on the shaping of Humboldt's thought. The Nazis twisted Humboldt into the adherent of an irrationalist strain of German idealism that they wished to cultivate in its modern form. The intellectuals of the GDR, by contrast, saw him as a champion of the progressive humanist thinking they associated with the French Revolution and the European Enlightenment.[34] Not surprisingly, this latter Humboldt is predominant in Hein's configuration of the man who emerges through the filter of Seifert's letters, with some exceptions. For example, he argues strongly against the rationalist technique of stuffing young students with knowledge, which he feels dulls their sensibility. Here, Humboldt boasts that he himself was a virtually unschooled child up to the age of 18, whom teachers saw as quite unpromising; his own early education was "naturhaft" [grounded in nature].[35] Humboldt thus appears to be an advocate of Rousseau's pedagogy, a pedagogy, of course, which had a seminal influence on the development of European Romantic thought. Seifert also cites Humboldt's advocacy for the progressive Young Germany movement in the 1830s, a movement that the servant associates with "JiddenBengel" [Jewish scoundrels].[36] On the other hand, as in Kehlmann's novel, Hein's Humboldt advocates human domination of nature,[37] revealing a negative Enlightenment tendency. Michael Dettelbach has noted that "like the historiography of natural science itself, historical assessments of Alexander von Humboldt have ever been pulled between the two poles of empiricism and idealism, Enlightenment and Romanticism,"[38] and that Humboldt's scientific work not only encompasses the priorities of both movements but highlights certain affinities between them. His argument is quite convincing, and it is safe to say that Hein's portrait of Humboldt is more nuanced in this regard than Kehlmann's.

Kehlmann's Humboldt is an avowed Kantian. Early in his travels with Bonpland, he catches the Frenchman in flagrante with a woman, and in upbraiding him for this deed, he asks him if he has never read Kant.[39] Shortly after completing his magnum opus, the *Disquisitiones Arithemeticae* as a young man, Gauß journeys to Königsberg to visit the famous philosopher, to whom he delivers a copy of the *Disquisitiones*. He explains in detail the book's complex hypothesis, and Kant's immediate response is to ask his servant Lampe to purchase some "sausages and stars" ["Wurst und Sterne"]. Realizing the hunched figure before him is an utterly senile old man, Gauß takes polite leave from Lampe and hears the song of male voices. Lampe says that this is the prisoners' choir, which always disturbs his master.[40] In creating this episode, Kehlmann may have drawn on Huizing's *Das Ding an sich*, where Kant's annoyance at the Königsberg prisoners' choir also comes up. Though Huizing's Kant is not the senile dwarf found in Kehlmann's novel, this definer of the Enlightenment also cuts a rather ridiculous figure (along with Lampe and Hamann) as one of Huizing's three chief protagonists. The "thing in itself" is a clay shard proffered to Hamann by a Russian courier in London. The Russian not only does not demand compensation for this mysterious artifact, but pays Hamann to take it off his hands because it has brought himself and his nation bad luck. He claims that the impression found on the shard is the handprint of the biblical Adam, who thereby sealed a pact with the devil. This Hamann is clearly naïve; he had been taken advantage of several times on his way to London from Riga and then in England's capital itself. Given his credulity and the debt he has incurred through this unfortunate trait, it is unsurprising that he agrees to the bargain with the Russian. A humorously ponderous prologue to the novel establishes that the shard had been found in Kant's tomb, along with his skull, by early forensic anthropologists who had wanted to study the skull to see if it could reveal the secret of Kant's genius. The fictitious narrator had come across the report of their findings, and, obsessed with discovering the truth behind the shard, he traces its progress from the time Hamann obtained it in London. The circumstance that the "thing in itself" is a physical object already parodies Kant's abstract signifier for the earth's phenomena, the noumenal essence of which cannot be grasped by humanity.

It soon becomes apparent to Hamann that the shard is indeed a sort of bad luck charm which seems responsible for his lack of personal and professional success. Prior to traveling to Königsberg, he describes the object in a letter to Kant as a "Skandalon" [snare] that he accepted from the "confused" elderly Russian (who mysteriously disappears into thin air once Hamann accepts the bargain) as an act of Christian charity. This explanation indicates that the seemingly guileless Hamann, who really needed the money, is also capable of duplicity.[41] In Königsberg, Hamann turns to Kant in the hope that the genius can rid him of the object, and the philosopher employs his servant, Lampe, to destroy the obviously durable shard by means of modern science, thereby also hoping to cure his brilliant friend of his apparent superstition. Indeed, Kant accuses Hamann of having become a religious fanatic and, in admonishing him, sings the praises of reason, virtue, and a belief in the progress of humanity.[42] Thus, Huizing's Kant constitutes the perfect Enlightenment role model for Kehlmann's Humboldt, who unwaveringly acts according to these dictates and tacitly admonishes men like Bonpland to do the same. Lampe, however, who seems a model of Prussian military rectitude, reflecting his career as a soldier in service to that country prior to his employment with Kant, fails in his missions to destroy the clay shard. Instead, Lampe himself is injured in these attempts, and they later bring misfortune to some of the individuals who used the most advanced contemporary scientific techniques to rid Hamann of the object. These techniques include electrocution through channeled lightening, steam cooking, artificially induced freezing, and an animal magnetism ceremony conducted by its celebrated inventor, Franz Mesmer. Hamann himself takes part in the journey to Braunschweig and the mesmerization procedure. All these undertakings fail to annihilate the ancient relic. Finally, an aesthetic approach in the form of a glass harmonica adagio composed and performed by Hamann, with hummed accompaniment by all three of the novel's chief protagonists, splits the shard into two pieces. But when Kant later discovers the object as a once again seamlessly reunified entity, he arranges on his deathbed, surreptitiously through his maid, to have it placed in his coffin prior to his burial. Between the chapters narrating the adventures of Hamann, Lampe, and the "thing in itself," Huizing inserts letters – primarily correspondence between Hamann and the physiognomist Johann Casper Lavater – in which Hamann reveals the arc of an increasing estrangement from Kantian philosophy and toward the mystically tinged anti-Enlightenment sensual linguistics that the historical Hamann indeed developed. Lavater's responses gradually reveal the mysterious history of the shard.

Gauß and Hamann do not have a great deal in common historically, and they cut quite disparate figures in the respective novels by Kehlmann and Huizing. Kehlmann's Gauß is a committed scientist who is able to establish a relatively stable life in Göttingen professionally, financially, and personally, despite the unhappiness that stresses and changes in all these domains cause him. Hamann, by contrast, is a rather unstable, itinerant philosopher who, goaded by his correspondence with Lavater, increasingly immerses himself in a seeming religious obscurantism, unthinkable for the Göttingen scientist, who tends toward both skepticism and scientific prophecy. Nevertheless, the fictional Gauß and Hamann play similar roles as everyman-like foils to their seemingly soulless, emotionally stunted counterparts, Humboldt and Kant, respectively. This character contrast in both novels enhances the anti-Enlightenment tenor in these works, because Humboldt and Kant come across as exaggerated specimens of unfeeling Enlightenment rationalism. This is particularly the case with respect to sexuality. Gauß, Hamann, and indeed the novels' respective chief "servant" or assistant figures, Bonpland and Lampe, emerge as relatively sensual, passionate men, and the portrayals of their relationships with women, while tinged by humor, are clearly designed to evoke empathetic identification on the part of the reader. Humboldt's homosexuality is revealed rather late in Kehlmann's novel,[43] though there are earlier hints. For the most part, he seems impervious to sensuality, or annoyed by it, when he finds Bonpland giving in to temptation. Kant, whom Humboldt cites in one of his admonitions to the Frenchman, is portrayed in *Das Ding an sich* as completely asexual. Indeed, the prologue, which parodies the scientific veneer of nineteenth-century phrenology, draws on one of the studies of Kant's skull to describe it as exhibiting both a dominant tendency toward "Vernünftigkeit" – an exaggerated propriety and rationalism – and a correspondingly extreme lack of development with respect to libido.[44] Huizing's Kant fully lives up to this phrenological report. In this respect, Kehlmann and Huizing employ similar character dialectics in the service of skewering the Enlightenment.

The Adamic shard driving the plot of *Das Ding an sich* almost literally embodies the impossibility of scientific reason's attempt to arrive at the unconditional through its own conditions, the aporia Blumenberg locates at the core of Kant's somatology. In yet another variation on the novel's employment of the corporeal in undercutting the Enlightenment, the shard as an irreducible and indestructible physical essence is seen to inspire the turn toward a sensual linguistics by the former Enlightenment adherent Hamann. Huizing uses a fictional device to motivate an intellectual transformation that the historical Hamann actually experienced. Indeed, with the exception of the fabulous shard, Huizing's delineation of Hamann's religious conversion in London closely follows the historical record, with a couple of notable exceptions. In both cases, Hamann was in London at the behest of Christoph Berens, also a friend of Kant, with whom Kant later tried to win Hamann back to Enlightenment rationalism. The historical Hamann did engage in a mission involving a Russian diplomatic official, though the nature of that mission, even whether it was mainly a political or commercial undertaking, remains unknown. As in *Das Ding an sich*, the historical Hamann, who enjoyed playing the lute, spent considerable time in London socializing with a professional lute player, but he broke off this relationship when his patron's homosexual activities became evident. In substantial debt and in poor health, Hamann isolated himself and intensely studied the Bible, resulting in his conversion to a form of Christianity somewhat tinged by Pietism. In *Das Ding an sich*, this new-found religiosity leads Hamann immediately to doubts concerning human progress and "proud" reason.[45]

Huizing's decision to have Hamann's initial response to his epiphany manifest itself as a refutation of Enlightenment reason, with its embrace of teleological human progress, underscores the anti-Enlightenment polemic inherent in his book. In their analyses of the London conversion, Hamann scholars James O'Flaherty and John Betz emphasize the intensely personal nature of his experience and the productive spur to the lyrical and philosophical writing it brought into being; but they do not suggest that its immediate result was a refutation of Enlightenment thought.[46] Huizing also employs poetic license in implying that Lavater had a significant role in the development of Hamann's theological perspectives. At the conclusion to his book, Huizing notes that: "Die Briefe sind Centonen aus Briefen und häufig freie Erfindungen" [The letters are centos from letters and frequently free inventions].[47] An example of such an approach can be seen in briefly comparing the novel's third "fliegender Brief" [flying roll], in which Hamann, among other things, attempts to ascertain the constitution of reason on the basis of Kantian doctrine, with its initial primary source, Hamann's letter to Lavater dated 18 January 1778. Some passages are virtually identical, as when Hamann notes a correspondence between Lavater's expressed need for courage in the face of an overwhelming burden created by the many tasks he faces and his own loss of courage under the burden of his idleness and boredom.[48] However, while Kant is nowhere mentioned in the original letter, Huizing uses the third "fliegender Brief" as the occasion to have Hamann praise Kant's attempt in the *Kritik der reinen Vernunft* [*Critique of Pure Reason*] (1781) to establish the sensual basis of all knowledge, while claiming, in rhetorical questions contra Kant, that even reason is dependent on language, and that such reason is perhaps still too "proud."[49] Of course, in evoking this key difference in the philosophies of the two men, Huizing adheres to intellectual history. Hamann did diverge from his friend in seeing the human capacity for reason as linked to the sensual imagery of rational language, and Kantian metaphysics as denuding language of its connection to the concrete, factual world.[50]

While the narrative in *Das Ding an sich* of Hamann's London sojourn largely adheres to history, and the letters, as Huizing himself notes, are a mélange of quotations, paraphrases from various sources, and pure invention, the body of the text, in which the shard and the attempts to destroy it are the centerpiece, is obviously the product of the author's imagination. In setting the stage for the shard adventures, Huizing maneuvers fact and fiction in a manner designed to heighten the effectiveness of the novel's anti-Enlightenment exposition. After Hamann's return to Königsberg, the historical Berens and Kant made two attempts to undo his conversion and win him back to Enlightenment ideals. These meetings inspired Hamann to write his most famous treatise, the "Sokratische Denkwürdigkeiten" [Socratic Memorabilia] (1759). Its subtitle concludes with the dedicatory missive "An Niemand und an Zween" [To Nobody and (the) Twain] and this "twain" consists of Berens and Kant.[51] As Betz remarks, Hamann's "message to them, wrapped behind many veils and symbolic allusions was simple: he was not to be reconverted to the ideals of the Enlightenment."[52] Huizing makes this work and its immediate successors the product of the walk during which Kant accuses his new friend of having become a religious fanatic and praises virtue, reason, and human progress.[53]

Huizing does not allude to the "simple message" in the "Sokratische Denkwürdigkeiten" as summarized by Betz. To have done so would have undermined the efficacy of the shard adventures in making such a reconversion impossible, for it is the shard that brings about the defeat of science and the Enlightenment, and the concomitant victory of art and emotion. This becomes evident with particular vividness in the chapter "Das Rohe und das Gekochte" [The Raw and the Cooked], an obvious allusion to the book with this title by structural anthropologist Claude Lévi-Strauss. The steam machine not only fails to damage the shard, but scalds Lampe's arm and is itself nearly destroyed in the process. It is made to sing. The result shocks the French team who attempt the pulverization and causes one of them, Jacques, to break into poetry. The shard's supernatural power confounds Enlightenment science and produces an aesthetic moment evocative of powerful feelings.[54] Ultimately, the shard inspires Hamann's own lyrical profusion, transforms him into the "vociferous" critic of Kant, and the "Seher der radikalen Aufklärung" [seer of the radical Enlightenment].[55] Spurred by Hamann's negative review of his *Kritik der reinen Vernunft*, Kant reverts to his typical coldness by allowing his relationship with this friend to taper off, despite the emotional bond the two shared in the wake of Hamann's successful musical undertaking, which temporarily split the shard in half.[56] Near the novel's conclusion, Kant orders his maid to weave the shard, hidden in a little packet, into his burial shroud, and then dies, "preußisch, müde und lebenssatt" [Prussian, tired, and fed up with life].[57] The contrast between the weary, resigned, expiring Kant and the revitalized Hamann evokes a victory of art over science, sensuality over abstraction, the "radical" Enlightenment over the "rational" Enlightenment. Huizing uses his fabulous Adamic shard to shatter Kantian reason and metaphysical idealism. *Das Ding an sich* closes with an ironic epilogue suggesting that perhaps someday science might develop a method for the shard's ultimate destruction, for which the scholarly narrator already has an idea.[58] The Enlightenment dream of domination over nature and mystery, which the narrator's remark reveals, is shown to transcend history.

In *Die Vermessung der Welt*, as we have seen, Kehlmann portrays Humboldt as Kantian in his perspectives, and most scholars agree that Kant's articulation of the domain of physical geography had a seminal influence on the explorer. Tang Chenxi provides a useful summary of Kant's chief tenets concerning physical geography: it should be strongly informed by contemporary climate theory; it should provide the educated public with practical and applicable insights into the globe's geographic constitution; and it should organize the knowledge it attains into a holistic totality. While organizing geographic space, the geographer remains detached from the object of his structuring endeavors. This allows for "man's theoretical as well as practical mastery of nature."[59] As I have observed, the Kantian goal of dominion over the natural world is the primary telos inspiring the Humboldt of Kehlmann's novel to undertake his dangerous expeditions. According to Hanno Beck, Humboldt's lifelong organization of geography into three discrete frames of reference – the concrete-systematic, the historical, and the chronological – was derived from Kant.[60] Nevertheless, Huizing's book underscores how Kant's adventures in space and time remained at the theoretical level; his famous unwillingness to travel beyond the town of Königsberg is a tacit theme in the novel. Only Lampe and Hamann venture beyond the town's confines in their quest to overcome the shard. Kehlmann's Humboldt, on the other hand, is shown to be an inveterate globetrotter; he is the man who puts Kant's theoretical cosmopolitanism and geographic mastery of nature into practice. While Kehlmann's Humboldt is not the tolerant and good-humored man of the world portrayed by Hein, *Die Vermessung der Welt* does show Humboldt to be the premier globalist *avant la lettre*, the role that has garnered him such high esteem in contemporary Atlantic studies.

Notes

1. Stahl, "Amazon-de. – Rezension."
2. Preußer, "Zur Typologie der Zivilisationskritik," 73.
3. See Blumenberg, *Der Prozeß*.
4. Ibid., 252.
5. Ibid., 256–7.
6. Hein, *Einladung zum Lever Bourgeois*, 82–103.
7. Ibid., 5–27.
8. Ibid., 104–83.
9. See Kellner, *Alexander von Humboldt*, 112, 225–7.
10. A recent detailed summary of Humboldt's Russian expedition is provided by Ette, *Alexander von Humboldt*, 319–64.
11. See Drommer, "Typische Bemerkungen," 187.
12. Hein, *Einladung zum Lever Bourgeois*, 122.
13. Ibid., 139–40.
14. Ibid., 110–1.
15. See ibid., 137, 145–6.
16. Blumenberg, *Der Prozeß*, 256–7.

17. See Krumrey, "Gegenwart," 144.
18. Hein, *Einladung zum Lever Bourgeois*, 180–1.
19. Such allusions to Hein's contemporary GDR in the tale have been noted by Fischer, who accurately claims that Hein's Humboldt "is faced with problems which simultaneously concretize the historical situation and make allusion to the present" – a GDR present marked by spying, all-encompassing state propaganda, and a repression of sexual behavior not in line with state mores. See Fischer, "*Einladung zum Lever Bourgeois*," 130.
20. Hein, *Einladung zum Lever Bourgeois*, 136.
21. Kehlmann, *Die Vermessung der Welt*, 285–6.
22. Ibid., 212–3.
23. See ibid., 104–5.
24. See, for example, ibid., 135–6.
25. Ibid., 268.
26. Anderson, "Der vermessende Erzähler," 64.
27. Kehlmann, *Die Vermessung der Welt*, 220.
28. Ibid., 196.
29. See Preußer, "Zur Typologie der Zivilisationskritik," 76–7.
30. Kehlmann, *Die Vermessung der Welt*, 70–1.
31. Tang Chenxi, *Geographic Imagination of Modernity*, 83–4, 197–8.
32. Goethe's poem, titled "Ein Gleiches" [Sameness] (1780), a pendant to "Wanderers Nachtlied" [Wanderer's Song at Night] (1776) and sometimes referred to as "Wanderers Nachtlied II," is one of the most famous poems in the German language. It reads as follows: "Über allen Gipfeln / Ist Ruh, / In allen Wipfeln / Spürest du / Kaum einen Hauch; / Die Vögelein schweigen im Walde. / Warte nur, balde / Ruhest du auch" (Goethe, *Gedenkausgabe*, 69). A possible translation would be: "Over all the hilltops / Is rest, / In all the treetops / You feel / Hardly a breath; / The little birds are silent in the forest. / Only wait / Soon you too will rest." In *Die Vermessung der Welt*, Humboldt's literalizing Spanish version is "translated" by the narrator into an equivalent German, provoking astonishment among Humboldt's auditors: "Oberhalb aller Bergspitzen sei es still, in den Bäumen kein Wind zu fühlen, auch die Vögel seien ruhig, und bald werde man tot sein" [Above all the mountain peaks it is still, in the trees there is no wind to be felt, also the birds are quiet, and soon one will be dead] (Kehlmann, *Die Vermessung der Welt*, 128).
33. See Ette, *Alexander von Humboldt*, 302–18.
34. See Rupke, *Alexander von Humboldt*, esp. 88–91, 116, 123, 138.
35. Hein, *Einladung zum Lever Bourgeois*, 163.
36. Ibid., 170.
37. Ibid., 150.
38. Dettelbach, "Alexander von Humboldt," 9.
39. Kehlmann, *Die Vermessung der Welt*, 48.
40. Ibid., 95–7.
41. Huizing, *Das Ding an sich*, 52–3.
42. Ibid., 55.
43. See Kehlmann, *Die Vermessung der Welt*, 264.
44. Huizing, *Das Ding an sich*, 14–5.
45. Ibid., 48.
46. See O'Flaherty, *Johann Georg Hamann*, 21–5; Betz, *After Enlightenment*, 29–32.
47. Huizing, *Das Ding an sich*, 237.
48. The passage in Hamann's collected letters reads as follows: "Sie beten um Muth, nicht unter der Last der Geschäfte zu sinken – und mir vergeht aller Muth, unter der Last langer Weile" [You pray for courage not to sink under the burden of tasks – and I am losing all courage under the burden of idleness] (Hamann, *Briefwechsel*, 3). Huizing modifies this line only slightly in *Das Ding an sich*: "Sie beten in Ihrem letzten Brief um Mut, nicht unter der Last der Geschäfte zu versinken – und mir vergeht aller Mut unter der Last langer Weile" [You pray in your last letter for courage not to sink to the bottom under the burden of tasks – and I am losing all courage under the burden of idleness] (119).
49. Huizing, *Das Ding an sich*, 121–2.

50. Metzke, "Kant und Hamann"; O'Flaherty, *Johann Georg Hamann*, 82–6.
51. Hamann, "Sokratische Denkwürdigkeiten."
52. Betz, *After Enlightenment*, 37.
53. Huizing, *Das Ding an sich*, 55.
54. Ibid., 114–6.
55. Ibid., 214–6.
56. Ibid., 209–11, 219.
57. Ibid., 229.
58. Ibid., 234.
59. Tang Chenxi, *Geographic Imagination of Modernity*, 100.
60. Beck, *Alexander von Humboldt*, 60–1. Citing Beck, among others, Tang Chenxi notes that Kant's ideas concerning geography influenced Humboldt (*Geographic Imagination of Modernity*, 276n2).

References

Anderson, Mark M. "Der vermessende Erzähler: mathematische Geheimnisse bei Daniel Kehlmann." *Text und Kritik*, no. 177 (2008): 58–67.

Beck, Hanno. *Alexander von Humboldt*. Vol. 1. Wiesbaden: Franz Steiner, 1959.

Betz, John R. *After Enlightenment: The Post-Secular Vision of J.G. Hamann*. Oxford: Wiley-Blackwell, 2009.

Blumenberg, Hans. *Der Prozeß der theoretischen Neugierde*. Frankfurt am Main: Suhrkamp, 1973.

Dettelbach Michael. "Alexander von Humboldt between Enlightenment and Romanticism." In "Alexander von Humboldt's Natural History Legacy and its Relevance for Today." Special issue, *Northeastern Naturalist* 8, no. 1 (2001): 9–20.

Drommer, Günther, ed. "Typische Bemerkungen zu untypischen Texten." In *Einladung zum Lever Bourgeois*, by Christoph Hein, 185–90. Berlin: Aufbau, 1980.

Ette, Ottmar. *Alexander von Humboldt und die Globalisierung: das Mobile des Wissens*. Frankfurt am Main: Insel, 2009.

Fischer, Bernd. "*Einladung zum Lever Bourgeois*: Christoph Hein's First Prose Collection." In *Studies in GDR Culture and Society 4: Selected Papers from the Ninth New Hampshire Symposium on the German Democratic Republic*, ed. Margy Gerber, Alexander Stephan, Duncan Smith, Volker Gransow, and W. Christoph Schmauch, 125–36. Lanham, MD: University Press of America, 1984.

Goethe, Johann Wolfgang. *Gedenkausgabe der Werke, Briefe und Gespräche*. Ed. Ernst Beutler. Vol. 2. Zurich: Artemis, 1949.

Hamann, Johann Georg. *Briefwechsel: 1778–82*. Ed. Arthur Henkel. Vol. 4. Wiesbaden: Insel, 1959.

Hamann, Johann Georg. "Sokratische Denkwürdigkeiten: für die lange Weile des Publikums zusammengetragen von einem Liebhaber der langen Weile. Mit einer doppelten Zuschrift an Niemand und an Zween." In *Sturm und Drang: eine Auswahl theoretischer Texte*, ed. Erich Loewenthal, 61–84. 3rd ed. Heidelberg: Lambert Schneider, 1972.

Hein, Christoph. *Einladung zum Lever Bourgeois*. Berlin: Aufbau, 1980.

Huizing, Klaas. *Das Ding an sich: eine unerhörte Begebenheit aus dem Leben Immanuel Kants*. Munich: Albrecht Knaus, 1998.

Kehlmann, Daniel. "Wo ist Carlos Montúfar?" In *Wo ist Carlos Montúfar? Über Bücher*, 9–27. Reinbek bei Hamburg: Rowohlt, 2005.

Kehlmann, Daniel. *Die Vermessung der Welt*. Reinbek bei Hamburg: Rowohlt, 2007. First published 2005.

Kellner, L. *Alexander von Humboldt*. London: Oxford University Press, 1963.

Krumrey, Marianne. "Gegenwart im Spiegel der Geschichte: Christoph Hein, *Einladung zum Lever Bourgeois*." *Temperamente* 6, no. 4 (1981): 143–7.

Metzke, Erwin. "Kant und Hamann." In *Johann Georg Hamann*, ed. Reiner Wild, 233–63. Darmstadt: Wissenschaftliche Buchgesellschaft, 1978.

O'Flaherty, James C. *Johann Georg Hamann*. Boston: Twayne, 1979.

Preußer, Heinz-Peter. "Zur Typologie der Zivilisationskritik: was aus Daniel Kehlmanns Roman 'Die Vermessung der Welt' einen Bestseller werden ließ." *Text und Kritik*, no. 177 (2008): 73–85.

Rupke, Nicolaas A. *Alexander von Humboldt: A Metabiography*. Frankfurt am Main: Peter Lang, 2005.

Stahl, Christian. "Amazon.de – Rezension." 15 December 2008. http://www.amazon.de/ Die-Vermessung-Welt-Daniel-Kehlmann/dp/3499241005/ref=sr_1_1?ie=UTF8&S=book& qid=1268837101&sr=8-1.

Tang, Chenxi. *The Geographic Imagination of Modernity: Geography, Literature, and Philosophy in German Romanticism*. Stanford: Stanford University Press, 2008.

Welcoming Alexander von Humboldt in Santa Fé de Bogotá, or the Creoles' self-celebration in the colonial city

Rodolfo Guzmán M.

On 8 July 1801, Alexander von Humboldt and Aimé Bonpland arrived in Bogotá. They were welcomed by a large parade that escorted them from the edges of the city to the house of José Celestino Mutis, director of the Royal Botanical Expedition of the New Kingdom of Granada and the first promoter of natural philosophy in this kingdom. This essay explores two main ideas from the perspective of political symbolism. First, the author argues that this magnificent welcome was a sign of respect and admiration for the German scientist, while at the same time serving as an opportunity for New Granada's educated Creoles to publicly call attention to their importance and prestige. Second, the author explores Humboldt's thoughts about the Creoles' social attitudes and the colony's potential emancipation from Spain.

In 1808, Alexander von Humboldt published his second volume of *Equinoctial Plants* to present to the European public the partial findings based on his observations of American flora. It was entitled *Plantes équinoxiales recueillies au Méxique, dans l'île de Cuba, dans les provinces de Caracas, de Cumaná et de Barcelone, aux Andes de la Nouvelle-Grenade, de Quito, et du Pérou, et sur les bords du Río Negro, de l'Orénoque et de la rivière des Amazones.* In addition to its vast taxonomic content, the book is unique in that it is dedicated to José Celestino Mutis (1732–1808), mathematician, botanist, and promoter of natural philosophy in the New Kingdom of Granada (see Figure 1).

Humboldt and Bonpland's dedication is adorned with a lithograph depicting the face of the botanist from Cádiz, below which one reads: "A Don José Celestino Mutis. Directeur en chef de l'Expédition Botanique du Roy de la Nouvelle Grenade, Astronome Royal à Santa Fé de Bogotá. Comme une faible marquée d'Admiration et de Reconnoissance" [To Don José Celestino Mutis, General Director of the Royal Botanical Expedition of the New Kingdom of Granada, Royal Astronomer in Santa Fé de Bogotá. As a small token of admiration and recognition].[1] In 1983, 175 years later, and also in homage to José Celestino Mutis, the Colombian government minted and put into circulation a 200-peso bill with his image. Not only does the artwork on the bill invoke the legacy of the Spanish scientist, it also refers back to the presence of Humboldt in New Granada. At the center of this bill are Mutis's effigy, the astronomical observatory in Bogotá, and Alexander von Humboldt's coat of arms (see Figure 2). Through the design and the minting of the new bill, the Colombian elite commemorated a very important piece of their cultural historiography: the

Figure 1.   Image courtesy of Missouri Botanical Garden.

arrival in New Granada of useful science, with Mutis as its principal proponent, and the cultural debt they owed to Humboldt.

The recognition to which the dedication refers has to do with the hospitality and the botanical information with which Mutis provided Humboldt. In studying the cultural context of the scientific development of the Creoles of New Granada and Peru and their influences on Humboldt's biogeography theories, Jorge Cañizares-Esguerra notes that: "Humboldt learned to read the Andes as a natural laboratory in which to study plant distribution from local colonial intellectuals."[2] Humboldt met Mutis and his Creole disciples in 1801, the year in which Humboldt and Bonpland visited New Granada. Arriving in Cartagena de Indias from Cuba on 30 March 1801, Humboldt and Bonpland remained there for almost 21 days and later continued, on the Magdalena River, to Santa Fé de Bogotá, capital of the New Kingdom of Granada, after a 45-day trip that Humboldt described as tortuous. Humboldt stayed as a guest in Mutis's house for two months (from July to September 1801), and what he saw of Mutis's work, and the scientific knowledge Mutis exchanged with him and many others, was extremely important for the development of some of Humboldt's theories about the distribution of plants, climates, and physical geography. During his stay in Bogotá, Humboldt also collected various plant specimens, measured the altitude of the mountains

Figure 2.   Image produced by author.

surrounding the city, and visited several small towns outside Santa Fé. Before his departure to Quito, Mutis made Humboldt the gift of 100 drawings.

Humboldt expressed his immediate admiration for Mutis in a letter to his brother, Wilhelm von Humboldt, dated 21 September 1801. Humboldt wrote that: "for more than 15 years, 30 painters worked in Mutis's studio, and Mutis possesses between 2000 and 3000 drawings in major folios. After [Joseph] Bank's library in London, I have not seen such a large botanical library."[3] Following Linnaeus's views on biodiversity and his system of botanical classification, Mutis had started the construction of this library as a personal initiative soon after his arrival in New Granada in 1760. Later on, beginning in 1783 when Mutis served as official director of the Botanical Expedition of New Granada, his collection received specimens from several regions of the viceroyalty. The full importance of Mutis's monumental achievement, and its significance for botanical science in the Americas, is revealed by the fact that, during Spain's military attempts to keep the New Kingdom of Granada from secession (1816–9), General Pablo Morillo confiscated all of Mutis's papers, works, and books and sent them to Spain. The confiscated material included 14 boxes filled with 5190 sheets (plates) and 711 drawings; 1 box of manuscripts and 48 boxes of plants; 15 boxes of minerals; 9 boxes of seeds; 6 boxes filled with knick-knacks; 8 boxes with various samples of wood; 1 box with cinnamon samples; 2 boxes of animal and other drawings; and 45 boxes containing Mutis's herbarium.[4]

In Colombian history, Mutis is remembered not only as the director of the Botanical Expedition and a promoter of the natural sciences; he also stands as the founder of a new cultural era in New Granada. Mutis was the first in Santa Fé de Bogotá to teach and sponsor instruction in mathmatics, physics, astronomy, medicine, and natural science from the perspective of the Enlightenment and natural philosophy. His efforts substantially modified the traditional scholastic education then available in New Granada. In the colleges and universities of the viceroyalty, where scholastic methods prevailed, teachings were based on the exaltation of and respect for the classics. The basic subjects in colonial education consisted of studies of grace, predestination, communion, and sin. Mutis was the first to publicly declare himself a Copernican and to introduce the experimental methods of Linnaeus and Buffon. Mutis directed the mathematics class for four years (1762–7), which inaugurated a new period in the New Kingdom of Granada's educational curriculum. Singificantly, Mutis educated a group of young Creoles, who began to understand and interpret natural phenomena within the new epistemological framework of natural philosophy.[5] By the beginning of the nineteenth century, these disciples of Mutis, all enlightened Creoles, constituted an intellectual elite of great importance and, by 1808, they would openly dedicate themselves to the struggle for independence in New Granada. The relationship between scientific knowledge and social critique embedded in the general principles of the Enlightenment and the "useful sciences" allowed these young Creoles to view the natural characteristics of their country from a new economic perspective and also to boost their Creole identity along with their old aristocratic aspirations for self-government. Given the international prestige of Humboldt as world traveler and man of science, for Mutis and his disciples, Humboldt's visit to the New Kingdom of Granada constituted a most important recognition of their scientific and cultural activities. Much has been said about what Humboldt represented for the post-independence Creoles in areas such as economic geography, the natural sciences, and literary production.[6] Far less attention, however, has been paid to how the Creoles actually received Humboldt, and how his visit served to further and enhance their own political aspirations in the years prior to the wars of independence. I argue that the celebration's symbolism was part of the Creoles' affirmation of self-identity.

By the end of the eighteenth century, Creoles had already accumulated important economic wealth and significant power in the social structure in New Granada and the rest of the New World viceroyalties. They were landowners, merchants, and bureaucrats, whose presence was prominent in colonial institutions such as the church, *cabildos* [municipal governments], and mercantile offices. They also had control over a vast labor force of indigenous and African slave populations.[7] Nevertheless, the Spanish political order, structured under corporate socio-racial privilege, made the Creoles second-class subjects of the king in relation to peninsular Spaniards. This cultural and political condition was always present in the discourse of the Creoles' collective identity. It is true that Creole self-identity in the Spanish-American possessions developed in different ways at different times, and in response to different circumstances. But by the time Humboldt arrived in Santa Fé de Bogotá, the New Granadine Creoles, like the British-American settlers and the rest of the Creoles of the Spanish-American territories, had already developed a strong sense of their cultural differences with respect to the imperial center. Most of the extensive and prolific scholarly work on the subject of Creole identity claims that the native

Euro-Americans of the colonial Atlantic world shared four major components to a greater or lesser degree: their sense of place; their conception of history; their aspirations to political autonomy; and an uncomfortable relationship with indigenous and African populations.[8]

In the pages that follow, I take Humboldt's arrival in Santa Fé de Bogotá as a point of departure for examining the social values and symbolic political actions discernable in the public celebration that the cultured Creoles organized in the capital to celebrate Humboldt's arrival. In the milieu of collective public celebrations in the colonial city, visitors were typically welcomed with parades, lavish receptions, and a vast mobilization of notables and ordinary residents. My main purpose here is to demonstrate that the "street theater" which was staged in Santa Fé upon the arrival of the distinguished German visitor surpassed mere etiquette and concentrated instead on the symbolic exhibition of a contest of political and cultural power between the Creoles and the Spaniards. I also highlight Humboldt's interpretations of the Creoles' political discontent with the Spanish Crown. Did he see the cultural and political differences between the Creoles and the Spaniards as decisive reasons for secession?

Humboldt's grand welcome in the capital of the New Kingdom of Granada has traditionally received little scholarly attention, largely because, in the Spanish colonies, an official welcome was to be expected for the most important natural scientist of a foreign country allowed by the king to visit his territories. As is well know, Humboldt, by direct order of the Spanish King, Charles IV, was permitted to move freely and conduct all types of measurements and observations during his travel to Spanish-American territories. He was also to be welcomed and helped by the local authorities in everything he needed: "todo favor, auxilio, y protección que necesite" [every favor, help and protection that he needs].[9] In most of the important Spanish cities and even in the mid-sized towns that Humboldt visited, he was welcomed and hosted with great courtesy by distinguished local Creole families or high-ranking colonial officials. In Cumaná, for instance, he was received by the governor of the province, Don Vicente Emparán. In Quito, he was first welcomed by the president of the Royal Audiencia, Don Luis Hector, Baron de Carondelet, and hosted in the private residences of the Marquis of Selva Alegre, Juan María Pío Montúfar y Larrea.[10] In Lima, he was received by none other than the Viceroy Don Gabriel de Avilés. At a cursory glance, Humboldt's welcome in Santa Fé was in keeping with this general custom of protocol and hospitality. Compared to how he was greeted in other cities, however, the personalities and number of residents who took part in the Santa Fé reception, and especially the cavalcade that escorted Humboldt from the edges of city to Mutis's residence, lent this occasion special significance.

Given that public rituals and celebrations were strictly regulated by local authorities, it is remarkable that a collective public event replete with symbolic messages took place in this colonial city.[11] Humboldt relates the event in the following way:

> Der in S[anta] Fé langerwartete Einzug war in der Tat sonderbar possi[e]rlich. Ich mit den Lozanos und dem Geistlichen Caicedo im sechsspännigen Wagen der Lozanos (eine in London verfertigte Kutsche mit ressorts in lat[titudo] 4° 30' und auf 1370 t[oisen] Höhe!). Bonpland in der ebenfalls sechsspännigen Kutsche des Erzbischofs und ein Schwarm von Reitern umher, der sich durch die von S[anta] Fé uns Entgegenkommen-den vermehrte. Alle Fenster waren voll Köpfen, die Gassenbuben und Schulknaben

liefend schreiend und mit Fingern auf mich weisend 1/4 M[eile] weit neben der Kutsche her. Alles versicherte, dass in dem toten S[anta] Fé seit zwanzig Jahren nicht mehr solche Bewegung und Aufstand stattgefunden habe. In Caracas wäre dies unmöglich gewesen. Dort ist man gewohnt, Fremde und Nicht-Spanier zu sehen. Aber im Inneren von Süd-Amerika und so wunderbare Ketzer, welche die Welt durchlaufen, um Pflanzen zu suchen und nun hier ankamen, um ihr Heu mit dem des D[o]n Mutis zu vergleichen! Das musste die Neugierde reisen. Dazu der Umstand, dass der Vice-könig unsere Ankunft mit Wichtigkeit behandelte, uns auf feinste zu behandeln befohlen.

[The long-awaited arrival in Santa Fé was indeed strangely droll. I with the Lozanos and the cleric Caicedo in the Lozanos' six-horse carriage (a London-made carriage with ressorts at latitude 4° 30' and an elevation of 1370 toises!). Bonpland was in the archbishop's carriage, also drawn by six horses, surrounded by a swarm of riders on horseback, whose numbers grew as people from Santa Fé joined up with them to meet us. All the windows were filled with faces, and street urchins and schoolboys were running alongside the carriage for a quarter of a mile, yelling, and pointing at me. Everyone assured us that the dead Santa Fé had not seen such an ado and excitement for the last 20 years. Such a thing would have been impossible in Caracas. There, people are used to seeing foreigners and non-Spaniards. But in the interior of South America, and such marvelous heretics who traverse the globe to collect plants, and now they had arrived here to compare their hay with that of Don Mutis! That had to provoke curiosity. Plus the circumstance that the viceroy treated our arrival with importance, and had ordered that we be made a fuss of.][12]

Humboldt also emphasized the event in a letter of 21 September 1801 to his brother Wilhelm:

Our arrival in Santa Fé looked like a triumphant march. The archbishop had sent us his carriage, in which the prominent members of the city arrived. We were offered a meal two miles from the city, and we arrived with an entourage of more than 60 people on horseback.[13]

At first, Humboldt did not seem to understand completely the reasons for such an elaborate welcome and attributed it to the novelty of a foreign traveler in the city, noting in his travel journal that:

Der alte Mutis erwartet uns hier mit seinem Freunden, eine ehrwürdige, geistreiche Gestalt in geistl[icher] Sotana. Er umarmete uns mit viel Herzlichkeit, lächelte, als er mich mit dem Baroemter in der Hand aussteigen sah und als ich das instrument niemandem anvertrauen wollte ... Mut[is] was in dieser eredsten Zusammenkunft fast verelgen bescheiden. Wir sprachen von wissenschftlichen Dingen, ... er lenkte das Gespräch geschickt aud allgemeinere Gegenstände, um es allgemein verständlicher zu machen; und auf Pflanzen und seine Pflanzen erpicht, enstand uns in den ersten Tagen der falsche Verdacht, man werde uns mit Höflichkeit abspeisen, sans enter dans des matièeres scientifiques. Aber nein, es war M[uti]s' Plan, die ersten acht Tage in Diners und Ceremonial zu verlieren, damit die Stadt sehe, wen er bewirthe und wir er bewirthen könne. Er wünschte daher, dass in dieser Zeit von Botanik fast gar nicht die Rede sein sollte. In den uns bereiteten Zimmern was ein prächtiges refresco bereitet, und hätte ich es glauben können, dass der berühmte Rizo, dem Cavanilles eine Pflanze gewidmet, uns bedientenartig aufwartete?

[The old Mutis and his friends were standing there (at his house) awaiting us; he was a venerable, witty presence in a clerical soutane. He embraced us very cordially and smiled when he saw me climb out with my barometer in hand and refuse to entrust the instrument to anyone ... During this first meeting, Mutis was almost bashfully modest. We spoke about scientific matters ... (but) he skillfully steered the conversation toward other things to make it more generally acessible; and since were were keen on plants, and on his plants, we developed, during those first days, the wrong impression that we would only be fed with politeness, without scientific subjects ever being broached. But no, it was Mutis's plan to spend the first eight days on dinners and ceremony, so that the city could see whom he hosted and how he could host them. He therefore desired that there would be almost no talk about botany during this time. In the rooms that had been prepared for us, spendid refreshments had been laid on, and could I really believe that the famous (Salvador) Rizo, to whom (José de) Cavanilles had dedicated a plant, appeared to serve us at table as if he were a waiter?][14]

Nonetheless, in the same letter to his brother Wilhelm, he gleaned the local meaning of what was taking place during his reception. After mentioning the exceptional parade, he writes:

It was well known that we were here to visit Mutis, who enjoyed a high degree of respect in the entire city, due not only to his advanced age, but also to his fame in the court, … thus our arrival was given more emphasis, so that through us, they could pay homage to this man.[15]

The parade, the procession into the capital, and the participation of distinguished personalities along with a crowd of regular spectators are all elements that must be included in the interpretive framework for this sort of event. Susan G. Davis writes:

Parades are public dramas of social relations, and in them performances define who can be a social actor and what subjects and ideas are available for communication and consideration. … People use street theater, like other rituals, as tools for building, maintaining and confronting power relations.[16]

In colonial society, such theatrical events were particularly charged with meaning because they were such an integral part of the Spanish courtly tradition. In the context of colonial cities, this tradition was emulated to an extreme as a way of maintaining and reproducing the imperial order. Because public ceremonies were crucial manifestations for modeling and acting out political and social concepts in local settings, it was immensely important for the eminent residents of the city not only to participate in them but also to be seen in public as outstanding and respected members of their communities. In fact, historians of courtly societies and colonial cultural history are familiar with many quarrels, confrontations, and legal battles between institutions and leading members of the city which were the result of breaches of etiquette during parades, public ceremonies, or even in the ordinary events of everyday activities.[17] About this hypersensibility surrounding respect for privilege, the German sociologist Norbert Elias concludes that the origin of these types of behaviors in courtly societies might be found in a social attitude characterized by people's constant search for "opportunities to affirm their status and power." In this search, the participants move through a series of reciprocal relationships of social prestige with respect both to their peers and to those who find themselves excluded. Prestige is meticulously ranked by way of social "steps," and constant quarrels and competitions for acquiring these ranks, or for holding on to them, are part and parcel of courtly society.[18]

In Santa Fé, as in any other society structured around corporative and socio-racial privilege, the ideal place to exhibit and protect these preferences and social pre-eminence was during public events. In them, the social and institutional hierarchies were organized according to rank and importance, and the inhabitants could collectively distinguish and exhibit the who's who of their city. It is easy to see this stratification in the colonies' iconography in paintings depicting religious processions, welcoming events, and civil celebrations, and official documents associated with colonial festivities. Both the artwork and the documents reflect and endorse the social hierarchical structure and political power.[19]

Except for religious celebrations and rituals, there were three reasons for staging processions or public parades in the streets of colonial Santa Fé:[20] (1) the celebrations organized by the royal spokesman to announce and proclaim a new king; (2) the arrival of a viceroy, an archbishop, or a high-ranking government official; and (3) receiving the Royal Seal. The latter was of the greatest importance of all, because it symbolized the arrival in the city of the king himself. It confirmed, in the city streets, the recognition of the king's role as the central figure, mediator, and unifier of the political order. In other words, through the power of the estate system, the regional and the imperial, the natural and the cultural, the past and the present, and the secular and the religious all came together and were celebrated in the welcoming acceptance of the Royal Seal. This tradition began in 1550 as a public ceremony for the colonial territories; the last such ceremony took place in Bogotá in 1817, when the independence movement was already underway. Given that this ceremony took place when the course of the movement toward independence was already irreversible, this was clearly the last attempt by the imperial powers symbolically to regain their former authority. This ceremony was described as follows:

> Al desfile concurrieron todos los grandes a caballo en ricos jaeces, todos los procuradores, receptores, porteros, escribanos, alcaldes, regidores y numerosos acompañantes. El sello iba en una salvilla de plata encima de un caballo provisto de riquísimo jaez; dos oidores a pie conducían el caballo por las riendas que eran de seda, plata y oro. El cortejo se detuvo en la real audiencia, una de cuyas salas estaba asignada a este representante de la autoridad real.

> [The parade was attended by all the dignitaries on horses with rich ornate trappings, lawyers for the Crown, municiple council members, debt collectors for the tribunals, ministers of justice, notaries, mayors all took part and many others accompanied them. The seal was carried on a silver tray on top of a horse adorned with a splendid harness; two judges on foot led the horse by its reins of silk, silver and gold. The entourage ended the procession at the Royal Hall of Justice, one of the rooms of which was assigned to house this representative of royal authority.][21]

If the importance of prestige and public exhibition was so great and so carefully regulated in colonial society, then why was Humboldt's welcome so extraordinary? There are three main historical and cultural aspects that lend this event particular symbolic and political significance. First, historically, the Creoles were in constant competition for political and cultural prestige with the *peninsulares*, and their public actions and activities cannot easily be separated from this context. For some historians, the Creoles' confrontations with imperial authority and its peninsular representatives in America began very early, even with the first conquest campaigns and the initial colonization. That is to say, Spain's authority was questioned at the very moment when the Crown refused to grant the conquistadores and their descendents the recognition of noble vassals perpetually entitled to the land [*encomiendas*] and the right to be their own masters.[22] After that, on both sides of the Atlantic, what followed was a long history of material ambitions, epic narratives, and political adjustments that manifested the desire on the part of Spain's royal authority and the colonial Creoles either to preserve old socio-political realities or create new ones. From the peninsular point of view, the Creoles' political loyalty and cultural capabilities were always in question.[23] From the perspective of the American territories, the Creoles were asking for political privileges and for cultural recognition of their unique history and what they had accomplished in the name of the king.

By the time Humboldt and Bonpland arrived in America, then, the cultural and political confrontations between Creoles and the *peninsulares* already had a long history. Spain's adherence to determinism based on astronomy, its cult of pure blood lines, and the rigidity of its social stratification served culturally to undermine the Creoles' aspirations and placed Creoles in an inferior position to subjects born in Spain. As the Creoles had been born far from the royal court and in close proximity to Native Americans, blacks, mestizos, and mulattos, it was said that, in America, the Creoles breathed unhealthy air, which affected their ability to think and understand. That is how the Franciscan Juan de la Puente expressed it in 1612, when he affirmed that it

> influye el cielo de la América, inconstancia, lascivia y mentira: vicios propios de los indios, y la constelación los hará propios de los españoles que allá se criaren y nacieren.

> [influences America's sky, leads to inconsistency, lasciviousness, and lies; vices characteristic of the indigenous Americans also influence the Creoles, given the effect of the constellations at the place of their birth.][24]

Before de la Puente, in 1574, the chronicler and cosmographer Juan López de Velasco (1530–98) had already noted in his *Geografía y descripción universal de las Indias* that:

> Los españoles que pasan a aquellas partes y están en ellas mucho tiempo, con la mutación del cielo y del temperamento de las regiones aun no dejan de recibir alguna diferencia en el color y calidad de las personas; pero los que nacen de ellos, que llaman criollos, y en todo son tenidos y habidos por españoles, conocidamente salen ya diferenciados en el color y el tamaño porque todos son grandes y la color algo baja declinando á la disposición de la tierra ... y no solamente en las calidades corporales se muda, pero en las del ánimo suelen seguir las del cuerpo, y mudando él se alteran también.

> [The Spaniards who move to that part of the world and who stay there for a long time, with the mutation of the heavens and the temperament of the regions, don't fail to receive some difference in the color and quality as persons; but those who are born of them, who are called criollos (Creoles), who in everything are considered Spaniards, it is well known they are different in color and in size because they are all large and their color darkening according to the disposition of the earth ... and not only do the qualities of the body change, but also does the spirit which follows the changes of the body, and once the body changes, so does the spirit.][25]

In response to this overwhelming negation, the Creoles' pursuit of their own standing in the world was not only focused on establishing their cultural uniqueness, but also on demonstrating their equal or even greater status with respect to Europe. Without abandoning the parameters of Iberian culture, the New World Creoles created an opposite version of themselves. Always with political and legal intent, but also motivated by the anxiety and desire to erase the stain of being the "bastard children" of the empire, the Creoles referred to their physical surroundings and historical experiences as evidence of their exemplary "greatness." For the Creoles, if it had not been for the political preference given to the Spanish-born, everything in America would have flourished with abundance and positive satisfaction.[26] Through their own history, chronicles, literature, and deeds, the Creoles demonstrated that material riches, religious piety, the grandeur of the cities, and even the cultural vitality of the overseas empire were all due to their efforts alone.[27]

Humboldt's arrival in Santa Fé coincided with a new stage of political tensions, this time promoted by the enlightened Creoles who ultimately ended Spanish rule. Humboldt was naturally aware of these tensions, for almost all the Creoles whom he met in America and in Europe, before and after his voyage, complained to him about the historical injustices that the metropolis was committing against them.[28] The greater part of the Creoles' complaints belonged to the commercial and political arena, and Humboldt's observations regarding these tensions also pertained to this sphere. His opinion was that the Creoles' grievances were justified; the Crown had been too rigid in not allowing them to hold important positions of political and commercial authority. But, in his view, reconciliation was possible without secession, and he did not see the colonies' independence as imminent. Humboldt thought that animosities would end by administering the American territories within the original framework of the beginning of the sixteenth century, when the *cabildos* and significant administrative centers overseas belonged to the colonizers. That was a time when peninsular Spaniards and American Creoles had been equals, and when the new overseas possessions had been administered in the same manner as the peninsular provinces, not as mere colonies. In his *Personal Narrative*, Humboldt wrote:

> Du temps de Charles-Quint et de Philippe II, l'institution des municipalités fut sagement protégée par la cour. Des hommes puissans, qui avoient joué du rôle dans la conquête, fondoient des villes et formoient les premiers *cabildos*, à l'instar de ceux d'Espagne. Il existoit alors une égalité de droits entre les hommes de la métropole et leurs descendans en Amérique.

> [In the time of Charles V and Philip II, the institution of municipalities was wisely protected by the court. Powerful men, who had acted a part in the conquest, laid the foundation of towns and formed the first *cabildos*, in imitation of those of Spain. An equality of rights then existed between the men of the mother country and their American descendants.][29]

Here, Humboldt echoed one of the Creoles' oldest political grievances since the establishment of the New Laws. That he also understood their bitterness and animosity against the *peninsulares* is clear from his comment that the administrative structure the Crown had established overseas had contributed to promoting the idea that "[l]'Européen le plus misérable sans éducation, sans culture intellectuelle, se croit supérieur aux blancs nés dans le nouveau continent" [the most miserable European, without education and without intellectual cultivation, thinks himself superior to the whites born in the new continent], and that "il peut un jour parvenir a des places dont l'accès est presque interdit aux natifs, même a ceux qui se distinguent par leurs talens, par leurs connaissances et par leurs qualités morales" [he may one day reach places to which access is almost interdicted to the natives, even to those distinguished for their talents, knowledge and moral qualities]. Humboldt knew that

> devant la loi, tout créole blanc est Espagnol; mais l'abus des lois, les fausses mesures du gouvernement colonial, l'exemple des états confédérés de l'Amérique septentrionale, l'influence des opinions du siècle, ont relâché les liens qui unissoient jadis plus intimement les Espagnols créoles aux Espagnols européens.

[in the eyes of the law, every white Creole was a Spaniard; but the abuse of the laws, the false measures of the colonial government, the example of the United States of America, and the influence of the opinions of the age, have relaxed the ties which formerly united more closely the Spanish Creoles to the European Spaniards.][30]

It was also clear to Humboldt that this political and cultural discrimination leveled against the descendents of the conquerors was the basis of their permanent discontent with the imperial authorities. This was what had contributed significantly to the consolidation of an *American* discourse of cultural uniqueness. Nevertheless, for him, the Creoles were Europeans, and because of that, he wished for

[u]ne sage administration [qui] pourra rétablir l'harmonie, calmer les passions et le ressentiment, conserver peut-être encore, pendant long-temps, l'union entre les membres d'une même et grande famille éparse en Europe et en Amérique.

[a wise administration (that) might re-establish harmony, calm their passions and resentments, and yet preserve for a long time the union among the members of one and the same great family scattered over Europe and America.][31]

In the context of public ceremonies in Santa Fé, the second aspect that contributed to the highly unusual connotations of Humboldt's staged welcome was that the Creoles who were present at and participated in the event were all involved with the natural sciences and the Botanical Expedition. Several other Creoles whom Humboldt met in New Granada, even though they were not present at the celebration of his arrival, were deeply critical of the imperial authorities and, nine years later, became openly involved in the secessionist cause. The most representative of these Creoles, who belonged to Mutis's circle, was Francisco José de Caldas, who would work with Humboldt in Quito in 1802.[32] About Caldas, Humboldt remarked:

Este Sr. Caldas es un prodigio en astronomía. Nacido en las tinieblas de Popayán y no habiendo viajado jamás más allá de Santa Fé, el mismo se construyó sus Barómetros;! Qué llegaría a hacer este muchacho en un país donde haya medios!

[This Mr Caldas is a prodigy of astronomy. Born in the fog of Popayán and having never traveled beyond Santa Fé, he built his barometers himself. The things this young man could have done in a country of means!][33]

The Royal Army executed Caldas in 1816 during the suppression of the Creoles who had participated in the so-called "Cry for Independence" of 1810.[34] Among the other Creoles whom Humboldt met in New Granada who were engaged in the "practical sciences" and also sympathized with the cause for independence, were Salvador Rizo, clerk and premier painter for the Botanical Expedition; Mutis's nephew, Sinforoso Mutis; and José Ignacio de Pombo, a close friend of Mutis and Caldas who was to become one of the first economists of the new republic. Since 1794, these and other Creoles had been under surveillance by the local imperial authorities as a consequence of their being associated with various seditious activities in the capital of the viceroyalty, such as the translation, printing, and distribution of the *Les Droits de l'homme* [*The Rights of Man*] and the clandestine posting of threatening circulars on the doors of the principal churches and homes in the downtown area.[35] One of the "infamous" pasquinades, written in verse, not only called the government "usurpers" and complained about taxes, but, even more shockingly for the authorities, threatened that the then government would end soon unless oppression ceased:

Si no quitan los estancos
si no cesa la opresión
se perderá lo ganado
tendrá fin la usurpación.

[If the taxes are not eliminated
if the oppression doesn't cease
what has been gained will be lost
the end of the usurpation will come.][36]

Although students of the Colegio del Rosario were found to be responsible for posting these circulars, Sinforoso Mutis was the one held under suspicion.

Any criticism of and threats against the local and imperial governments were seen as dangerous attempts to promote the North American and French model in the Spanish colonies. These activities certainly alarmed the authorities, which did not delay in repressive means, immediately investigating, accusing, arresting, or condemning many prominent Bogotá Creoles. Among those investigated, who had also been part of the Botanical Expedition, were Francisco Antonio Zea, Enrique Umaña, and Sinforoso Mutis. Camilo Torres, a Creole from Popayán who resided in Santa Fé as a lawyer and professor at the Colegio del Rosario, assisted Zea in his defense when the latter was connected with Nariño and his translation of the Declaration of the Rights of Man. In a letter to his parents about the events of 1794, Torres remarked bitterly on the disproportionate despotism by the local authorities, who considered him suspicious only because he spoke French; they even searched his office in the Colegio del Rosario. Torres was very concerned about the authorities' attitudes toward the educated Creoles. In his letter to his father, he wrote that

> lo menos que se decía era que todos los criollos eran unos herejes y sublevados que habían adoptado las máximas de la Francia y trataban de sacudir el yugo del Soberano … Comenzaron a aprender a unos, a registrar a otros y ya no había hombre que temiese su arresto, así como no había un Americano a quien no creyesen o fingiesen creer delincuente.

> [the least they said was that all the Creoles were heretics and promoted sedition, adopted the French dictums and intended to overthrow the royal authority. … They started to arrest some, register others, and there was not a man who was not afraid of being arrested. Likewise, there was not an American whom the Spaniards did not see as delinquent.][37]

Although Torres was never involved with any clandestine events, the suspicions of the local authorities were nonetheless correct: by 1810, he would be one of the first intellectual leaders of the independence movement. In fact, his execution in 1816 made him, along with Caldas, one of the first martyrs of New Granada's independence.

Another account that eloquently illustrates the serious tension between the cultured Creoles and *peninsulares* during the years prior to Humboldt's arrival in Santa Fé de Bogotá is that of Manuel del Socorro Rodríguez. Originally from Cuba, Rodríguez had settled in Santa Fé in 1789, when he arrived there as part of Viceroy José Manuel Espeleta's entourage (Espeleta governed New Granada from 1789 until 1797). Rodríguez is remembered as the founder of the press in what is today's Colombia; in 1791, Rodríguez founded *El Papel Periódico de Santafé de Bogotá*, the first weekly newspaper in the New Kingdom of Granada, which remained in circulation for five years. He was also the director of the Royal Library of Bogotá. Even though Rodríguez's activities contributed to bringing the ideas and literature of the Enlightenment to New Granada, he was not sympathetic to the Creoles' "infidelities." In a secret report on the state of affairs in New Granada, which he signed on 19 April 1793, Rodríguez lamented the large number of students then educated in Santa Fé and who, rather than spreading throughout the kingdom as lawyers or priests, decided to remain in Bogotá, "llenando de vicios la república y formando las torpes asambleas del libertinaje, de la independencia y demás desórdenes que no se pueden escribir" [promoting vices in the republic and forming clumsy assemblies of licentiousness, independence, and many other disorders of which I cannot even write].[38] In keeping with the old peninsular discourse of disqualifying the Creoles because of their character, Rodríguez asserted that licentiousness was so prevalent in New Granada because of "el genio americano, cuyo carácter por lo general es más inconstante que el hebreo, má amigo de la singularidad que el griego y mas idólatra de su libertad que el antiguo romano" [the American temperament, whose character in general is more erratic than the Jews, more a friend of uniqueness than the Greeks and more idolatrous of his liberty than the ancient Roman].[39] Nevertheless, his main concern and principal warning was to be vigilant and alert regarding the literary and academic societies because

En reuniéndose los hombres (principalmente los americanos) en estas asambleas científicas, se dejan transportar demasiado del emtusiasmo patriotico y llega a tanto la extravagancia ... que se olvidan de que hay soberano, leyes y religion.

[In gathering men together (mainly Americans) in these scientific assemblies, they overstated their patriotic enthusiasm and arrived with such extravagance ... that they forgot that there is a king, laws and religion.][40]

The dangerous scientific assemblies to which Rodríguez refers could be none other than the ones formed by the members of the Botanical Expedition, whose patriotic exaltation was boosted by natural philosophy and its new way of seeing and interpreting one's natural surroundings.

By the time Rodríguez wrote his secret report, the Creoles, thanks to the new scientific precepts, were already revising the descriptions of New World nature put forth by the first chroniclers and historians of the Indies, whose classifications seemed lacking because they depended on similarities with Old World nature. For the "practical sciences," by contrast, the purpose of classifying, measuring, and ordering was to underline the uniqueness in the composition of living things and their habitat. In studying New Granada's Andean formation, the Creoles not only confirmed its natural exceptionality but also became aware of its magnificent economic potential. For them, New Granada would have access to unimaginable prosperity as soon as its abundant and prodigious natural wealth was to become known, classified, system-atized, and, more importantly, commercialized.

This set of ideas, perceptions of nature, and the cultural context gave rise to the Creoles' narrative that Jorge Cañizares-Esguerra identifies as the "political economy of paradise"; that is, the belief of the Creoles involved in the study of the natural sciences that "thanks to the providential microcosmic and ecological attributes of the Andes, [their] kingdom could become commercial emporiums, supplying the consumers of the world with all they need."[41] Francisco José de Caldas, Francisco Antonio Zea, and Pedro Fermín de Vargas were among the cultured Creoles who believed that, because of its privileged geographical and astronomical position, the New Kingdom of Granada was destined to become a great commercial and economic center. In *Estado de la geografía del virreinato de la Nueva Granada*, published in Santa Fé de Bogotá in 1808, Caldas presented his "patria" in the following manner:

> La posición geográfica de la Nueva Granada parece que la destina al comercio del universo. Mejor situada que Tiro y que Alejandría, puede acumular en su seno los perfumes del Asia, el marfil africano, la industria europea, las pieles del Norte, la ballena del medio día y cuanto produce la superficie de nuestro globo ... Convengamos; nada hay mejor situado en el Viejo ni en el Nuevo Mundo que la Nueva Granada ... Volvamos ahora nuestros ojos sobre nosotros mismos, registremos los departamentos de nuestra propia casa, y veamos si la disposición interna de esta Colonia corresponde al lugar afortunado que ocupa sobre el globo.

> [The geographic position of New Granada seems to destine it to the commerce of the universe. Better situated than Tiro and Alexandria, it can gather in its bosom the perfumes of Asia, the African ivory, the European industry, the furs of the North, the whale of midday, and everything produced by the surface of our globe ... Let's agree; there is no place better situated either in the Old or in the New World than New Granada ... Let us now turn our eyes onto ourselves, let's organize the rooms of our own home, and let's see if the internal disposition of this Colony corresponds to the fortunate place that it occupies on the globe.][42]

Cañizares-Esguerra is no doubt correct in regarding Caldas's words as a good example of the discourse of the "political economy of paradise." But these exaltations of the privileged kingdom and riches of the patria also belong to the Creoles' old discourse about America as a place of wealth and *grandeza* [greatness]; that is, a city and its hinterland surrounded with extraordinary natural and cultural abundance. As mentioned above, the Creoles developed this discourse as a response to the peninsular Spaniards who questioned their ability to produce civilization, knowledge, and culture. During the first decade of the nineteenth century, these ideas were incorporated into the discourse of the practical sciences, accompanied by strong political and economic thoughts of autonomy; this is clear from Caldas's call to "turn our eyes onto ourselves" and "organize the rooms of our own home."

Along with the historical confrontations between Creoles and *peninsulares*, and the prolific flow of ideas about the uniqueness and natural wealth of the patria, the third aspect that illustrates the political character that was present at Humboldt's arrival has to do with the secular nature of this welcoming. It was the first time in Santa Fé de Bogotá that the Creoles had organized a public event of this magnitude which did not have religious connotations or implied imperial obedience. The motives for the parade, as well as the use of space, were not traditional, and in the city's milieu of collective public celebrations, one would expect that a parade which was both official and popular would have ended at the prominent main square, the cathedral, or the *real audiencia* [Royal Hall of Justice] – not at the house of a private citizen, no matter how well respected he was. In addition, when symbols are altered in public parades by changing the use of space and the relative importance of the participants, the hierarchical order is also changed and, most importantly, so is the message transmitted. This message was none other than to endorse the significance of the practical sciences, which Mutis had been fomenting in New Granada for almost 40 years, and, at the same time, the Creoles who courted him.

It is because of these ideas and activities of the cultured Creoles that the adoption of natural philosophy and the movement toward independence appear linked together as part of the same process in New Granada's cultural history. As I mentioned above, one of the first martyrs in the fight for independence was Francisco José de Caldas, Mutis's most significant disciple. This was not because Mutis had advocated this movement (he was always loyal to the Crown), but because the "practical sciences" provided the Creoles with new conceptual tools to reaffirm themselves. This cultural and political context explains why one of the first acts of the imperial army, during its failed attempt to contain the independence movement in Santa Fé de Bogotá, was to dismantle Mutis's library. This also allows us to understand that the spatial and symbolic center of this welcoming is not to be found exclusively in Humboldt himself, nor in the main square of the city, nor in the king's direct representatives, but rather in the space and prestige of the ideals that the Creoles represented. To legitimize this prestige politically required nothing less than a public exhibition, and the arrival of Humboldt in Santa Fé de Bogotá provided them with that opportunity. Being under close scrutiny by the imperial authorities, the pre-independence Creoles used this welcoming festivity as a sophisticated way in which symbolically to deliver their message: they were ready to embrace a new era.

Notes

1. All translations are mine unless otherwise noted.
2. Cañizares-Esguerra, *Nature, Empire, and Nation*, 5; see also chap. 6.
3. Humboldt, *Cartas americanas*, 85.
4. The bibliography related to Mutis and his Botanical Expedition in the New Kingdom of Granada is abundant. Some of the most relevant studies are: Amaya, *Mutis, Apóstol de Linneo*; Frías Núñez, *Tras el dorado vegetal*; Hernández de Alba, *Historia documental*; San Pío Aladrén, *Mutis*; and Soto Arango, *Mutis*.
5. For the incorporation of Newtonian philosophy in Santa Fé, see Hernández de Alba, "Humboldt y Mutis." On the history of education in the New Kingdom of Granada, see Silva, *Universidad y sociedad*. On Mutis and his pedagogical and educational influence, see Soto Arango, *Mutis*, and Nieto Lozano, *La educación*. On education during colonial times in general, see Gonzalbo, *Historia de la educación*, and Lanning, *Academic Culture*.
6. One can discern three different periods with respect to the importance of Humboldt in Latin American cultural production. The first period starts with his visit to the Caribbean and South America (1799–1804) and covers the process of independence. The Creoles who welcomed Humboldt in the various Spanish-American cities, and Simón Bolívar himself, were the first to announce and promote the value of the new dimension that Humboldt's work gave to American geography and its cultural past. In 1824, in a letter advocating for the freedom of Bonpland, who was jailed in Paraguay under the tyranny of Dr Francia, Bolívar began his missive to the tyrant by affirming that "[d]esde los primeros años de mi juventud tuve la honra de cultivar la amistad del señor Bonpland y del barón de Humboldt, cuyo saber ha hecho más bien a la América que todos los conquistadores" [During the very early years of my youth, I had the honor of nurturing a friendship with Mr Bonpland and with the Baron Humboldt, whose knowledge has benefited America more than all the Conquistadors] (Bolívar, *Cartas de Bolívar*, 54). The beginning of the twentieth century, until the decade of the eighties, marked a second important period in

Latin American and Iberian Humboldt studies, with works produced on both sides of the Atlantic (see Miranda, *Humboldt y México*; Ortega y Medina, *Humboldt desde México*; and Pereyra, *Humboldt en América*). The most comprehensive and contentious study of Humboldt in America published during this time was Minguet's *Alejandro de Humboldt*. For Colombia, see, for example, the magazine of Colombian culture, *Bolívar*, vols 52–4, which are dedicated to the memory of Humboldt in honor of the centenary of his death (1959). Also published in 1959 was Pérez Arbeláez's *Alejandro de Humboldt en Colombia*, an extract of Humboldt's works. The third period of studies covering the presence of Humboldt in America has offered readings of his cultural and ideological influence (see Pratt, *Imperial Eyes*). For Atlantic perspectives on Humboldt, see Pagden, "Identity Formation," and Cañizares-Esguerra, *Nature, Empire, and Nation*.

7. For the socio-economic conditions of the Creoles in New Granada during Humboldt's visit, see McFarlane, *Colombia before Independence*, and Jaramillo Uribe, "La sociedad colombiana."

8. For a recent study about Creoles' identity formation from a transatlantic perspective, see Bauer and Mazzotti, *Creole Subjects*. For seminal works on the topic of Creoles' identity formation, see Lafaye, *Quetzalcóatl and Guadalupe*; Lavallé, *Las promesas ambiguas*; Phelan, *People and the King*; and especially Brading, *First America*, and Pagden, "Identity Formation."

9. See Humboldt, *Personal Narrative*, I.15. See also the letter from Humboldt to Baron von Forrell (without a date but probably from January or February of 1799), in which Humboldt outlined the specific privileges of mobility and courtesy that he wanted during his travel to South America and Cuba (Humboldt, *Cartas americanas*, 3–4).

10. It was in Quito where Humboldt met Carlos Montúfar, the son of the Marquis of Selva Alegre, who accompanied Humboldt and Bonpland for the rest of the expedition and even returned to Europe with them. Both Juan María Pío Montúfar and his son Carlos became heroes of the independence movement in Ecuador.

11. For pertinent studies of Spanish colonial public celebrations and their relation with political and social concepts, see Curcio-Nagy, *Great Festivals* and Valenzuela Márquez, *Las liturgias del poder*.

12. Diary entry, 23 June to 7 August 1801, in Humboldt and Faak, *Reise*, 93; translated by Vera Kutzinski. Botting, paraphrasing Humboldt to some extent, gives the following account: "The arrival of the expedition had been expected and the day after their arrival on the great plain before the city a cavalcade of finely dressed horsemen rode out to greet them and lead them, as distinguished visitors of the highly respected Mutis, in a triumphal procession into the capital. Humboldt was invited to sit in the archbishop's six-horse, London-built carriage, and behind him came Bonpland following in another carriage, while on either side of them trotted a large escort of sixty or more of the leading citizens of Bogotá – an escort which increased considerably in numbers as they drew near to the city. Few scientists can have been accorded such a popular civic reception and Humboldt found the whole thing almost comical. A great crowd of schoolboys and street urchins, running, shouting and pointing, stretched for a quarter of a mile behind the coaches, and every window of every house was crowded with spectators" (Botting, *Humboldt and the Cosmos*, 146).

13. Humboldt, *Cartas americanas*, 85.

14. Diary entry, 23 June to 7 August 1801, in Humboldt and Faak, *Reise*, 93; translated by Vera Kutzinski. See also Botting, *Humboldt and the Cosmos*, 146. In 1801, Santa Fé de Bogotá had approximately 21,000 inhabitants, and the city's urban development was not comparable to the wealth and cultural activities of Quito, Lima, or Mexico. For a solid study of the political and economic conditions of the New Kingdom of Granada during the eighteenth century, see McFarlane, *Colombia before Independence*. See also Jaramillo Uribe, "La sociedad colombiana." For statistical information regarding population, ethnic composition, and cultural activities in Santa Fé de Bogotá between 1778 and 1806, see Vargas Lesmes, *La Sociedad de Santa Fé*.

15. Humboldt, *Cartas americanas*, 85.

16. Davis, *Parades and Power*, 6.

17. For the New Granada, Ramos studied these themes in relation to the concept of institutional pre-eminence in a legal case between the ecclesiastic members of the Santo Oficio and civil authorities in Cartagena in 1729. See Ramos, "Competencias."
18. Elias, *Court Society*, 130.
19. For an in-depth study of the iconography and representations of colonial cities and events, see Kagan and Marias, *Urban Images*, and Phelan, *Ceremonial and Political Roles*.
20. For a detailed list and comments on public festivities and celebrations in colonial Santa Fé, see Vargas Lesmes, *La sociedad de Santa Fé*.
21. Quoted in Martínez, *Bogotá*, 60. For a detailed account of the public festivities and celebrations in Santa Fé de Bogotá during the last decades of the eighteenth and beginning of the nineteenth century, see Vargas Lesmes, *La sociedad de Santa Fé*.
22. These measures taken by the Crown were put into effect in 1542 under the famous Leyes Nuevas [New Laws] of Carlos I. They were created as a reform of the previous laws of Burgos issued by Ferdinand II (the Catholic) in 1512. The New Laws were created to prevent the exploitation of the indigenous people by the *encomenderos* [landowners] by strictly limiting their power during the colonization process. The insubordinations of Gonzalo Pizarro against the viceroy Blasco Nuñez de Vela in 1544 in Peru and the rebellion of Cortez's brother in 1565–8, who wanted to establish an independent kingdom in Mexico, are representative cases of disobedience and political confrontation to the Crown's authority in the early stages of the conquest. See Brading, *First America*, and Pagden, *European Encounters*.
23. As Pagden has noted, a good example of this Creole uneasiness with the Crown was the *relación* that a commission sent to Peru in 1556 to investigate the Creoles' feelings regarding their *encomiendas*. The report noted that "when the *encomienda* had been made perpetual, would the loyalty of the criollos [Creoles] be assured, 'for as they are feudatories they will thus quench the fires of rebellion … which until now has not been the case, rather some of them have taken some pleasure in these disturbances because they are not holders of perpetual *encomiendas*'" (Pagden, *European Encounters*, 53).
24. Quoted in Brading, *First America*, 298. Interracial mixing in the Spanish-American colonies created a different form of racism. On the complexities and treatment of the discourse of race in the New Granada during the nineteenth century, see Lasso, "Race War and Nation."
25. Quoted in García Avilés, *El tiempo*, 19–20.
26. For this discourse on abundance in Creole historiography and iconographies, see Ortega, *El discurso*.
27. We can find this Creole inversion of negative European classifications in Bernardo de Balbuena's *Grandeza mexicana* (1604), Antonio de la Calancha's *Crónica moralizada* (1639), Carlos de Sigüenza y Góngora's *Paraíso occidental* (1684), and (for the specific case of the New Kingdom of Granada) Juan de Castellanos's *Elegías de varones ilustres de Indias* (1595) and Lucas Fernández de Piedrahíta's *Historia general de las conquistas del Nuevo Reino de Granada* (1681, but written in the 1640s). See also Guzmán, "La representación."
28. The most representative was, of course, Bolívar, whom Humboldt met in Paris in 1804. José Ignacio Pombo, a close friend of Mutis's and one of the first Creoles of New Granada to write and propose serious commercial reforms for the colonies, was one of the first to welcome Humboldt in Cartagena in March 1801. There is no question that Pombo informed Humboldt about the Creoles' complaints regarding the Crown's tight commercial regulations and policies restricting their direct administration of the political life in the colonies.
29. Humboldt, *Voyage*, 52; Humboldt, *Personal Narrative*, IV.103.
30. Humboldt, *Essai politique*, 2–3; Humboldt, *Political Essay*, 206.
31. Humboldt, *Essai politique*, 3; Humboldt, *Political Essay*, 206.
32. The encounter and subsequent relationship between Humboldt and Caldas was very problematic. Caldas, a strong admirer of Humboldt's, was waiting for him with enthusiasm and with the hope of traveling with him to Mexico and even Europe. Humboldt recognized the intelligence and value of this young Creole but decided not to take him, even though Mutis offered to cover all the expenses. See Caldas's correspondence in Castrillón Arboleda, *Biografía*; see also Hernández de Alba, "Humboldt y Mutis," and Bateman, "Caldas y Humboldt."

33. Castrillón Arboleda, *Biografía*, 160.
34. The year 1810 was when the political and military process of independence began in the Spanish-American possession. It was a process completely consolidated by 1819 after the definitive expulsion of the imperial army that intended to reconquer these territories between 1816 and 1819. Beginning in 1810, the viceroyalties of New Granada, New Spain, and Rio de la Plata, as well as the captaincy generals of Chile, Caracas, Quito, Santo Domingo, Guatemala, and Yucatán, all undertook efforts to establish a republican system of self-government in their respective territories. For a comparative history of the revolution in the Americas, see Langley, *Americas*. For New Granada, see Safford and Palacios, *Colombia*.
35. A prominent Creole from Santa Fé, José Antonio Nariño, was the author of the translation of the Declaration of the Rights of Man, which cost him imprisonment and banishment from the New Kingdom of Granada in 1795. Humboldt met him in 1795.
36. Quoted in Hernández de Alba, "El 20 de Julio," 232.
37. Quoted in Garrido, "Precursores de la independencia," 220.
38. Cacua Prada, *Don Manuel*, 120.
39. Ibid., 119.
40. Ibid., 121.
41. Cañizares-Esguerra, *Nature, Empire, and Nation*, 121.
42. Caldas, "Estado de la geografía," 276–7.

References

Amaya, José Antonio. *Mutis, Apóstol de Linneo: historia de la botánica en el virreinato de Nueva Granada, 1760–1783*. Bogotá: Instituto Colombiano de Antropología e Historia, 2005.

Balbuena, Bernardo de. *La grandeza mexicana*. Ed. Luís Adolfo Domínguez. Mexico: Porrua, 1971. First published 1604.

Bateman, Alfredo D. "Caldas y Humboldt." *Revista de la Academia Colombiana de Ciencias Exactas, Físicas y Naturales* 10, no. 41 (1959): 59–67.

Bauer, Ralph, and José Antonio Mazzotti, eds. *Creole Subjects in the Colonial Americas: Empires, Texts, Identities*. Chapel Hill: University of North Carolina Press, 2009.

Bolívar, Simón. *Cartas de Bolívar, 1825, 1826, 1827*. Ed. R. Blanco-Fombona. Madrid: Editorial America, 1992.

Botting, Douglas. *Humboldt and the Cosmos*. New York: Harper & Row, 1973.

Brading, David A. *The First America: The Spanish Monarchy, Creole Patriots, and the Liberal State, 1492–1867*. Cambridge: Cambridge University Press, 1991.

Cacua Prada, Antonio. *Don Manuel del Socorro Rodríguez: itinerario documentado de su vida, actuaciónes y escritos*. Bogotá: Banco de la República, 1966.

Calancha, Antonio de la. *Crónica moralizada del Orden De San Agustín en el Perú*. Ed. Ignacio Prado Pastor. 6 vols. Lima: Universidad Nacional de San Marcos, 1974. First published 1639.

Caldas, Francisco José de. "Ensayo sobre el estado de la geografía en el virreinato de Santa Fé de Bogotá con relación a la economía y al comercio." In *Francisco José de Caldas: un peregrino de la ciencia*, ed. J. Chenu, 269–98. Madrid: Historia 16, 1992.

Cañizares-Esguerra, Jorge. *Nature, Empire, and Nation: Explorations of the History of Science in the Iberian World*. Stanford: Stanford University Press, 2006.

Castellanos, Juan de. *Elegías de varones ilustres de Indias*. Ed. Gerardo Rivas Moreno. Bogotá: Gerardo Rivas Moreno, 1997. First published 1589.

Castrillón Arboleda, Diego. *Biografía del "sabio" Caldas*. Bogotá: Fondo de Publicaciónes, Universidad Sergio Arboleda, 2008.

Curcio-Nagy, Linda Ann. *The Great Festivals of Colonial Mexico City: Performing Power and Identity*. Albuquerque: University of New Mexico Press, 2004.

Davis, Susan G. *Parades and Power: Street Theatre in Nineteenth-Century Philadelphia*. Berkeley: University of California Press, 1988.

Elias, Norbert. *The Court Society*. Trans. Edmund Jephcott. New York: Pantheon Books, 1983.

Fernández de Piedrahíta, Lucas. *Noticia historial de las conquistas del Nuevo Reino de Granada*. Ed. Sergio Elías Ortiz. 2 vols. Bogotá: Kelly, 1973. First published 1681.

Frías Núñez, Marcelo. *Tras el dorado vegetal: José Celestino Mutis y la Real Expedición Botánica del Nuevo Reino de Granada (1783–1808)*. Seville: Diputación Provincial de Sevilla, 1994.

García Avilés, Alejandro. *El tiempo y los astros: arte, ciencia y religión en la alta Edad Media*. Murcia: Universidad de Murcia, 2000.

Garrido, Margarita. "Precursores de la independencia." In *Gran Enciclopedia de Colombia*, ed. Jorge Orlando Melo, 211–22. Vol. 1. Bogotá: Circulo de Lectores, 1991.

Gonzalbo, Pilar. *Historia de la educación en la época colonial: la educación de los criollos y la vida urbana*. Mexico: Colegio de México, Centro de Estudios Históricos, 1990.

Guzmán M., Rodolfo. "La representación de la ciudad en Lucas Fernández de Piedrahíta como expresión de identidad y transformación sociocultural en el criollo preilustrado de la Nueva Granada." *Cuadernos de Literatura* 6, no. 12 (2001): 42–70.

Hernández de Alba, Guillermo. "El 20 de Julio de 1810." In *Gran Enciclopedia de Colombia*, ed. Jorge Orlando Melo, 223–42. Vol. 1. Bogotá: Circulo de Lectores, 1991.

Hernández de Alba, Guillermo. *Historia documental de la Real Expedición Botánica del Nuevo Reino de Granada después de la muerte de su director Don José Celestino Mutis, 1808–1952*. Bogotá: Fundación Segunda Expedición Botánica, Instituto Colombiano de Cultura Hispánica, 1986.

Hernández de Alba, Guillermo. "Humboldt y Mutis." *Revista de la Academia Colombiana de Ciencias Exactas, Físicas y Naturales* 10, no. 41 (1959): 48–57.

Humboldt, Alexander von. *Cartas americanas*. Ed. Charles Minguet. Trans. Marta Traba. Caracas: Biblioteca Ayacucho, 1980.

Humboldt, Alexander von. *Essai politique sur le royaume de la Nouvelle-Espagne*. Vol. 2. Paris: Schoell, 1811.

Humboldt, Alexander von. *Personal Narrative of Travels to the Equinoctial Regions of the New Continent*. Trans. Helen Maria Williams. 7 vols. London: Longman, Hurst, Rees, Orme, & Brown, 1814–29.

Humboldt, Alexander von. *Political Essay on the Kingdom of New Spain*. Trans. John Black. Vol. 1. London: Longman, Hurst, Rees, Orme, & Brown, 1811.

Humboldt, Alexander von. *Reise auf dem Río Magdalena, durch die Anden und Mexico*, ed. Margot Faak. Part 1. Berlin: Akademie Verlag, 1986.

Humboldt, Alexander von. *Voyage au régions équinoxiales du Nouveau Continent*. Vol. 2. Paris: Maze, 1819.

Humboldt, Alexander von, and Aimé Bonpland. *Plantes équinoxiales recueillies au Méxique, dans l'île de Cuba, dans les provinces de Caracas, de Cumaná et de Barcelone, aux Andes de la Nouvelle-Grenade, de Quito, et du Pérou, et sur les bords du Río Negro, de l'Orénoque et de la rivière des Amazones, ouvrage rédigé par A. Bonpland*. 2 vols. Paris: Levrault et Schoell, 1808.

Jaramillo Uribe, Jaime. "La sociedad colombiana en la época de la visita de Humboldt." In *La personalidad histórica de Colombia*, 132–44. Bogotá: Instituto Colombiano de Cultura, 1977.

Kagan, Richard, and Fernando Marias. *Urban Images of the Hispanic World, 1493–1793*. New Haven, CT: Yale University Press, 2000.

Lafaye, Jacques. *Quetzalcóatl and Guadalupe: The Formation of Mexican National Consciousness, 1531–1813*. Chicago: University of Chicago Press, 1976.

Langley, Lester D. *The Americas in the Age of Revolution, 1750–1850*. New Haven, CT: Yale University Press, 1996.

Lanning, John Tate. *Academic Culture in the Spanish Colonies*. London: Oxford University Press, 1940.

Lasso, Marixa. "Race War and Nation in Caribbean Gran Colombia, Cartagena, 1810–1832." *American Historical Review* 111, no. 2 (2006): 336–61.

Lavallé, Bernard. *Las promesas ambiguas: ensayos sobre el criollismo colonial en los Andes*. Lima: Pontificia Universidad Católica del Perú, Instituto Riva-Agüero, 1993.

Martínez, Carlos. *Bogotá: sinopsis sobre su evolución urbana*. Bogotá: Escala Fondo Editorial, 1976.

McFarlane, Anthony. *Colombia before Independence: Economy, Society, and Politics under Bourbon Rule*. New York: Cambridge University Press, 1993.

Minguet, Charles. *Alejandro de Humboldt historiador y geógrafo de la América española*. Trans. Jorge Padín Videla. Mexico: Universidad Nacional Autónoma de México, 1985. First published 1969.

Miranda, José. *Humboldt y México*. Mexico: Universidad Nacional Autónoma de México, 1962.

Nieto Lozano, Danilo. *La educación en el Nuevo Reino de Granada*. Bogotá: Editorial Santa Fé, 1955.

Ortega, Julio. *El discurso de la abundancia*. Caracas: Monte Ávila, 1992.

Ortega y Medina, Juan Antonio. *Humboldt desde México*. Mexico: Universidad Nacional Autónoma de México, 1960.

Pagden, Anthony. *European Encounters with the New World*. New Haven: Yale University Press, 1993.

Pagden, Anthony. "Identity Formation in Spanish America." In *Colonial Identity in the Atlantic World, 1500–1800*, ed. Nicolas Canny and Anthony Pagden, 51–93. Princeton: Princeton University Press, 1987.

Pereyra, Carlos. *Humboldt en América*. Madrid: Editorial América, 1917.

Pérez Arbeláez, Enrique, ed. *Alejandro de Humboldt en Colombia: extractos de sus obras compilados, ordenados y prologados, con ocasión del centenario de su muerte, en 1859*. Bogotá: Empresa Colombiana de Petróleos, 1959.

Phelan, John Leddy. *The Ceremonial and Political Roles of Cities in Colonial Spanish America*. Milwaukee: University of Wisconsin-Milwaukee, 1972.

Phelan, John Leddy. *The People and the King: The Comunero Revolution in Colombia, 1781*. Madison: University of Wisconsin Press, 1978.

Pratt, Mary Louise. *Imperial Eyes: Travel Writing and Transculturation*. London: Routledge, 1992.

Ramos, Arístides. "Competencias de jurisdicción en la Inquisición de Cartagena de Indias." *Dossier Virreinatos* 3, no. 14 (2008): 326–34. http://www.destiempos.com/n14/dossier_n14.htm (accessed October 24, 2009).

Safford, Frank, and Marco Palacios. *Colombia: Fragmented Land, Divided Society*. New York: Oxford University Press, 2002.

San Pío Aladrén, Pilar. *Mutis and the Royal Botanical Expedition of the Nuevo Reyno de Granada*. Bogotá: Villegas Editores, 1992.

Sigüenza y Góngora, Carlos de. *Paraíso occidental*. Ed. Margarita Peña. México: Consejo Nacional para la Cultura y las Artes, 1995. First published 1684.

Silva, Renan. *Universidad y sociedad en el Nuevo Reino de Granada: contribución a un análisis histórico de la formación intelectual del la sociedad colombiana*. Bogotá: Banco de la República, 1992.

Soto Arango, Diana. *Mutis: educador de la élite neogranadina*. Tunja: Universidad Pedagógica y Tecnológica de Colombia, 2005.

Valenzuela Márquez, Jaime. *Las liturgias del poder: celebraciónes públicas y estrategias persuasivas en Chile colonial, 1609–1709*. Santiago, Chile: LOM Ediciónes, Centro de Investigaciónes Diego Barros Arana, 2001.

Vargas Lesmes, Juli án. *La sociedad de Santa Fé colonial*. Bogotá: Centro de Investigación y Educación Popular, 1990.

Reading Juan Francisco Manzano in the wake of Alexander von Humboldt

Marilyn Grace Miller

Colonial scholars have recently begun to pay closer attention to the traffic of the work of Cuban poet Juan Francisco Manzano between the Caribbean and Europe, pointing out that the first version of his so-called slave narrative, along with a selection of his poetry, was first published in English translation in London in 1840. This recent shift in Manzano studies signals a growing recognition of the Cuban poet's circulation in an international abolitionist discourse, despite the fact that he himself never left Cuba or even denounced slavery explicitly. By situating Manzano temporally and spatially in relation to Alexander von Humboldt and his comments on Cuban slavery, we can better understand the participation of both in transatlantic efforts to expose and question colonial servitude in the Americas.

Opposites attract

No two lives would appear to be more different than those of the German scientific explorer Alexander von Humboldt (1769–1859) and the Cuban slave poet Juan Francisco Manzano (c.1797–c.1854).[1] The first was a nonpareil transatlantic explorer whose international importance can hardly be overestimated, and whose far-flung research exploits earned him the moniker of "second discoverer of America" from the lips of no less a personage than Simón Bolívar. The second was an item of property in the households of the wealthy Cuban families of Beatriz de Jústiz, Marquise of Santa Ana and María de la Concepción Valdés, Marquise of Prado Ameno. In these reduced (and virtually enclosed) domestic settings, Manzano wrote a handful of poems and a drama in verse hardly anyone has read even today – hardly a writing career to be compared with Humboldt's staggering textual output, so vast that editors have yet to publish a complete collection of his correspondence alone. And while Humboldt, whom Charles Darwin judged to be "the greatest scientific traveler that ever lived,"[2] is revered and remembered as well in a vast array of buildings, institutions, monuments, and municipalities that bear his name, Manzano would no doubt be a "dead being" to contemporary publics, were it not for the fact that he is the author of the only known slave narrative written in Spanish before emancipation.[3] Nonetheless, despite the enormous differences in these two lives in terms of personal experiences and historic prominence, they share some surprising affinities. Both men penned narratives in which the portrayal of colonial slavery in Cuba became perhaps the most hotly debated aspect.[4] Both authors saw the products of their textual labor edited, translated, modified, and even "mutilated" by men with political agendas very different from their own. The great Cuban ethnographer Fernando Ortiz, in his study of John Thrasher's 1856 English translation of the *Essay politique sur l'île de Cuba* [*Political Essay on the Island of Cuba*] (1826), wrote that "the mutilations of Humboldt's text are neither few nor insignificant."[5] Both Humboldt and Manzano produced documents that circulated as part of an international and multilingual abolitionist debate, and their portrayals of slave life in Cuba, though radically different, were both deemed dangerous to interests in the island and censored by colonial authorities.[6] Thus, despite working in different genres from extraordinarily dissimilar backgrounds, educations, and everyday experiences, Humboldt and Manzano are both treasured and sometimes criticized by contemporary readers for the unique perspectives they provide on the conditions of slave life in early nineteenth-century Cuba.

Born in Berlin to a Prussian army officer and a wealthy widow, Alexander von Humboldt was educated by private tutors and began studying classics, languages, mathematics, political history, and economics at an early age. During his university studies, he expanded his interests and knowledge in such fields as botany, geology, and mineralogy, and the death of his mother in 1796 provided him with the financial resources necessary to pursue his dream of combining world travel with scientific exploration. Encouraged to engage his prodigious curiosity in geomagnetism, volcanology, climatology, and astronomy, Humboldt soon set out on an epic journey that would last five years and take him to a territory more vast than that covered by perhaps any of the early "discoverers," including the prolific Dominican friar and "defender of the Indians," Bartolomé de las Casas.[7] Before returning to enormous fanfare and fame in Europe after his legendary sally into the known and uncharted territories of the Americas, Humboldt met with United States President Thomas Jefferson, that same president who had earlier doubted that a slave woman named Phillis Wheatley could, in fact, be the author of a series of verses carefully composed in the tradition of Alexander Pope.[8] Following his celebrated return to Europe, Humboldt lived for two decades in Paris, where he worked on his writing, continued his scientific experiments, and participated in a rich social and intellectual life, attending the most important Paris salons and mentoring promising young scientists. In 1827, he accepted a position in the court of Frederick William III, the King of Prussia, in Berlin; he lived there until his death in 1859. Humboldt's *Essai politique sur l'île de Cuba* was just one piece of a writing career that spanned seven decades and produced the multivolume scientific findings, the three-volume *Relation historique*, the five-volume *Examen critique de l'histoire de la géographie du Nouveau Continent et des progrès de l'astronomie nautique au quinzième et seizième siècles*, another three-volume work on Russia and Central Asia, and his famous five-volume *Kosmos*, published from 1845 to 1862. In the midst of all this writing, Humboldt managed to entertain a steady stream of international visitors and to maintain an active correspondence with family members, political figures, and friends from his travels, though he complained that attending to these responsibilities left him only the night-time to do his own work. Of the 50,000 letters he wrote, we still have access to about 15,000.[9]

It was in the same final years of the eighteenth century when Humboldt was just embarking on his extraordinary quest that, historians believe, Juan Francisco Manzano was born in the island of Cuba to María del Pilar Manzano, a hand servant to Beatriz de Jústiz de Santa Ana.[10] Forbidden from learning to read and write and from mixing with other slave children, Manzano gained his literacy and much of his knowledge of the world on the sly, first memorizing sermons and theatrical performances he had attended with members of the family who owned him, composing poems in "one of those notebooks of the imagination," and eventually learning to read and write by studying the exercises cast off by his young masters.[11] Manzano's "modest" dreams of participating in the intellectual and literary life of his white contemporaries and of securing his freedom were repeatedly frustrated and realized only partially.[12]

Though we have no proof that Manzano knew of Humboldt's visit to Cuba at the turn of the nineteenth century or had any access to the texts which documented that experience, or that Humboldt was ever acquainted with Manzano's story or read his works, Humboldt's influence on the men of letters who surrounded Manzano and aided his literary efforts suggests a shared historical and literary genealogy. I suggest reading Manzano in the wake of Humboldt in two senses, then. First, we can read Manzano's works temporally within a thematic trajectory that follows on the heels of Humboldt's observations penned during and after visits to Cuba at the turn of the nineteenth century, a moment contemporary with Manzano's birth. But since we have yet to establish a direct connection between the two authors or their works, I suggest that we also examine their writings within a *network* of circulation, one that implicates not only a Cuban poet and a German scientific traveler, but also the Cuban man of letters Domingo Del Monte and the Irish diplomat Richard Robert Madden, as well as such tangential figures as Scottish abolitionist David Turnbull and Victor Schoelcher, the French statesman credited with championing and heralding the end of slavery in the francophone Caribbean.

Fionnghuala Sweeney's essay, "Atlantic Countercultures and the Networked Text: Juan Francisco Manzano, R.R. Madden and the Cuban Slave Narrative," reveals how Manzano's notorious narrative of his life in slavery passed from Cuba to Britain, from Spanish to English (and later to other languages), and from his own handwritten account to a hybrid early publication that did not even bear his name. Sweeney urges us to read the early edition of Manzano's "autobiography" as both a "networked" text and a "borderland" text rooted in the Cuban experience but transiting a broader, Atlantic circuit.[13] Indeed, Manzano's life and oeuvre, and their connections to Humboldt and other leading nineteenth-century Atlantic figures, beg for a methodological approach informed by the notions of the *histoire croisée*, which focuses on the "empirical intercrossings consubstantial with the object of study, as well as on the operations by which researchers themselves cross scales, categories, and viewpoints."[14] If reading Manzano's memoir within the frames of the slave narrative and as the nascent voice of Afro-Cuban identity and anti-slavery rhetoric is bound to disappoint us, since Manzano never condemns slavery explicitly, then studying his diverse works in the larger context of far-reaching anti-colonial and anti-slavery discourses that also include Humboldt can help us better understand his unprecedented and precedent-setting story.

Ambivalent abolitionists

Both Humboldt and Manzano have been accused of addressing the matter of slavery with a measure of ambivalence, and both have also been trumpeted as key voices of abolitionist literature. How have critics arrived at these seemingly contradictory conclusions? While Humboldt's writings on slavery in the *Essay politique sur l'île de Cuba* and elsewhere, and the glaring absence of any systematic discussion of the subject in Manzano's work, have both been construed to support the first contention, it is clear that, despite these charges of ambivalence, both authors' works were enlisted as important tools in abolitionist campaigns and anti-slavery rhetoric. To understand better the charge of ambivalence, then, we must reconsider the role played by the topic of Cuban slavery in relation to the entire oeuvre of each author. Oliver Lubrich's "In the Realm of Ambivalence: Alexander von Humboldt's Discourse on Cuba" reminds us that the *Essai politique sur l'île de Cuba* was originally part of the *Relation historique du voyage aux régions équinoxiales du Nouveau Continent* (translated by Helen Maria Williams as the *Personal Narrative*). It was thus a case study, as it were, of a specific Spanish colony in relation to the whole of Spain's American empire, still over a decade away from any successful independence drive when Humboldt visited the Caribbean in 1801 and 1804.

Indeed, while what Humboldt saw in Cuba perhaps provoked the German explorer to denounce slavery most vociferously in a section of the *Essai politique sur l'île de Cuba* which other hands would later title "The Nature of Slavery," Humboldt's observations on slavery are woven throughout this and other texts. A study of the personal diaries Humboldt wrote in "real time" during his 1799–1804 American sojourn also show that – as he himself would insist again many years later when he defended his work against treasonous translation – he arrived in the Americas as an enemy of both slavery and of revolution, which, to him, meant radical revolution, as in the case of the French Jacobins.[15] But while "all of Humboldt's diaristic observations confirm that he was an enemy of slavery,"[16] they also indicate that he consistently rejected violent revolution as a means to reaching full abolition, judging instead that slavery could be eradicated through legislative means and governmental measures by the second quarter of the nineteenth century. According to Michael Zeuske:

> If we analyze Humboldt's relationship with the local slave-holding elite, however, another account comes to light. While being a lifelong friend of members of the reformist elite in Havana (the group around Francisco Arango y Parreño, among whom were the largest slaveholders in all of the Americas at that time), Humboldt had a far more conflicted relationship with the Venezuelan elites who worked toward a revolution and the establishment of a "white republic." He had especially strained relationships with those men who became military leaders during the revolution for independence: the Bolívars, the Ibarras, and the Peñalvers, among others. An enemy of violent revolutions, Humboldt himself preferred slave emancipation that was controlled by the slave holders to the slaves' self-emancipation.[17]

Despite a clear anti-slavery stance, then, Humboldt's travels in Cuba and elsewhere in Latin America brought him into contact with many of the principal slaveholding families and made him a first-hand witness to their fears that what had happened in Haiti from 1789 to 1804 could happen on the continent and in other parts of the Caribbean as well. Humboldt was convinced – at least early on – that "the condition of free men of colour is happier at the Havannah, than among nations which boast during ages of the most advanced civilization," thanks to higher rates of manumission and Spanish legislation that favored the attainment of freedom through the process of *coartación*, in which slaves could purchase their freedom over time.[18]

Of course, the end of slavery that Humboldt predicted proved to be much more elusive, and slaves' access to their own emancipation in fact became more difficult by the 1830s, when Juan Manzano's attempts to secure his freedom, even after it had been promised him, were repeatedly thwarted. It is important to signal this historical shift not only to show how repression of enslaved and free populations of color had become much more sinister by this later date, but also because the question of resistance is key to a consideration of Manzano's own "ambivalence" on the slavery question.[19] Just as has happened with his North American counterpart Phillis Wheatley, readers have hoped to find in Manzano righteous condemnation of slavery and all its evils, as well as outright rejection of the "white" aesthetic values espoused and practiced by the slaveholding educated elite. Both writers have disappointed contemporary readers on both counts, Wheatley most famously in her poem "On Being Brought from Africa to America," which begins:

'Twas mercy brought me from my Pagan land,
Taught my benighted soul to understand.[20]

Manzano, in turn, disappointed readers in his attempts to: (1) emphasize his proximity, both racial and relational, to whites and white privilege, noting that he called his slave mistress "mamá mía";[21] (2) distance himself from other slaves and from blacks in general as a "mulatto among blacks";[22] and (3) defer to his white benefactor Domingo Del Monte, who is credited with convincing Manzano to commit his sordid life story to paper, despite Manzano's preferences for penning poetry.

Key benefactors

Born in 1804 in Venezuela as the son of a functionary of the Spanish Crown, Domingo Del Monte's name would later become synonymous with the emergence of a Creole-Cuban identity and its corresponding literary production.[23] While he spent most of his youth in the island, Del Monte also traveled in Spain and the United States, forming friendships with prominent writers in Madrid and Philadelphia before returning to Cuba in 1829. By 1835, Del Monte was well established in transatlantic literary circles and something of a celebrity in Cuba: he was the publisher of *El puntero literario* (1830) and *La moda o Recreo semanal del bello sexo* (1829); he directed the *Revista Bimestre Cubana* (1831–4) and was a member of the influential Sociedad Económica de Amigos del País. But Del Monte was most famous, probably, for his *tertulias*, or literary salons, in both Havana and Matanzas. Like Humboldt, he had a remarkable talent, according to his contemporaries, for inspiring those around him to conceive of and practice culture "as a perennial dialogue."[24] Arguably, it was under Del Monte's tutelage that Manzano first enjoyed limited success as a writer, publishing poetry from as early as 1821 in venues such as the *Diario de la Habana* and Del Monte's own *La moda*. In a letter from December 1834, when Manzano was still a slave, it is difficult to separate his delight in Del Monte's efforts to publish his works from his absolute dependence on his mentor for exposure to a wider circle beyond the limitations of the Havana or Matanzas salons:

Mi querido y Sr. Don Domingo: no puedo pintar a su merced la grande sorpresa que me causó cuando supe por su merced mismo la dirección que piensa dar a mis pobres rimas: cuando las considero navegando a climas tan distantes par aver la luz pública en el emporio de la ilustración europea, donde tantos vates con razón se disputan la primacía. Todo me parece sueño. Nacidos en la Zona tórrida bajo la oscuridad de mi destino, vuelan desde el seno de mis infortunios, llevando el nombre de su infeliz autor, más allá de donde merece ser oído: a la verdad, señor.
¡Mucho bien esperé, pero no tanto!

[My dear Señor Don Domingo: I can't paint for your grace, Sir, the great surprise it caused me when I found out from you yourself, Sir, the direction you hope to give my poor rhymes: when I consider them navigating such distant climes to see the public light in the emporium of the European Enlightenment, where so many wise poets vie for primacy. It all seems to me a dream. Born in the torrid zone under the darkness of my destiny, they fly from the breast of my misfortunes, carrying the name of their unhappy author beyond where they should be heard; in truth, Sir:
I had hopes, but never this high!][25]

While Manzano adopts the stance of the humble and grateful protégé here, he also forecasts the circulation of his texts beyond the confines of the island, within the "emporium of the European Enlightenment." He marks himself, then, as a bona fide, if undeserving, contender in the literary marketplace of the day, in which value and merit were still ascribed, for the most part, using European texts and authors as models. For Jerome Branche, Manzano's "excessive" expression of gratitude to Del Monte no doubt is a product of the poet's temperament and weaknesses; it should also be read, though, as a strategy of self-preservation and self-censoring in the face of very real threats to his life and person.[26] Manzano knew that without the *appearance* of acquiescence and subservience to white power which is so off-putting to contemporary readers, his literary abilities would have gone unnoticed and his poems would have languished unpublished.

But if, in this letter from late 1834, Manzano was moved to see how Del Monte's assistance had resulted in the circulation of his poetry amongst distant publics, subsequent correspondence with his mentor suggests a variety of frustrations, as well as a nasty case of writer's block when it came to putting on paper the life story upon which his fame – and perhaps his very freedom – would ultimately hinge. In a letter from 25 February 1835, Manzano tells Del Monte of his hopes that his recent marriage will afford him the solace and inspiration he so seeks, but admits that his new wife's family "groans" at the union. Why? Manzano writes at the end of the letter that he (and presumably the new in-laws) can never be happy while still awaiting his elusive liberty, marked cautiously in the text only by the first letter of the word, and referring to himself only by the initials of his name:

No se olvide su merced de que J.F. no será de ningún modo feliz, si no siendo *L*: y ahora con más razón; ¡ojalá que así como las musas me han dado una joven, que dicen no la merezco, me dieran contar conmigo mismo y poder ofrecer mis servicios a quien tan altamente me favorece!

[Don't forget, Sir, that J.F. will never in any way be happy without having my *L*: and now more than ever. How I wish that just as the muses have given me a young woman who they say I don't deserve, they would give me the chance to be on my own, and thus offer my services to this one who so highly favors me!][27]

Manzano's fear that Del Monte might forget the matter of his liberty (with a capital "L"), so poignant and so thinly veiled in this letter, makes much more sense if we consider it in relation to a letter from exactly four months later, in which he responds to Del Monte's request for the finished manuscript of a "history" that his benefactor had apparently asked for four or five months earlier. Manzano protests that the same day that he received the request, "me puse a recorrer el espacio que llena la carrera de mi vida y cuando pude me puse a escribir" [I set about reviewing the space that fills the course of my life, and when I could, I started writing].[28] Though he assures Del Monte that he hopes to finish soon, he admits that, on more than four occasions, he has been unable to complete the task. "Un cuadro de tantas calamidades no parece sino un abultado protocolo de embusterías; y más cuando desde tan tierna edad, los crueles azotes me hacían conocer mi humilde condición" [A description of so many calamities seems like nothing more than a bulky report of mistruths, and even more so since the cruel lashes of the whip have reminded me of my lowly condition from such a young age], he confesses. "Me abochorna el contarlo y no sé cómo demostrar los hechos, dejando la parte más terrible en el tintero y ¡ojalá tuviera otras con que llenar la historia de mi vida...!" [It embarrasses me to recount this, and I don't know how to demonstrate the facts while leaving the most terrible part in the inkwell; oh, how I wish I had other facts with which to fill the history of my life...!]. To retell such experiences is, of course, to relive them, and Manzano recoils from the task, as well as from the self-portrait that emerges from it, which he is sure will lower Del Monte's estimation of him "one hundred percent": "Así idos preparando par aver a una débil criatura, rodando en los más graves padecimientos ... el blanco de los infortunios" [So prepare yourselves to see a weak creature, reeling under the most severe suffering ... the target of misfortunes].[29] "I am a slave," he bluntly reminds Del Monte, and "a slave is a dead being for his master."[30] All the more reason, then, that his task "of daring to speak up" will be a delicate and terrifying one, especially since the slave mistress who most abused him is still living as he doggedly, but fearfully, continues with his assignment.

In a letter from September of that same year, Manzano responds again to correspondence from Del Monte, complaining: "La prometida libertad, que tenía en esta casa, parece que se la va llevando el viento, como se llevó la palabra" [The liberty I had promised to me in this house seems to have been carried away by the wind, just as the promise was carried away];[31] in an October letter, he writes again of a frustrated attempt to change masters, and thus secure the funds necessary to buy his freedom.[32] But the man he had hoped would be his new master at least offered hope that, with Del Monte's help, a subscription could be taken up to purchase Manzano's freedom, thus releasing him from his unbearable situation, made all the worse by the fame he was now enjoying in Matanzas as a poet.[33] As this paper trail suggests, Del Monte is the key, the linchpin, in a complex series of struggles, first for exposure and recognition and, finally, for freedom itself. Or perhaps not so finally, if we take into account a letter Manzano wrote to Rosa Alfonso, Del Monte's wife, from a prison cell in October of 1844.

Already a "free" man for some eight years by that time, Manzano was imprisoned for his suspected role in the so-called Ladder Conspiracy, an uprising to which the colonial government of Capitán-General Leopoldo O'Donnell had responded by interrogating, torturing, and imprisoning many blacks, both free and enslaved, and by expelling white Cubans and foreigners considered sympathizers. Fearing for his very life, Manzano writes to Doña Rosa to insist that despite all the injustice and treachery he had endured, he himself had never betrayed Del Monte or his reputation.[34] And once again, Manzano demonstrates his dependence on Del Monte and his family, pleading with Rosa Alfonso to provide his wife and young daughters with something to eat, since he himself cannot attend to their needs.[35] In the Franco manuscript version of this letter included in the most recent complete editions of Manzano's works compiled by both Abdeslam Azougarh (2000) and William Luis (2007), Manzano signs this letter as "su criado" [your servant], suggesting the terrible irony of finding himself in such deplorable conditions several years after having obtained his longed-for freedom.[36] Burton ties Manzano's silence from 1844 to his death in 1853 to his prison experience and the torture he endured there.[37]

Manzano's impassioned correspondence with Del Monte and later Del Monte's wife, in which his emotional register seems to oscillate between encouragement/ delight and discouragement/despair, prompts us to frame the *Autobiography* in a nuanced intertextual context that takes into account the conflicts in interest between the author as a man who sought recognition primarily as a poet and Del Monte as a procurer and agent with more than literary acclaim on his mind. As we shall soon see, the early publishing history of the *Autobiography* leads us directly down this path, showing that the same painful past the poet recoiled from recounting would serve as a "perfect picture" of slavery for abolitionists and slavery reformers following on the heels of Humboldt.

Although the biographical details already mentioned in relation to our two authors make clear the gulf that separated Humboldt and Manzano in terms of their access to and exercise of personal agency, Humboldt's relationships with certain key cultural figures also determined, to a significant extent, the direction his travels and his writings would take. In 1798, Humboldt arrived in Madrid with Aimé Bonpland, the botanist who would accompany him on his scientific sojourns in the Americas. There, he was introduced to Mariano Luis de Urquijo, a foreign minister in the Spanish court who, upon discovering Humboldt's desire to travel to the Spanish colonies at his own expense, got him an audience with King Carlos IV, which was then followed by not one passport but two: one from the Secretary of State and one from the Council of the Indies. "Never had a traveler been granted greater concessions and never before has a Spanish Government placed greater confidence in a foreigner," Humboldt wrote.[38] Urquijo, a fascinating and controversial character in his own right, was a diplomat and Francophile, whose translation of Voltaire's *La mort de Cesar* was condemned by the Spanish Inquisition. Despite a series of political problems related to his attempts to limit the long arm of the Inquisition, Urquijo successfully promoted many cultural and scientific efforts during his two tenures as Secretary of State (1799–1800 and 1808–13). The first of these periods coincided with Humboldt's arrival in the court of Carlos IV, an understudied moment that Miguel Ángel Puig-Samper examines with considerable detail in "Humboldt, un prusiano en la corte del Rey Carlos IV." He notes that Urquijo was ideologically related to a group of Humboldt's friends in Madrid who frequently met at the *tertulia* of the Countess of Montijo, María Francisca de Sales Portocarrero. "The gentleman Urquijo aided my request and managed to smooth out all the obstacles," Humboldt would later recall.[39] Though Urquijo might be considered a minor detail in Humboldt's far-ranging story, it is worth pointing out that the Spanish politician who would help launch him on his Latin American adventure was himself an abolitionist.[40] Also, as a man who had lived for a time in Great Britain and was forced to repeatedly defend himself against the Spanish Inquisition, Urquijo exhibited the same Atlanticist sensibility that Humboldt would soon come to epitomize.

In a situation not entirely alien to the fundamental role Del Monte played in Manzano's "career," Humboldt's audiences with Urquijo and Carlos IV would prefigure later relationships with monarchs and other well-placed cultural agents. Aaron Sachs addresses this issue in *The Humboldt Current*, and while his claim that "Humboldt's compromises with dictatorial rulers, his practice of dedicating books to them, his direct employment in the Prussian court, all cast doubt on his ultimate integrity and radicalism" perhaps overstates the case,[41] especially since such dependence on the court was only the case late in the great explorer's life, the fact remains that both Manzano and Humboldt – from within utterly different contexts and experiences – understood that champions of their work were the key to needed resources and to various kinds of freedom. Certainly, Manzano's dependence on others was nearly absolute, while Humboldt's was rarely, if ever, so. Their stories also feature very different chronologies in relation to the freedoms each sought. The timely intervention of Urquijo and others before Humboldt even embarked on his legendary American foray is emblematic of the freedoms (of movement, of access, etc.) that would characterize all the scientific explorer's subsequent ventures and efforts, whereas Manzano's reiterated acknowledgment and obeisance of his patron's wishes only gained him deferred, and ultimately uncertain, freedom. Nonetheless, it is instructive to see how *both* men insisted on the autonomy of their postures and projects, despite external pressures. While Sachs's comment that Humboldt used his sponsors to virtually the same extent that they used him may be an overstatement, it points to similar strategies employed by Manzano, whose surrender of his writings and his own personal fate to Del Monte, Madden, and others ultimately gained him a measure of freedom that could not be bound even by slavery itself.

Words become flesh, flesh becomes words

Although Manzano was probably only an infant when Humboldt traveled in Cuba at the end of 1800, the European's words regarding the "torments and debasements"[42] of people of African descent would seem to eerily prefigure Manzano's plight and fight to be considered not a brutish slave, but a poet and a full peer of the men who gathered in Del Monte's *tertulias*. Humboldt wrote in the *Political Essay on the Island of Cuba*:

> It is in vain that writers of ability, in order to veil barbarous institutions by ingenious fictions of language, have invented the terms of *negro peasants of the West Indies, black vassalage*, and *patriarchal protection:* it is to profane the noble qualities of the mind and the imagination, to exculpate by illusory comparisons, or captious sophisms, excesses that afflict humanity, and for which they prepare violent commotions.[43]

Besides declaring famously that "Slavery is no doubt the greatest of all the evils that afflict humanity," Humboldt described colonial servitude in Cuba as a catalogue of human deprivation, providing a list of the various forms of psychological control and physical abuses that slaves faced in both urban and rural settings, a list that uncannily foreshadows Manzano's tortured and torturous recall of the results of such punitive measures in his own body and soul.[44] Humboldt also understood, more than eight decades before complete and final emancipation in 1886, that "a real amelioration of the captive caste ought to extend over the whole moral and physical position of man."[45]

Nonetheless, Humboldt perhaps could not have imagined the degree of degradation, both physical and metaphysical, that Manzano had to revisit as he struggled to compose the personal history Del Monte had requested of him. Manzano literally embodied many of the "abominable practices" to which Humboldt had referred, and he embodied them as a privileged house slave whose exceptional verbal gifts, and thus possibilities for "genuine improvement," had been duly noted.[46] It was Manzano's own shameful life story, rather than a series of observations compiled by a scientist, that Irish diplomat Richard Robert Madden carried to London and published in an abridged version in English in 1840. Manzano's remarkable skills in both writing and declaiming poetry, Del Monte's recognition and cultivation of those skills, and Madden's efforts in publishing the slave's life story abroad converted Manzano into a minor cause célèbre for reformers on both sides of the Atlantic. It is this insertion in international debates related to slavery and abolition that places Manzano in unlikely proximity to Humboldt. The two men's observations of slave life in Cuba, so unalike, would soon be subjected to similar "surgeries" at the hands of their translators, although these translators' political postures could hardly have been more dissimilar.

Richard Robert Madden, the man to whom we owe the first translation and publication of Manzano's paradigmatic narrative, served Britain as the Super-intendent of Liberated Africans in Cuba from 1836 to 1840, following the 1835 signing of the Anglo-Spanish Treaty that established Mixed Commission Courts in eastern and western Atlantic sites such as Sierra Leone and Angola, as well as in Kingston and Havana.[47] Madden is a figure closely associated with the over-whelming failure of such agreements to enforce the reduction or cessation of slave traffic, particularly in Cuba, as his later involvement in the plight of the Africans aboard the *Amistad* would demonstrate.[48] By the time he arrived in Cuba, Madden had already served in several other international settings as a physician or diplomat, including in the Middle East and the Ottoman Empire where he had witnessed slavery at first hand.

Madden was both a contemporary of and heir to Humboldt, and his central role in Manzano's story suggests a single degree of separation between the German and the Cuban, with Madden, rather than Del Monte, serving as mediator. We might assume that the most obvious place to look for parallels between Humboldt and Madden would be in the latter's *The Island of Cuba: Its Resources, Progress, and Prospects*, published in London in 1849, a work whose title suggests close parity with Humboldt's *Political Essay*, also called *The Island of Cuba* in John Thrasher's edition (see Figure 1).[49] But unlike his earlier two-volume *A Twelvemonth's Residence in the West Indies, during the Transition from Slavery to Apprenticeship* (1835), in which Madden demonstrates how well he knew Humboldt's works by citing him some 12 times, *The Island of Cuba* does not mention the German explorer. Nevertheless, the transatlantic aspects of Humboldt's earlier work are echoed in Madden's explicit desire

> to state facts, and to leave his readers to form their own opinions with respect to them, and to place before the public the results of his own experience in the British West Indies, in Cuba, and on the western coast of Africa, in various official situations – and in the United States, in a private capacity.[50]

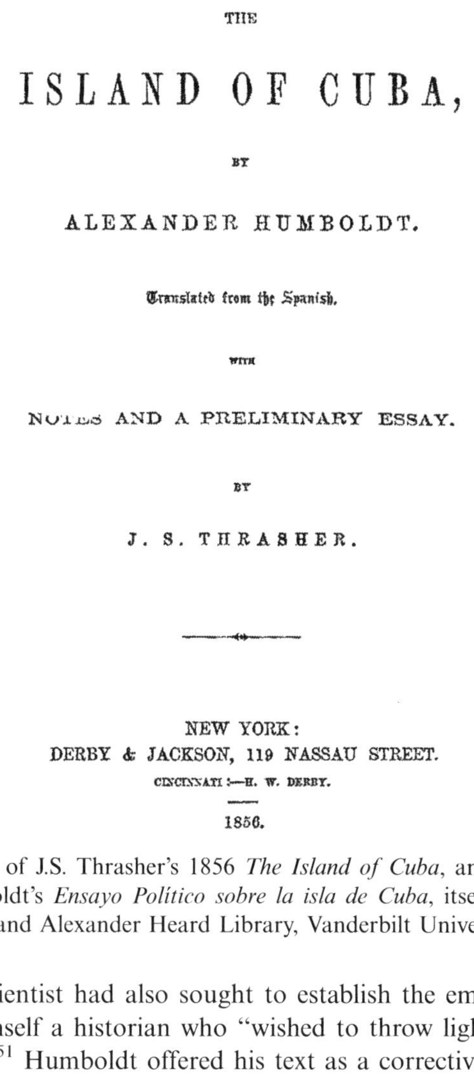

THE

ISLAND OF CUBA,

BY

ALEXANDER HUMBOLDT.

Translated from the Spanish,

WITH

NOTES AND A PRELIMINARY ESSAY.

BY

J. S. THRASHER.

NEW YORK:
DERBY & JACKSON, 119 NASSAU STREET.
CINCINNATI :—H. W. DERBY.

1856.

Figure 1. Title page of J.S. Thrasher's 1856 *The Island of Cuba*, an unauthorized English translation of Humboldt's *Ensayo Político sobre la isla de Cuba*, itself an 1827 translation. Courtesy of the Jean and Alexander Heard Library, Vanderbilt University.

The Prussian scientist had also sought to establish the empirical nature of his essay, declaring himself a historian who "wished to throw light on facts, and give precision to ideas."[51] Humboldt offered his text as a corrective to the "benevolent credulity" and "passionate animosities" that had resulted in "the most vague and erroneous statements" regarding conditions in Cuba.[52]

Both Humboldt and Madden were consummate Atlanticists who presented their experiences in Europe and the Americas as eyewitness accounts; they were in agreement as to slavery's immorality. Humboldt had repudiated the use of such terms as "peasants," "vassals," and "patriarchal protection" to mask the abuses of commerce in human flesh;[53] Madden would later use language reminiscent of Humboldt's as he took issue with the ideas of Joseph Hume, a fellow physician and politician who advocated for free trade in labor, rather than the "premature" abolition of slavery. For Madden, such ideas were old pleas, of good intentions towards the people of Africa; old pretexts for man robbing; old plans for peopling plantations under colour of zeal for the promotion of the interests of civilisation and religion; the old spirit of fraud and cupidity embodied in another form of hypocrisy.[54]

There are also some surprising parallels between Humboldt's and Madden's frames of reference as they tackled the subject of Cuban slavery. Both used experience and data from other parts of the Caribbean to examine the case of the Spanish colony, and both also drew comparisons between oriental and American slavery. As Lubrich has noted: "[t]he imagining of the Orient in the travel writings of Humboldt is ambiguous." However, conflicts between the West and East serve repeatedly as a historical backdrop and point of comparison for reading the contemporary situation in America, and Cuba in particular. "Humboldt refers on several occasions to events occurring in southeast Europe," Lubrich continues, and "[h]e associates the colonial slavery that he observes in Cuba ('le commerce des nègres') with the Turkish dominion over contemporary Greece."[55] As a medical doctor, Madden was also a man of science, one who had observed slavery in the Ottoman Empire before arriving in the Caribbean.[56] Excerpts of his observations, included in works such as *Travels in Turkey, Egypt, Nubia and Palestine* (1829), found their way into the Cuban newspapers of the late 1830s, offering a veiled criticism of Spanish colonial rule in the island.

Both men found that their Latin American sojourns only confirmed their repugnance at slavery in Europe; Humboldt wrote: "I preserved, on quitting America, the same horror of slavery which I had felt in Europe."[57] In Madden's *Memoirs*, which his son edited and which were published in London in 1891, the Irishman even brings Humboldt into the frame of his own self-portrait. In a composition that begins, "This here is a portrait of one Mister Madden," the writer paints himself as one who wrote much

> of rebels and wrongs, and endeavored to touch
> Men's hearts with their sufferings; but none except fools
> Would feel any pity for Irish or Poles,
> As Albert to Humboldt observed very cutely,
> And argued indeed for a Prince most astutely.
>
> Who ought many battles for slaves he could boast,
> In Cuba, Jamaica, on Africa's coast.[58]

Where Madden really parts ways with Humboldt is in terms of focus, emphasis, and rhetorical zeal. Whereas, for Humboldt, slavery in Cuba and elsewhere in Latin America was a topic he took up for consideration as he ostensibly brought his masterful essay to a close (though the text, in fact, continues well beyond this point of "termination"), when Madden wrote his *Island of Cuba* in 1849, "the extinction of the slave-trade in the Spanish colonies and the Brazils" was the central concern and the central aim of his text; any other proposed solution to the complex problems within and betwixt the colonies and former possessions of England, Spain, and Portugal was "illusory."[59] Madden's mission in Cuba was radically different from Humboldt's 35 years earlier. No longer could slavery be considered a flawed feature of the socio-political, economic, and physical landscape, and the improvement of the slaves a worthy goal on the road to its gradual dissolution, as Humboldt had suggested.[60] Frustrated time and again in his efforts to enforce laws that were more often disregarded than respected, and repudiated by powerful interests for whom his intervention in Cuban affairs was a constant thorn in the side, Madden doggedly continued with his duties. He disputed official reports, refused to rubber-stamp activities he considered illicit, and visited *ingenios* [plantations] unannounced, and all of these activities confirmed his suspicions that the benign picture of Cuban slavery endorsed by so many, including – to a certain extent – Humboldt himself, was the product of dishonesty, hypocrisy, and greed.[61] "So transcendent the evils I witnessed, over all I had ever heard or seen of the rigor of slavery elsewhere, that at first I could hardly believe the evidence of my senses."[62] Burton writes: "he could not be cajoled, coerced or intimidated."[63] It should hardly surprise us, then, that Madden made such a concerted effort to obtain a first-hand account of the Cuban slave experience or that he notably doctored that same text to serve his own political ends.[64]

Traduttore, traditore

Critics speculate that Madden met Manzano in one of the famous *tertulias* of Del Monte, Manzano's Cuban mentor, perhaps even on the same occasion in 1836 when the Creole poet's declamation of the sonnet "Mis treinta años" [My Thirty Years] compelled those present to collect the funds necessary to purchase his freedom.[65] At least one important Cuban historian, Juan Pérez de la Riva, in fact credits Madden with the arrangements for Manzano's manumission.[66] As I have argued elsewhere, the relationship between poetry and narrative is crucial here, since the worthiness of Manzano's life story or autobiography rested in large part on his success as a recognized poet.[67] Indeed, the title Madden affixed to the 1840 English version of the text we read as Manzano's *narrative* of Cuban slavery was, in fact, *Poems by a Slave in the Island of Cuba* (see Figure 2).

Madden inserted Manzano's narrative between his own writings, thus establishing an explicit intertextual relationship. As the table of contents demonstrates more clearly, he wagered that both Manzano's poetry and his narrative would be potent proof for his own multi-genre anti-slavery arguments, which took shape in fiery poems such as "Slave-Trade Merchant" and "The Sugar Estate," and in a series of essays that, together, constitute an appendix of more than 60 pages to Manzano's life story, the latter covering only half as many pages in the 1840 publication. The book's essays, which bear titles such as "Evils of the Cuban Slave-Trade," "Conditions of Slaves in Cuba," and "Emancipation of Slaves in Cuba," demonstrate the degree to which Madden was committed to full and immediate abolition. They show us as well the very different conditions for publishing such ideas that one could find at that time in London, versus Havana. As we see on the cover of the publication, the book could be obtained at the offices of the Anti-Slavery Society in London.

Madden's version of Manzano's story (which had already been revised and corrected by Cuban proofreader Anselmo Suárez y Romero) omitted certain key passages that Madden deemed deleterious to the aims of the British abolitionist effort, such as Manzano's account of his close intimacy with and love for his first mistress. Ironically, then, the first version of Manzano's remarkable "autobiography" does not bear that title or even his own name. It was staged by mentors and handlers hailing from both sides of the Atlantic who commissioned, edited, corrected, extracted, translated, and otherwise manipulated his life story, publishing it, at least initially, in a country and language not his own.[68]

Like Humboldt, Madden denounced slavery in Cuba as an evil and, like Humboldt, he read Cuban slavery against or alongside slavery in the Orient and elsewhere. In his essay "Evils of the Cuban Slave-Trade," Madden wrote:

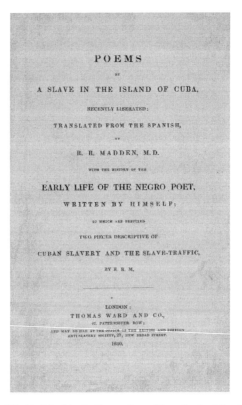

Figure 2. Title page of R. R. Madden's *Poems by a Slave in the Island of Cuba*, published in London in 1840, containing his translations of several of Juan Francisco Manzano's poems and portions of his life story, as well as several poems and essays by Madden. The title page does not identify Manzano as the author. Reproduced with permission from Wilson Library, University of North Carolina, Chapel Hill.

> All that I have ever seen of slavery – and I have seen some of its horrors in various countries – in Africa itself, in Asia likewise, and in America ... falls infinitely short of the terrible evils of the slave-trade, that is now carried on in Cuba.[69]

In an attempt to complement his moral outrage with the proofs of science, he cites Humboldt's calculations on slave mortality in Cuba:

> It is little to say, that 25,000 human beings are annually carried into Cuban slavery; that at the expiration of thirty years from the date of the abolition of the slave-trade on the part of Great Britain, the odious traffic continues in full force; that no small amount of foreign capital is invested in this trade; that British subjects, now that slavery is put down in our colonies, are embarking their means with impunity in slave properties in Cuba, are buying their slaves of necessity in the slave market, for there is no natural increase of the slave population of Cuba, but a terrible decrease by deaths; which, at the ordinary mortality on the sugar plantations, would sweep away the race in slavery, in ten years, and, according to Humboldt's calculation, in much less, for he states this mortality to vary from ten to eighteen per cent per annum.[70]

But Madden was by no means servile to the purportedly empirical findings of earlier observers, including Humboldt. In an essay titled "Laws for the Protection of Slaves in Cuba," he lambastes Alexis de Tocqueville's portrayal of Spanish slavery as relatively benign, noting that while pleasure-seeking visitors who sat down with the owners of opulent plantations over good Spanish wine often came to this conclusion, his own experience had taught him otherwise: "Perhaps this extensive acquaintance with slavery in various countries during the last ten years, may have qualified me to form some opinion of the relative evils or advantages of slavery in a Spanish colony."[71]

Madden's experiences with slavery in other settings included a stint in Jamaica, where, in 1834, he had observed the declaration of emancipation, an event he recalled as one of the finest moments of his life.[72] He was aware that his ideas went against the grain and were anathema to many. In the preface to his two-volume *A Twelvemonth's Residence in the West Indies, during the Transition from Slavery to Apprenticeship*, published in London in 1835, Madden wrote:

> I do not expect my work will please any political party; – that it will not serve my interests, I am well assured. That it may serve the interests of that great question which is now solving in the West Indies, is the first and most ardent of my wishes.[73]

Planters had reacted with violence and hostility to his activities in Jamaica, and he had learned that "[w]hoever is popular with the negroes must of necessity be in a degree of disfavor more than unpopular with the white people."[74]

The bookending of Manzano's life story by Madden's poetic and apologetic writings graphically demonstrates its shared fate with later Latin American *testimonios* such as Esteban Montejo's post-emancipation account of Cuban slavery "authored" by the ethnographer Miguel Barnet in 1964, and Rigoberta Menchú's account of military violence in Guatemala, first published with the assistance of Elizabeth Burgos Debray in 1983. All three texts were commissioned and/or vetted by well-trained and well-intentioned men and women of science and/or moral conscience but present thorny problems in terms of narrative authority and reliability as documentary sources, and the problems of limited access to publishing venues for the same populations they attempt to represent.

The radical changes Madden made to Manzano's narrative and poetic texts, including, but by no means limited to, the translation itself, might also be compared to the liberties J.S. Thrasher took with Humboldt's text when he published the third English version of the *Essai politique sur l'île de Cuba* in 1856, even if Madden and Thrasher were at absolute cross purposes on the slavery question.[75] While Madden had excised those parts of Manzano's recollection of his experiences that seemed to paint slavery in a favorable light and had sandwiched the "slave poet's" narrative between strident essays and zealous verses from his own pen, Thrasher added to and omitted from Humboldt at will, niftily purging that part of his essay which most cogently damned slavery and its continuation, and adding a hefty dose of his own pro-slavery commentary in the form of a preliminary essay. Like Madden, Thrasher envisioned a different function for the text than that expressed by its author.

In the essay accompanying his 1930 translation of Humboldt's famous text on Cuba, in which he also included a translation of Thrasher's preliminary essay, Fernando Ortiz wrote that:

> What the translator Thrasher did with Humboldt could not possibly have been any more disloyal, since he mutilated those important observations without the author's permissions and without even apologizing in the short preface where, on the contrary, he gives the impression that the translation is complete. Let me stress this traitorous sin not just by evoking the worn phrase *traduttore, traditore*, although there is an element to it

that is very important for understanding the meaning of Thrasher's *Preliminary Essay* and the twisted spirit of those times, during which the most inhumane despotisms paraded as legal institutions in this part of the world.[76]

Scholars are familiar with Humboldt's rejoinder to the liberties Thrasher took with his text. While Humboldt acknowledged the pro-slavery advocate's embellishment of the essay with updated data on commerce, agriculture, and geography, he also accused him of arbitrarily omitting the very portion of the work to which he attached "greater importance than to any other."[77] Thrasher responded with another letter to the newspaper's editor, insisting that he did not "willfully mutilate" Humboldt's text but only left out the anti-slavery material because it was a "distinct essay" in which Cuba was only alluded to incidentally.[78] This exchange between two men from opposing camps on the slavery question shows the degree to which all texts from the period, but especially translations, were susceptible to manipulation and even "mutilation" as they were reinvented for ulterior purposes. Of course, the case of Manzano's life story, which he reluctantly completed only because his future as a published poet and a free man seemingly depended on it, further illuminates the degree to which a slave author – even after obtaining his freedom – might still find himself silenced and muzzled, unable to defend his own text or his own self-portrait.

Painting a perfect picture

A full text of Manzano's manuscript, which had been reduced and radically altered in Madden's edition, would not appear in Spanish until almost a century later. That 1937 Cuban edition, prepared from the original manuscript, was a response to new interest in Afro-Cuban history and creative production ushered in by the early twentieth-century vanguard of *negrismo*, which critics, in turn, sought to legitimate by pointing to earlier projects by authors of color such as Manzano.[79] But the content of the restored *historia*, so painstakingly recounted by Manzano as he struggled simultaneously to secure his freedom and to retain his standing as a poet, earned him praise from some twentieth-century readers and condemnation from others.[80] Some have read the *Autobiography* as the prostrate but ultimately selfish plea of a man who wanted to distance himself as much as possible from other slaves so as to be accepted by his white literary peers as an equal and a confidant, rather than a curiosity. Others credit him with initiating a discourse of Afro-Cuban resistance.[81] There is still ongoing debate as to whether Manzano's fame, even in his own day, had anything at all to do with literary acumen or poetic ability, or was, in fact, the result of a shared agenda amongst abolitionists and slavery reformers, for whom aesthetics mattered little and Manzano was reduced to a poster child for the merits of their respective campaigns.

This seemingly unsolvable tension threatens to leave the matter of Manzano's value to contemporary readers eternally hanging: was Manzano a model of black resistance whose verses, however rough, are the expression of an unusually fine, if untrained, mind? Or do his poems, modeled on now forgotten eighteenth-century poets, merely prove the extent to which he subscribed to white values, acquiesced to white standards, and coveted whiteness itself? The circuitous publishing history, *histoire croisée* par excellence, of his textual production – a body of work that admittedly seems inconsequential next to Humboldt's – at the very least confirms that Manzano's was an exceedingly complex case in terms of voice, agency, and reception.

Perhaps more careful assessment of his "collected works," which takes into account how poetry and drama served Manzano as both refuge and subterfuge in the midst of such tautly lived tensions – including the dilemma of how to write his own life story – will bring readers around to the ultimate "unspeakability" of the poet's writerly task.[82] Whatever decision contemporary readers make about Manzano, however, it should matter that he himself claimed that poetry provided him "in all the labors of life" with lines analogous to his situation,[83] and it was perhaps to poetry that he owed his long sought-after emancipation, since it was following the declamation of one of his compositions that a collection was taken to buy his freedom.

The poetics of slavery

Despite the tragic loss of those parts of Manzano's original manuscript, which ended up on the cutting room floor (including a second part referring to his adult life that was either lost, suppressed, or destroyed),[84] the 1840 publication of *Poems by a Slave* alerts us to how, within the context of literary romanticism that characterized the mid nineteenth century, poetry might be combined with the more "empirical" genres such as the essay and the autobiography to "prove" the humanity of a given individual and the inhumanity of slavery itself, in a way that narrative or scientific writing alone could not. Just as the teenage Wheatley had done a half-century earlier in North America and Britain, Manzano provided evidence in the form of poems to readers on both sides of the Atlantic that Americans of African descent possessed spiritual and creative faculties which marked them as fully human.

It was Manzano's poetry, not the autobiography, that French abolitionist Victor Schoelcher seized upon and translated when he alluded to the Cuban writer in his *Abolition de l'esclavage, examen critique du prejugé contre la couleur des africains et des sans-mêlés*, also published in 1840 and included in the second volume of the 1979 compilation *Polemique Coloniale*.[85] By then, the French statesman had been busy with anti-slavery projects for some 12 years, following initial observations of slavery in New Orleans and Cuba in 1828.[86] During that period, Schoelcher moved from a posture favoring the gradual eradication of slavery to one insisting on complete emancipation, a platform notably not shared by most of his Cuban contemporaries, including Del Monte. In *Abolition de l'esclavage*, Schoelcher included translations of several of Manzano's poems in a fiery, Franco-Atlantic anti-slavery campaign that culminated in April of 1848 when Schoelcher himself formally announced the abolition of slavery in France and its colonies.[87] Like Madden, Schoelcher judged poetic texts by writers of color as strong arguments for the full personhood of the writer as well as for the immorality of those who continued to question his humanity.

Though Madden rhapsodized that Manzano's autobiographical account provided readers with the "most perfect picture of Cuban slavery that has been given to the world,"[88] we must recall that he too included Manzano's verse in that first publication. More importantly, Manzano, time and again in that same narrative for which he is now mostly known, portrays himself as a poet and lays claim to the special power poetry possessed to both console and inspire him. On balance, then, the two things that most distinguish the representation of Cuban slavery in the writing project of Manzano versus that of Humboldt are: (1) the centrality of poetry to that project and (2) the centrality of the self as the principal subject of study. Whereas Humboldt's aperture is frequently very wide, directed outward toward ever fuller heights, depths, and horizons, Manzano turns inward, making his own experience the chief object of reflection and study, fear and hope.

Both of these differences are very much in evidence in the sonnet usually titled "Mis treinta años" [My Thirty Years], which Manzano recited in Del Monte's parlor in 1836, apparently so moving the men assembled there that they together bought him his freedom:[89]

> Cuando miro el espacio que he corrido
> Desde la cuna hasta el presente día,
> Tiemblo y saludo a la fortuna mía
> Más de terror que de atención movido:
>
> Sorpréndeme la lucha que he podido
> sostener contra suerte tan impía,
> Si así puede llarmse la porfía
> De mi infelice ser al mal asido;
>
> Treinta años ha que conocí la tierra:
> Treinta años ha que en gemidor estado,
> Triste infortunio por doquier me asalta,
>
> Mas nada es para mí la dura guerra
> Que en vano suspirar, he soportado,
> Si la comparo ¡oh Dios! con la que falta.[90]

Madden's translation of "Thirty Years" in *Poems by a Slave* not only changes much of the sense of Manzano's poem, tying it much more explicitly to the "chains" of slavery, but it also changes the form itself, sacrificing the classical integrity of the 14-line Castilian sonnet for a square structure of four stanzas of four verses each:

> WHEN I think on the course I have run,
> From my childhood itself to this day,
> I tremble, and fain would I shun,
> The remembrance its terrors array.
>
> I marvel at struggles endured,
> With a destiny frightful as mine,
> At the strength for such efforts:–assured
> Tho' I am, 'tis in vain to repine.
>
> I have known this sad life thirty years,
> And to me, thirty years it has been
> Of suff'ring, of sorrow and tears,
> Ev'ry day of its bondage I've seen.
>
> But 'tis nothing the past–or the pains,
> Hitherto I have struggled to bear,
> When I think, oh, my God! on the chains,
> That I know I'm yet destined to wear.[91]

However faithful or unfaithful a translator we judge Madden to be, his version of the poem retains certain key elements, including the autobiographical voice, the speaker's stance at the threshold between the early and latter parts of his life (it is, of course, no coincidence that the speaker's age reflects that of Jesus Christ at the moment he took up his earthly ministry), his reaction of fear and trembling as he looks back on that life, his sense of marvel at his ability to have sustained so much suffering, and, finally, the open mouth of the "oh" with which he invokes the ear of

God Himself as he anticipates his bleak future. In the original Spanish, "Mis treinta años" is a poem that speaks of trembling, terror, struggle, misfortune, unhappiness, and of being reduced to a state of groaning and vain sighing, but it is a poem in which slavery itself is never mentioned explicitly. And yet, with this poem and the amazing story of its role in finally joining Manzano to his long sought-after freedom, we may gain an understanding of nineteenth-century Cuban slavery only suggested by Humboldt, however passionately he might have denounced the "unjust institutions" that had assumed an "appearance of legitimacy" in the "lands of slavery."[92] For all its susceptibility to external control and manipulation as part of a game of transatlantic hopscotch in which the author himself was not invited to play, Manzano's poetics of slavery provides us with a picture of the Cuban slave experience that in certain regards surpasses that of Humboldt, and that compels us to reach beyond sheer data to the improbable irrefutability of a single life story. Reading his life story and the verses Manzano crafted to console himself and convince others of his full measure as a man alongside Humboldt's monumental work will help us to rebalance the asymmetries of the historical record.

Acknowledgements

I would like to thank my colleagues at the conference on Atlantic Emancipations (Philadelphia, April 2008) and the symposium on Humboldt's Transatlantic Personae: Plotting the Imaginaries (Louisiana State University, May 2009), at which many of the central ideas of this essay were first presented.

Notes

1. Historical uncertainty as to the exact dates of Manzano's birth and death contrasts with the immense amount of biographical information for Humboldt, much of which is provided in his own writings, both scientific and personal. The most careful of Manzano's biographers, Roberto Friol, acknowledges the dearth of documentation faced by historians: without a birth certificate having been located, "one must accept the date Manzano himself indirectly points to, 1793, confirmed date of the birth of Nicolás de Cárdenas y Mazano" (*Suite*, 49). This date precedes that suggested by Francisco Calcagno in his 1878 work *Poetas de color*, which includes a study of Manzano.
2. Cohen, *Mapping the West*, 100.
3. In June 1835, Manzano wrote to his benefactor Domingo Del Monte, reminding him: "Yo soy esclavo; y que el esclavo es un ser muerto ante su señor" [Don't forget that I am a slave; and that for his master the slave is a dead being] (Manzano, *Autobiografía*, 125). I take up this point again later in this essay. For commentary on the difficulties of enunciating the experience of slavery and its multiple forms of violence, including expressive violence, see Barrett, "African-American Slave Narratives"; Bontemps, *The Punished Self*; Davis and Gates, *Slave's Narrative*; DuBois, *Torture and Truth*; Rushdy, *Neo-Slave Narratives*; and Scarry, *Body in Pain*. Despite early examples by Madden and

Schoelcher, translators have rarely taken up Manzano's poetry alongside the autobiographical writing. See, for example, King, *Autobiography*, and Yacou, *Un Esclave-poète.*

4. Scholars of the works of both authors continue to debate the correct classification of these texts within a specific genre, as well as the degree of "literariness" versus historical value of each work. While Manzano did not call his memoir of early life in slavery an autobiography, nor was it published as such in its first version of 1840, it has now become canonized as the *Autobiography.* Humboldt's reflection on Cuba, published in 1826 as the *Essai politique sur l'île de Cuba,* first saw light as chapter 28 of his *Relation historique* (Paris, 1825–31), which itself was part of the weighty collection of 30 volumes titled *Voyage aux régions équinoxiales du Nouveau Continent fait en 1799, 1800, 1801, 1802, 1803 et 1804* (Paris, 1805–29), thus establishing early on the problem of relegating the text to a specific generic classification.

5. Ortiz and Kutzinski, "Humboldt's Translator," 337; see also Luis, introduction to *Autobiografía,* 19–20.

6. Havana's City Council deemed Humboldt's *Political Essay on the Island of Cuba* "extremely dangerous among us because of its author's opinions about slavery and even more so because of the terrible, albeit accurate, picture it presents about the population of color and its immense strength on the island" (Martínez-Fernández, "Introduction," 10). Manzano's story and his text documenting it was apparently considered so dangerous in Cuba that it was secretly smuggled out of the country and first published without attribution of the author, though Friol argues that Madden himself should be censured for the method he used to hide Manzano's identity: "The Spanish authorities did not identify him simply because they chose not to. Manzano was the only ex-slave poet that there was in the Island in that moment. The same goes for using only the initials of the poet on some pages of the book, and the fact that the name Juan appears before some of the poem translations" (*Suite,* 34).

7. Thrasher, in his preliminary essay to *The Island of Cuba,* uses the history of Las Casas's defense of the Indians – at the expense of the Africans, who he recommended replace them in their unjust slavery – to chide Humboldt's abolitionist stance: "Las Casas, bishop of Chiapas, moved by the deepest compassion for the native races, urged, upon the ground of humanity, the substitution of African slaves for the natives in the labor of the new communities. The hardships of the poor Indian were dwelt upon with the same fervor and zeal, the same heedless inconsistency, that characterizes the appeals of the humanitarians of the present day in behalf of the negro, and the conscience of Europe gave an energetic impulse to the new institution ... If we could have an impartial view of the condition of the great mass of negroes in Africa, of their social and military slavery from the earliest ages, subject to the sway of barbarous native chiefs, it might be found that his argument in favor of the change from a savage to a civilized master, was not so inconclusive as is now supposed; and that the step itself was not so cruel as it has been, and still is painted" (Thrasher, "Preliminary Essay," 43–4).

8. See, in particular, Gates, *Trials of Phillis Wheatley.*

9. Ette, "'Espíritu de inquietude moral,'" 25.

10. As indicated, there is debate concerning the poet's birth date: Manzano's description of his birth in the *Autobiography* situates the event in relationship to the birth of his "young master" Nicolás de Cárdenas, for whom varying birth dates have also been suggested. See, for example, the introduction to the 1962 Cuban edition of Manzano's *Zafira.*

11. Manzano, *Autobiografía,* 84–5, 89–90.

12. Franco cites communication between Manzano and a fellow poet of color, in which Manzano attests to having hoped for "moral and material improvement" when he left behind the life of servitude, but finds instead that he has become a pariah and victim of colonial society for being an intellectual and black ("Juan Francisco Manzano," 26).

13. Sweeney, "Atlantic Countercultures," 402.

14. Werner and Zimmermann, "Beyond Comparison," 30.

15. Zeuske, "Humboldt, esclavitud, autonomismo," 260–1.

16. See Zeuske, "Alexander von Humboldt and Slavery."

17. Ibid. Zeuske reiterates certain elements of this argument in "Comparing or Interlinking?"

18. Humboldt, *Personal Narrative,* 127–8.

19. Martínez-Fernández agrees with Humboldt's characterization, noting: "At the time of Humboldt's scientific tour slavery had not reached the appalling intensity and extreme brutality that it would during the apogee of sugar in the middle decades of the nineteenth century ... As the century unfolded and as King Sugar spread its wicked mantle across Cuba's plains this picture yielded to a far more sinister scenario with higher rates of enslavement, higher rates of plantation slavery, lower rates of manumission, and growing oppression of blacks and mulattos, both free and slave" ("Introduction," 9).
20. Marable and Mullings include Wheatley's poem in their collection, acknowledging that while many critics have accused her for her "weak stance on slavery," more recent interpretations have been more sympathetic, recognizing that "Wheatley was a product of her times" (*Let Nobody*, 8).
21. Manzano, *Autobiografía*, 84.
22. See Branche, "'Mulato entre negros.'"
23. Before he was 20, Del Monte wrote a piece for *El Revisor Político y Literario*, announcing a poetry collection soon to be published by a young author who for the first time had achieved an "authentic Cuban lyric" style (Bueno, *Domingo Del Monte*, 8). That poet was José María Heredia, considered the inaugural voice of Cuba's national literary tradition, despite the fact that some 70 years would pass before Cuba would gain its independence from Spain in 1898.
24. Bueno, *Domingo Del Monte*, 9.
25. Manzano, *Autobiografía*, 122. All translations are mine unless otherwise noted.
26. Branche, *Colonialism and Race*, 136.
27. Manzano, *Autobiografía*, 125.
28. Ibid.
29. Ibid.
30. "Temo desmerecer en su aprecio un ciento por ciento pero acuérdese su merced, cuando lea, que yo soy esclavo; y que el esclavo es un ser muerto ante su señor, y no pierda en su aprecio lo que he ganado" (Manzano, *Autobiografía*, 125).
31. Ibid., 127.
32. For an excellent review of a Cuban slave's right to seek a new master in cases of mistreatment, as well as *coartación*, the means by which a slave could purchase his or her own freedom, see Fuente, "Slaves."
33. Manzano, *Autobiografía*, 128.
34. For an excellent study of Manzano's intellectual milieu, see Labrador-Rodríguez, "La intelectualidad negra."
35. Manzano, *Autobiografía*, 128.
36. See Azougarh, *Juan Francisco Manzano*, 117, and Manzano, *Autobiografía*, 129.
37. Burton, *Ambivalence*, 63.
38. De Terra, *Humboldt*, 84.
39. Humboldt, *Ensayo*, II.44–5; also cited in Puig-Samper, "Humboldt," 335.
40. See, for example, "Mariano Luis de Urquijo (1768–1817)," Centro Virtual Cervantes, http://cvc.cervantes.es/ciencia/humboldt/contactos_03.htm, which states: "Urquijo fue el prototipo de político ilustrado, enemigo de los privilegios de la Iglesia, defensor del progreso científico y social (promovió la abolición de la esclavitud en España)" [Urquijo was the prototype of the enlightened politician, enemy of the privileges of the Church, defender of scientific and social progress (he promoted the abolition of slavery in Spain)].
41. Sachs, *Humboldt Current*, 84.
42. Humboldt, *Political Essay*, 260.
43. Humboldt, *Personal Narrative*, 260–1.
44. Ibid., 261, 263–5.
45. Ibid., 264.
46. Humboldt, *Political Essay*, 261.
47. Burton, *Ambivalence*, 20.
48. For Madden's role in the abolition of slavery in Cuba, see Quintana García, "Madden."
49. Madden, *La Isla de Cuba*.
50. Madden, *Island of Cuba*, vi.
51. Humboldt, *Personal Narrative*, 259.

52. Ibid., 260.
53. Ibid., 260–1.
54. Madden, *Island of Cuba*, xix–xx.
55. Lubrich, "'Egipcios por doquier.'"
56. See Madden, *The Turkish Empire*.
57. Humboldt, *Personal Narrative*, 260.
58. Madden, *Memoirs*, 129. I have not been able to identify with certainty the "Albert" referred to in these verses, but it may very well be Albert Gallatin, the Secretary of the Treasury in the United States when Humboldt visited in 1804, a visit Gallatin referred to as an "exquisite intellectual treat." See "Humboldt as a Resource of Information about the West," Alexander von Humboldt Digital Library Project, http://www2.ku.edu/ ~ maxkade/humboldt/subwashington.htm.
59. Madden, *Island of Cuba*, vii.
60. Humboldt, *Personal Narrative*, 266–7.
61. See Burton, *Ambivalence*, 30–1.
62. Madden, *Memoirs*, 77; also quoted in Burton, *Ambivalence*, 30.
63. Burton, *Ambivalence*, 31.
64. Arguably, Manzano's little-known play in verse, *Zafira*, published in Havana in 1842, is in some sense much more an example of his authorship than is the *Autobiography*, since it bears his name and was hailed by his contemporaries as the first work of its genre published by an Afro-Cuban. But given that it is set in Algeria in the sixteenth century, it is hard for modern-day readers to understand just why such a text should matter, since it gives us little or nothing of the first-hand account of Cuban slavery so poignantly recounted in the *Autobiography*. As I have tried to demonstrate in a longer essay, Manzano's *Zafira* was heralded in the Cuban press, it represented an early milestone in the development of a "minority" literature in the island, and its setting, though remote in time and geography, was read – at least by some – as an allegory of Cuba's colonial condition. I suggest that Manzano drew on the historical precedent of the sixteenth-century Arab King Selim's defense of his territory from the incursions of the Turkish despot Barbararoja, as well as the fresher, first-hand experiences of Madden in Turkey and the Middle East, to dramatize and re-present conflicts familiar to mid-nineteenth-century Cubans engaged in independence struggles, a device many readers would have recognized from Humboldt's writings (see Miller, "Imitation").
65. Burton, *Ambivalence*, 24. Burton draws on post-colonial theory, particularly Homi Bhabha's notion of ambivalence, to explore affinities and tensions between the two men.
66. Ibid. This is not corroborated by Roberto Friol, Manzano's chief biographer.
67. See Miller, "Rebeldía narrativa."
68. Add to this circuitous and uncertain publication history another glaring paradox: the second part of Manzano's autobiographical account, alluded to in the first, disappeared soon after it was written in 1839. What might part two of the *Autobiography* tell us of Manzano's fate after his early runaway attempt, the point at which the preserved segment of his story abruptly breaks off? While Friol and a handful of other historians have done admirable work tracing Manzano's trajectory in the years between that early flight and his death in 1853 (Friol, *Suite*, 165), very little is known of the details of Manzano's life in his adult years, particularly after his manumission in 1836.
69. Madden, *Poems by a Slave*, 156.
70. Manzano, *Poems by a Slave*, 156. The full text reads: "And surely, a cause like this whose efforts are directed to the removal of ills, terrible beyond all other evils, that involves the question of life and death – that treats, not of the doom of one man, or ten thousand, but of the destiny of the whole people of a quarter of the globe – whose business is with the wrongs and sufferings of stolen men, and whose denunciations are for the atrocious deeds of Christian brokers in the trade of blood, who roll in riches and move in the goodly circles of Cuban society – surely it requires no exaggeration of the evils of Cuban slavery. They are great, indeed, beyond the power of imagination to picture to itself. All that I have ever seen of slavery – and I have seen some of its horrors in various countries – in Africa itself, in Asia likewise, and in America, even in as bad a form as in either of these regions – all that Clarkson ever penned of the magnitude of its evils, when this trade was at its height,

or that Sturge or Scoble recently witnessed of its mitigated atrocities, in the transition from slavery to freedom, in the British colonies – and mitigated as they were, God knows they were bad enough to be witnessed even by those already acquainted with all the evils of this system, but still worse to be seen by persons whose eyes were not accustomed to the practical horrors of slavery; yet all that these gentlemen witnessed or described in our colonies, or that I have myself seen there of cruelties inflicted or endured, falls infinitely short of the terrible evils of the slave-trade, that is now carried on in Cuba. It is little to say, that 25,000 human beings are annually carried into Cuban slavery; that at the expiration of thirty years from the date of the abolition of the slave-trade on the part of Great Britain, the odious traffic continues in full force; that no small amount of foreign capital is invested in this trade; that British subjects, now that slavery is put down in our colonies, are embarking their means with impunity in slave properties in Cuba, are buying their slaves of necessity in the slave market, for there is no natural increase of the slave population of Cuba, but a terrible decrease by deaths; which, at the ordinary mortality on the sugar plantations, would sweep away the race in slavery, in ten years, and, according to Humboldt's calculation, in much less, for he states this mortality to vary from ten to eighteen per cent per annum" (156).

71. A more extensive citation bears including: "Tolerably well acquainted with some of the British West India islands, with one of them, both previously and subsequently to the act of emancipation, and having seen something of slavery in many eastern countries, I brought perhaps some little knowledge of the condition of men held in slavery to the subject, which has been the object of anxious inquiry with me, during a residence of upwards of three years in a Spanish colony, where slavery flourishes, and where upwards of four hundred thousand human beings, exist in that condition. Perhaps this extensive acquaintance with slavery in various countries during the last ten years, may have qualified me to form some opinion of the relative evils or advantages of slavery in a Spanish colony" (Manzano, *Poems by a Slave*, 171).

72. Madden, *Memoirs*, 86; also cited in Burton, *Ambivalence*, 19.

73. Madden, *Twelvemonth's Residence*, vi.

74. Ibid., II.32.

75. I am indebted to Vera Kutzinski for bringing this parallel to my attention. See Kutzinski, "Translations of Cuba."

76. Ortiz and Kutzinski, "Humboldt's Translator," 337.

77. Humboldt, "Baron von Humboldt's Political Essay," cited in Ortiz and Kutzinski, "Humboldt's Translator," 337.

78. Thrasher, "Baron Humboldt and Mr. Thrasher," cited in Ortiz and Kutzinski, "Humboldt's Translator," 339–40.

79. Friol, *Suite*, 41–5.

80. The other single most important first-hand account of slavery in the Latin American canon is, of course, Miguel Barnet's *Biografía de un Cimarrón* [Autobiography of a Runaway Slave] (1968), which was based on a series of interviews in which the centenarian Esteban Montejo recounted his life during slavery and after its abolition in Cuba. While Montejo's story is compelling, it presents several thorny problems in terms of questions of authorship and its categorization as biography or autobiography, and even as history or fiction – see, for example, Sklodowska, "Testimonio mediatizado." Both texts attest to the ways in which slave narrative was a genre indeed characterized by fictionality and derivative material.

81. Gomáriz, for example, writes that Manzano constructs a "poetics of codified resistance through diverse anti-hegemonic strategies, such as the 'conscious interpretation of a role,' escape from the sugar plantation, and a confrontation with hegemony" ("La poética," 115; my translation). Providing a counterpoint, Branche's essay shows how Manzano makes a concerted effort in his life story to project a self that is fundamentally *different* from the rest of the slave body; that is, his text does not develop a common cause with other enslaved individuals (see "'Mulato entre negros,'" 79).

82. See Williams's excellent chapter, "Juan Francisco Manzano's *Autobiografía*: Narrating the Unspeakable," in *Representation*, 21–51. Like most critics, Williams ignores, in large part, Manzano's poetic production. On attempts to compile the collected works of Manzano in

different eras, see the 1852 manuscript version of the *Obras completas* at Yale and the 1972 *Obras* published by the Instituto Cubano del Libro in Havana.

83. Azougarh, *Juan Francisco Manzano*, 89. This phrase does not appear in the Luis edition of the *Autobiografía* (see Manzano, *Autobiografía*, 104).

84. Madden claimed that the second part of the *Autobiografía* came into the hands of the poet's cruel *ama* [slavemistress] by way of Ramón de Palma, who was given the task of correcting and copying the manuscript (Burton, *Ambivalence*, 63).

85. Schoelcher, *Polemique Coloniale*, 89–93.

86. Welborn, "Victor Schoelcher," 95.

87. Despite the fact that he never left Cuba, Manzano's persona and behavior were linked early on to two French Enlightenment thinkers when an observer remarked of the young slave, "Mire Ud. que éste va a ser más malo que Rousseau y Voltaire" [Watch out, this one is going to be worse than Rousseau and Voltaire] – a comment that propelled the young slave to ascertain "quienes eran estos dos demonios" [who were those two devils] (Azougarh, *Juan Francisco Manzano*, 82). In chapter 4 of *The Social Contract*, written in 1762, Rousseau had argued: "To renounce liberty is to renounce being a man, to surrender the rights of humanity and even its duties ... Such a renunciation is incompatible with man's nature; to remove all liberty from his will is to remove all morality from his acts" (*Du Contrat social*, Essai I.iv, 239). Voltaire decried the religious defense of slavery: "We tell them that they are men like us, that a God died to redeem them, and then we make them work like beasts of burden," he wrote in his *Essai sur les moeurs et l'ésprit des nations*, a text first published in 1753, with later editions containing new chapters on European colonies in the Americas (Voltaire, 380; also quoted in Hunting, "Philosophes," 409).

88. Madden, *Island of Cuba*, iv.

89. Manzano, *Autobiografía*, 137–8. Scholars have arrived at varying conclusions regarding the relationship between Manzano's emancipation and (1) his recital of the sonnet "Mis treinta años" in Del Monte's *tertulia* and (2) his writing of the *Autobiography*. The most recent timeline of these events, included in Luis's 2007 introduction to Manzano's writings, dates the composition of the *Autobiography* to 1835 and the declamation of the sonnet and the purchase of his freedom by members of the Del Monte *tertulia* to 1836 – both events prior to Madden's arrival that same year in Havana. Nonetheless, many critics tie the freedom papers to the completion of the life story, which Manzano was reluctant to write and repeatedly stymied from finishing, when the painful recollections of his early years in slavery forced him to relive those traumatic events. Brickhouse affirms, for example, that "he produced the autobiography in exchange for his freedom" ("Manzano," 210).

90. Various versions of this famous sonnet exist, including one that Friol claims is written in Manzano's own hand. The differences in the two versions point once again to the intervention of editors and correctors in Manzano's textual production (and authority), even in the original Spanish (Friol, 12).

91. Manzano, *Autobiografía*, 84.

92. Humboldt, *Island of Cuba*, 265.

References

Azougarh, Abdeslam. *Juan Francisco Manzano: esclavo poeta en la isla de Cuba*. Valencia: Ediciones Episteme, 2000.

Barnet, Miguel. *Biografía de un cimarrón*. La Habana: Academia de Ciencias de Cuba, Instituto de Etnología y Folklore, 1966.

Barrett, Lindon. "African-American Slave Narratives: Literacy, the Body, Authority." *American Literary History* 7, no. 3 (1995): 415–42.

Bontemps, Alex. *The Punished Self: Surviving Slavery in the Colonial South*. Ithaca, NY: Cornell University Press, 2001.

Branche, Jerome C. *Colonialism and Race in Luso-Hispanic Literature*. Columbia and London: University of Missouri Press, 2006.

Branche, Jerome. "'Mulato entre negros' (y blancos): Writing, Race, the Antislavery Question, and Juan Francisco Manzano's *Autobiografía*." *Bulletin of Latin American Research* 20, no. 1 (2001): 63–87.

Brickhouse, Anna. "Manzano, Madden, 'El Negro Mártir,' and the Revisionist Geographies of Abolitionism." In *American Literary Geographies: Spatial Practice and Cultural Production, 1500–1900*, ed. Martin Brückner and Hsuan L. Hsu, 209–35. Newark: University of Delaware Press, 2007.

Bueno, Salvador. *Domingo Del Monte. ¿Quién fue?* Havana: Ediciones Unión, 1986.

Burton, Gera C. *Ambivalence and the Postcolonial Subject: The Strategic Alliance of Juan Francisco Manzano and Richard Robert Madden*. New York: Peter Lang, 2004.

Calcagno, Francisco. *Poetas de color*. Havana: Imp. Militar de la V. de Soler y Compañía, 1878.

Cohen, Paul. *Mapping the West: America's Westward Movement, 1524–1890*. New York: Rizzolli, 2002.

Davis, Charles T., and Henry Louis Gates, Jr., eds. *The Slave's Narrative*. Oxford: Oxford University Press, 1985.

De Terra, Helmut. *Humboldt: The Life and Times of Alexander Von Humboldt, 1769–1859*. New York: Knopf, 1955.

DuBois, Paige. *Torture and Truth*. New York: Routledge, 1991.

Ette, Ottmar. "Un 'espíritu de inquietud moral.' *Humboldtian Writing*: Alexander von Humboldt y la escritura de la modernidad." In *Humboldt y la modernidad*, Leopoldo Zea and Hernán Taboada, 25–50. Mexico, D.F.: Fondo de Cultura Económica, 2001.

Franco, José Luciano. "Juan Francisco Manzano, el poeta esclavo y su tiempo." In *Autobiografía, cartas y versos de Juan Francisco Manzano*, 9–32. Havana: Municipio de la Habana, Administración del Alcalde Beruff Mendieta, 1937.

Friol, Roberto. *Suite para Juan Francisco Manzano*. Havana: Editorial Arte y Literatura, 1977.

Fuente, Alejandro de la. "Slaves and the Creation of Legal Rights in Cuba: *Coartación* and *Papel*." *Hispanic American Historical Review* 87, no. 4 (2007): 659–92.

Gates, Henry Louis, Jr. *The Trials of Phillis Wheatley: America's First Black Poet and Her Encounters with the Founding Fathers*. New York: Basic Books, 2003.

Gomáriz, José. "La poética de resistencia de Juan Francisco Manzano." *Casa de las Américas*, no. 219 (2000): 115–20.

Humboldt, Alexander von. *Ensayo político sobre la isla de Cuba*. Trans. D.J.B. de V. y M. Paris: Casa de Jules Renouard, 1827.

Humboldt, Alexander von. *Essai politique sur l'ile de Cuba*. 2 vols. Paris: Gide Fils, 1826.

Humboldt, Alexander von. *The Island of Cuba: A Political Essay by Alexander von Humboldt*. Trans. J.S. Thrasher. Introd. Luis Martínez-Fernández. Princeton, NJ: Markus Wiener, 2001.

Humboldt, Alexander von. *Personal Narrative of Travels to the Equinoctial Regions of the New Continent by Alexander de Humboldt and Aimé Bonpland*. Trans. Helen Maria Williams. Vol. 7. London: Longman, Rees, Orme & Brown, 1814.

Humboldt, Alexander von. *Relation historique du voyage aux regions equinoxiales du Nouveau Continent fait en 1799, 1800, 1801, 1802, 1803, et 1804 par Al. de Humboldt et A. Bonpland redige part Alexandre de Humboldt*. Paris, 1814–25.

Humboldt, Alexander von. *Voyage aux regions equinoxales du Nouveau Continent fait en 1799, 1800, 1802, 1803, et 1804, par Al. de Humboldt et A. Bonpland*. 30 vols. Paris: F. Schoell, 1805–29.

Hunting, Claudine. "The Philosophes and Black Slavery 1748–1765." *Journal of the History of Ideas* 39, no. 3 (1978): 405–518.

King, Lloyd. *The Autobiography of a Cuban Slave*. St. Augustine: University of the West Indies, 1990.

Kutzinski, Vera M. "Translations of Cuba: Fernando Ortiz, Alexander von Humboldt, and the Curious Case of John Sidney Thrasher." *Atlantic Studies* 6, no. 3 (2009): 303–26.

Labrador-Rodríguez, Sonia. "La intelectualidad negra en Cuba en el siglo XIX: el caso de Manzano." *Revista Iberoamericana* 62, no. 174 (1996): 13–25.

Lubrich, Oliver. " 'Egipcios por doquier'. Alejandro de Humboldt y su visión 'orientalista' de América." *HiN. Alexander von Humboldt im Netz* 3, no. 5 (2002). http://www.uni-potsdam.de/u/romanistik/humboldt/hin/hin5/inh_lubrich_2.htm.

Lubrich, Oliver. "In the Realm of Ambivalence. Alexander von Humboldt's Discourse on Cuba (*Relation historique du voyage aux régions équinoxiales du Nouveau Continent*)." *German Studies Review* 26, no. 1 (2003): 63–80.

Luis, William. Introduction to *Autobiografía del esclavo poeta y otros escritos*, by Jaun Francisco Manzano, 13–69. Madrid: Iberoamericana, 2007.

Madden, Richard R. *A Twelvemonth's Residence in the West Indies, during the Transition from Slavery to Apprenticeship*. 2 vols. London: James Cochrane, 1835.

Madden, Richard R. *La Isla de Cuba*. Trans. Sarah Méndez Capote. Havana: Consejo Nacional de Cultura, 1964.

Madden, Richard R. *Poems by a Slave in the Island of Cuba*. London: Thomas Ward, 1840.

Madden, Richard R. *The Island of Cuba: Its Resources, Progress, and Prospects*. London: Charles Gilpin, 1849.

Madden, Richard R. *The Memoirs (Chiefly Autobiographical) from 1798–1886 of Richard Robert Madden*. London: Ward & Downey, 1891.

Madden, Richard R. *The Turkish Empire: In Its Relations with Christianity and Civilization*. 2 vols. London: T.C. Newby, 1862.

Madden, Richard R. *Travels in Turkey, Egypt, Nubia, and Palestine, in 1824, 1825, 1826, and 1827*. London: Henry Colburn, 1829.

Manzano, Juan Francisco. *Autobiografía del esclavo poeta y otros escritos*. Ed. and introd. William Luis. Madrid: Iberoamericana, 2007.

Manzano, Juan Francisco. *Obras*. Havana: Instituto Cubano del Libro, 1972.

Manzano, Juan Francisco. *Obras completas*. Manuscript volume signed by Nicolás de Azcárate, dedicated to the Academia de Estudios, 1852. Beinecke Rare Book & Manuscript Library, Yale University.

Manzano, Juan Francisco. *Poems by a Slave in the Island of Cuba, Recently Liberated; Translated from the Spanish, by R. R. Madden, M.D. with the History of the Early Life of the Negro Poet, Written by Himself; to Which are Prefixed Two Pieces Descriptive of Cuban Slavery and the Slave-Traffic, by R. R. M.* London: Thomas Ward, 1840.

Manzano, Juan Francisco. *Zafira: tragedia en cinco actos*. Havana: Consejo Nacional de Cultura, 1962. First published 1842.

Marable, Manning, and Leith Mullings, eds. *Let Nobody Turn Us Around: An African-American Anthology: Voices of Resistance, Reform and Renewal*. Lanham, MD: Rowman & Littlefield, 2009.

Martínez-Fernández, Luis. "Introduction: The Many Lives and Times of Humboldt's *Political Essay on the Island of Cuba*." In *The Island of Cuba*, by Alexander von Humboldt, 1–18. Princeton, NJ: Markus Wiener, 2001.

Menchú, Rigoberta. *Me llamo Rigoberta Menchu y asi me nació la conciencia/Elisabeth Burgos*. Barcelona: Argos Vergara, 1983.

Miller, Marilyn. "Imitation and Improvisation in Juan Francisco Manzano's *Zafira*." *Colonial Latin American Review* 17, no. 1 (2008): 49–71.

Miller, Marilyn. "Rebeldía narrativa, resistencia poética y expresión 'libre' en Juan Francisco Manzano." *Revista Iberoamericana* 71, no. 211 (2005): 417–35.

Ortiz, Fernando, and Vera M. Kutzinski, trans. "Humboldt's Translator in the Context of Cuban History." *Atlantic Studies* 6, no. 3 (2009): 327–43.

Puig-Samper, Miguel Ángel. "Humboldt, un prusiano en la corte del Rey Carlos IV." *Revista de Indias* 59, no. 216 (1999): 329–55.

Quintana García, José Antonio. "Madden and the Abolition of Slavery in Cuba." *Irish Migration Studies in Latin America* 7, no. 1 (2009): 81–4.

Rousseau, Jean-Jacques. *Du Contrat social, ou, Principes du droit politique*. Amsterdam: Chez M.M. Rey, 1762.

Rushdy, Ashraf. *Neo-Slave Narratives: Studies in the Social Logic of a Literary Form*. New York: Oxford University Press, 1999.

Sachs, Aaron. *The Humboldt Current: Nineteenth-Century Exploration and the Roots of American Environmentalism*. New York: Penguin, 2006.

Scarry, Elaine. *The Body in Pain: The Making and Unmaking of the World*. New York: Oxford University Press, 1985.

Schoelcher, Victor. *Polemique Coloniale*. Vol. 2. Fort-de-France: Éditions Désormeux, 1979.

Sklodowska, Elzbieta. "Testimonio mediatizado: ¿ventriloquia o heteroglosia? (Barnet/ Montejo; Burgos/Menchú)." *Revista de Crítica Literaria Latinoamericana* 19, no. 38 (1993): 81–90.

Sweeney, Fionnghuala. "Atlantic Countercultures and the Networked Text: Juan Francisco Manzano, R.R. Madden and the Cuban Slave Narrative." *Forum of Modern Language Studies* 40, no. 4 (2004): 401–14.

Thrasher, J.S. "Baron Humboldt and Mr. Thrasher." *New York Daily Times*, August 17, 1856, 1.

Thrasher, J.S. "Preliminary Essay." In *The Island of Cuba: A Political Essay by Alexander von Humboldt*, 19–66. Princeton, NJ: Markus Wiener, 2001.

Voltaire. *Essai sur les moeurs et l'ésprit des nations et sur les principaux faits de l'histoire depuis Charlemagne jusqu'à Louis XIII*. Paris: Garnier Frères, 1963.

Welborn, Max. "Victor Schoelcher: A Superior Breed of Abolitionist." *Journal of Negro History* 54, no. 2 (1969): 93–108.

Werner, Michael, and Bénédicte Zimmermann. "Beyond Comparison: Histoire Croisée and the Challenge of Reflexivity." *History and Theory* 45, no. 1 (2006): 30–50.

Williams, Lorna. *The Representation of Slavery in Cuban Fiction*. Columbia: University of Missouri Press, 1994.

Yacou, Alain. *Un Esclave-poète a Cuba au temps du péril noir: autobiographie de Juan Francisco Manzano (1797–1851)*. Paris: Éditions Karthala and Centre d'études et de recherches caribéennes, 2004.

Zeuske, Michael. "Alexander von Humboldt and Slavery." Alexander von Humboldt im Netz. http://www.uni-potsdam.de/romanistik/ette/projekte/humboldt/de/forschung_ms.html.

Zeuske, Michael. "Comparing or Interlinking? Economic Comparison of Early Nineteenth-Century Slave Systems in the Americas in Historical Perspective." In *Slave Systems: Ancient and Modern*, ed. Enrico Dal Lago and Constantina Katsuri, 148–83. Cambridge: Cambridge University Press, 2008.

Zeuske, Michael. "Humboldt, esclavitud, autonomismo y emancipación en las Américas, 1791–1825." In *Alexander von Humboldt: estancia en España y viaje americano*, coord. Mariano Cuesta Domingo and Sandra Rebok, 257–77. Madrid: Real Sociedad Geográfica/ Consejo Superior de Investigaciones Científicas, 2008.

Humboldt's translator in the context of Cuban history[1]

By Fernando Ortiz
Translated by Vera M. Kutzinski

Alexander von Humboldt's *Political Essay on the Island of Cuba* was published in English after it had already appeared in other languages.

In 1856, a North American, Mr. John S. Thrasher, put into print in New York an English-language version of the *Political Essay*; he based it on the Spanish version and changed the work's title: *The Island of Cuba, by Alexander von Humboldt. Translated from the Spanish, with notes and a preliminary essay, by J.S. Thrasher.*[2]

This English edition includes an interesting *Preliminary Essay* and numerous *notes* by J.S. Thrasher. The footnotes reflect on the various social and statistical changes that had occurred during the thirty years that intervened between the first edition and the English version that then appeared.

The *Preliminary Essay* follows the same goal. But, above all, it prepares the North American reader to align his judgments and opinions, not so much about Humboldt's work, but, rather, about the Cuban situation, with those of the translator, who was very careful and interested, as were many northern neighbors then, in Cuba's fate – her slavery regime, her revolutionary convulsions, the annexationist conspiracy, and the timorous intrigues on the parts of Britain and France.

Thrasher wrote that his long stay in Cuba and his knowledge of the island's resources and conditions had prepared him to pronounce with certainty that the *Political Essay on the Island of Cuba* was the best work about this country and that, with his translation, he had responded concretely to the oft-repeated question his fellow countrymen asked him about what might be the best book on this Antillean island.

The time that has passed since 1855, when Thrasher penned that translation and his preliminary essay, and the various profound changes that Cuba, like the rest of the world, has experienced in all areas since then, make his *essay* and his *notes* less current. But both retain a documentary value for appreciating the viewpoints about Cuban issues which North America, who personally took part in events that were then unfolding in our country, held in those dark times. For this reason, I believe it to be worthwhile to print this new Spanish edition of Humboldt's work, reproducing his text as it was published in 1827 but also adding Thrasher's notes and his *Preliminary Essay*, which can be found in this edition's appendix. Both have been especially translated for these volumes by our collaborator, Mr Adrián Valle, so that Cuban readers will have available to them Thrasher's essay, which had not been translated until today and which has been completely forgotten.

But Thrasher's essay must be read keeping in mind the times when it was written and only as a document of socio-historical reflections. I believe that the essay will contribute to making us duly understand those terrible times with their inhuman harshness. This is why I am writing these paragraphs.

Readers interested in a better explanation of the meaning of Thrasher's essay can acquaint themselves with the profound worries that afflicted Cubans during the middle of the nineteenth century in the partial anthology by José Antonio Saco, whose work, under the title *Contra la anexión* [Against annexation], encompasses volumes V and VI of our *Libros Cubanos* series. The prologue and the epilogue that accompany these volumes, edited by the author of these pages, provide an ample overview of that historical period.

But I cannot reprint Thrasher's proslavery writings without referring to the circumstances of their initial publication and to the stance that Humboldt adopted before the inaccuracies of his faithless translator. This is of vital interest for Cuban history, revealing all of a period's darkness. And the underhanded and intense personal participation of Thrasher in Cuba's turbulent life during the middle of the nineteenth century brings renewed interest to the narrative of this episode in Humboldt's life, which is directly related to his work as a Cubanist.

The English edition is preceded by the following dedication: *To the Members of the American Press, this work is respectfully dedicated in grateful acknowledgment of their sympathy and protection in a time of peril, by their obliged colaborer, J.S. Thrasher*. What exactly were the dangers to which Thrasher refers in his dedication? What secret does it contain?

Let me recount an interesting episode in Cuban history.

Who was J.S. Thrasher, Humboldt's translator? He was an American journalist, who came to Cuba to take advantage of the waters churning with Cuban agitations against Spanish rule and to channel these waters toward the annexation of Cuba's bright star to the federated constellation of the United States of America, as one more star among many.

According to *El Lugareño* [Gaspar Betancourt Cisneros], annexationism in Cuba was "a calculation not a sentiment." But it was an insistent calculation and the only one that then seemed viable to Cubans, disenchanted as they were by the severity and incomprehension of Spanish absolutism. At the time, many North Americans shared their annexationist sentiments. The United States, which saw annexationism primarily as a strategic matter, also began to regard it as an economic benefit; in this, the continental annexationists coincide at times with the insular annexationists.

For many Cubans and foreigners alike, annexation meant the consolidation of slavery, which even Spain could not support for much longer, they thought, against pressure from Britain; and this was of interest to plantation owners and slave traders in both Cuba and the US South. A Cuban proclamation from 1848 read: "Uniting Cuba with this strong and respected nation, whose interests in the South will be identical with our own, means to strengthen her peacefulness and future fate; it will increase her wealth, doubling the value of her plantations and her slaves, tripling the value of her land; it will give liberty to individual action and get rid of this hateful and pernicious system of restrictions that paralyzes trade and agriculture."[3]

Even the conservative Spaniards themselves accepted the real economic potential of annexation for Cuba. One of them wrote: "The pine forests of Carolina, the steppes of Florida, and the swamps of Louisiana prove to what heights of grandeur the island of Cuba could have been lifted, with its virgin lands and its countless ports, under a more intelligent and conscientious administration."[4]

A *report* secretly sent to the Spanish government in those days confessed the following: "Within two months in these parts, things have gone from bad to worse; malcontent has given way to disaffection with the government of the Motherland; there are, as they had been before, no disagreements over the means through which to effect emancipation: all are unanimously determined to unite the fortunes of the Island with the United States. The general opinion of the day is that separation from Spain is necessary and inevitable, and that total independence is impractical; that a union with the Republic of the United States is essential to their interests. [...] Everyone, all the classes of criollos [Creoles] agree that Cuba has no other choice but to belong to the United States; and that the differences in habits, customs, religion, and language are minor inconveniences that will disappear before circumstances essential to the cultivation and development of sugar: the joint interest in favor of the slave trade."[5]

At the time, annexationist beliefs were widespread, and the Cuban *intelligentsia*, disaffected with Spanish rule, shared them. The same report reveals that

> among the criollos, there is a small number of influential and prominent persons, who publicly speak out and write against black slavery; but although they are opposed to slavery in theory, they put reality and their comfort before abstract principles, and they do not embrace the idea of exposing their luck to the risks that would come with a change in the system of cultivation that currently exists. for some years now, the criollo landowners of the island have considered this group, made up especially of writers and professors, as hostile to the interests of their compatriots because of their fanatical and dangerous ideas; but they now see that they need their ideas and abilities and that, belonging to the center of the government is indispensable for an effective cooperation that would bring their visions to fruition. All this has unified their different opinions, some realizing the justice of the abstract principles that the others profess and leaving their application for a later time. All agree that they must work together for the benefit of a single objective: Cuba's separation from Spain and its union with the Republic of the United States. Today, there is no one among the members of that group, nor among those who had more strongly declared their opinion in favor of the protection of Great Britain not so long ago, who does not speak out, now convinced of the major advantages that will accrue to the Island of Cuba under the protection of the United States and of the need for putting this plan in action. To the arguments against this opinion they reply: "We would prefer above all the protection of Great Britain, if it were not for the law that abolishes slavery which will take hold here before long and ruin our sugar factories."[6]

Cuba's separatist conspiracy had its roots in the United States.

> In 1848, in the month of January, the annexationists founded the journal *La Verdad* in New York, and one of the leaders of this group, *El Lugareño*, wrote to José Antonio Saco, the famous exile from Bayamó, offering him the journal's editorship. But Saco declined in a personal letter, which seriously affected those who thought him in favor of his country's *manifest destiny*, based on what he had said on another occasion: that if Cuba were swept away by circumstances to hurl herself in foreign hands, there would be no hands better, more honorable, and more glorious than those of the great confederation of North America, where Cuba would find peace and solace, strength and protection, justice and liberty.[7]

In 1848, the conspiracy also extended to Cuba, headed up by the Venezuelan Narciso López, a General in the Spanish army.

The thinking of the Cuban annexationists had two aspects: one, negative, of loathing for Spain; the other, positive, of attraction to the United States.

In 1849, J[osé] L[uis] Alfonso expressed the Anti-Spain sentiment when he wrote to Saco with reference to Cuba: "*I don't say go to the United States; I would throw myself to the devil to get away from Spain.*"

In 1848, Saco himself wrote to *Narizotas*: "Does it make sense for Cuba to become part of the United States? Given what we are today under Spain, there is no Cuban who would not want that union."

A manifesto from April 20, 1848, signed by "*several Cubans,*"[8] read:

> With respect to the population, let us consider first what a Cuban is, physically, morally, and politically. Nothing more than a slave. He has no right to speak or to write; he cannot, in any way, criticize the operations of his government; he cannot tell anyone of his complaints when his rights are abused; he cannot leave the country, nor can he go from one city to another, from the city to the countryside, from one plantation to another, etc. without a permit; nor can he walk around at odd hours of the night without exposing himself to abuse. *Whether innocent or guilty*, he can be arrested and jailed, tied up and buried in a dungeon, *without being told why*. His home can be raided, and he can be dragged away at the point of bayonets and, in this manner, taken to a prison and jailed, *all without any form of judgment and without appearing before a judge*, and this on the basis of a mere suspicion, of slander, either because a crime was committed in the house where he lives or because it was his luck to have been in the wrong place at the wrong time. With the same arbitrariness, the government seizes, confiscates, and appropriates the goods of any person.[9]

In their bitter anti-Spanish pessimism, some annexationists confirmed privately Cubans' powerlessness vis-à-vis their own government, based precisely on their being the descendents of Spaniards: "Do you really think that the children of the Spaniards' slaves can be free men?" *Narizotas* wrote to *Saquetes*, pointing to the example of the tyrannies and upheavals in the continental Spanish republics.

People had lost any hope that the Spanish metropole could become more liberal. In 1849, Gaspar Betancourt Cisneros wrote to Saco:

> Domingo [Delmonte] and you and all those who have any hope that Spain might grant Cuba freedom, equality, national representation, and all those things that you would expect from the *derechos de raza y paternidad* [rights of descent and paternity] – to me, you are Jews, whom I would have plant cedar stakes, promising you that they would bear oranges.

The attraction to the United States was, on the other hand, rooted in political values (liberty, democracy, republic, equality, suffrage) and in economic ones (market, capital, industrialism, technology), which Cuba lacked and which Spain did not provide; nor could it provide because it itself lacked them.

In 1850, Narciso López embodied Cubans' separatist ideals and led the revolution. In the conspiracy, he offered General John A. Quitman, the Major-General of the US army, the command of the Cuban revolutionaries. But the proposal was rejected, and Quitman promised his help, if the armed rebellion were to break out and if it was organized and supported by Cubans. As Villanova points out, Mr J. S. Thrasher was General John A. Quitman's private secretary.[10]

On May 19, 1850, General Narciso López arrived in Cárdenas with some 500 men; he landed and took the city, flying for the first time in Cuba the same flag that, half a century later, would be raised in Morro Castle in Havana as a symbol of a new

State. But Narciso López's separatist goals were later foiled and, together with the invaders, he was forced to return to the safety of the United States.

Easy suspicions would suggest that the North Americans pursued the same politics in Cuba that they had in Texas (1845); the same as Cavour and Garibaldi did with the *mil de Marsala*; the same astute politics that Spain attempted unsuccessfully (1787–89), according to General James Wilkinson, when it tried to annex the state of Kentucky to Spain or else to make it independent as a sovereign republic allied to and protected by Spain.[11]

Those conspirators did not back down when faced with defeat. Narciso López armed another expedition and prepared an uprising in Cuba. But, also at this time, Fillmore, the then-President of the United States, officially threatened the delinquents should they persist in their conspiracy. In spite of this, the expedition was armed in the US, and a revolt broke out in Cuba. It broke out in Camagüey and Trinidad but without success; on August 12, 1851, Joaquín Agüero and other patriots were shot in Puerto Príncipe, and Isidro Armenteros and two others on the 18th of the same month in Trinidad. The armed expedition arrived in Cuba, organized with a Cuban regiment, a Magyar regiment, another German and nine North American regiments, under the command of Narciso López and the Hungarian General John Pragay. After shooting Agüero, the so-called filibusters landed in Playitas. Five days later, they were beaten back, and on September 1, the leader Narciso López died in the gallows, and at least fifty unfortunate soldiers were executed in the Atarés castle, together with their leader, Colonel Crittenden.

What happened to Thrasher in the midst of all this?

> On December 1, 1841, the first issue of a journal entitled *Faro Industrial de la Habana* [Havana's Industrial Beacon] appeared in Cuba's capital. Despite its title, this was not a paper whose purpose was to train its lens on the problems and interests of industry but to report on economic and literary subjects without entering the territory of political ideas, and to publish special announcement and resolutions by the authorities. Carlos del Castillo, Ildefonso Vivanco, Fernando del Castillo, and Antonio Bachiller formed a society for publishing this journal, whose royal license Carlos del Castillo had secured. *El Faro Industrial de la Habana* was always owned by its founders; but it was leased out at different times. Thrasher was the last lessee; but to avoid the obstacle that came with his being a foreign citizen – he had never wanted to give up his citizenship –, he suggested that the journal be given to Don José Ramón Ariza.[12]

From the position of directing the *Faro Industrial*, Thrasher shrewdly reported on events with the sparkle of his annexationist principles, even when the Spanish authorities allowed him only an area that was too limited for his propaganda to be able to take hold. Thrasher was acting, then, with unquestionable duplicity. We can see that, in 1850, the *Faro Industrial* published under its imprint a factitious pamphlet entitled "Memoria y recolección de documentos para la historia de la ridícula invasión" [Report and collection of documents about the history of the ridiculous invasion] (Havana, 1850), with which Thrasher tried to mislead the authorities by throwing them this bit of public support.

According to information obtained by Herminio Portell Vilá, Thrasher was really a Havana correspondent of Narciso López's, and his code name in the conspiracy was *El Yankee*.[13]

The events of 1851, when Cuban unease exploded violently, also swept up Thrasher and brought the *Faro Industrial* to its collapse.

On August 13, 1851, General Narciso López repelled the attacks of the regiment under the command of General Enna in the Pozas. And on the 15th, the *Faro Industrial* gave an account of this event, copying from the *Gaceta Oficial* the narrative of the combat, printing in the same column the announcement of a literary work with the title *La Risa* [The Laugh]. The *laborantes* spread a seemingly veiled joke … and Cubans laughed.

On the 17th, in a scuttle between the Spanish General and the invaders on the coffee plantation of Frías, Enna was dealt a fatal wound, and on the 20th, he was solemnly interred in Havana, where his body had been taken.

In the issue of the 21st, the *Faro* simply reprinted from the *Gaceta Oficial* the obituary for General Enna, followed by an article by F. Henriet, entitled *Monografía de la sonrisa* [Essay on Laughter].[14] Now the sarcasm was clear. In this way, the *Faro*'s mocking attitude reappeared, now very visible and very irksome to the Spanish, whose passions were extremely excited. And on the 23rd, on the occasion of the accursed general's funeral, the *Faro* repeated its mockery with a sequel to the *Monografía de la sonrisa*.

It is not difficult to recall how censored the press was in those days. A separatist reported years later that

> [o]ne could ill-afford to censor or impugn any resolution, even when dictated by the most ignorant and greedy of the group's captains, when it was not even possible for a city council to express its opinions in obsequious and humble ways. The Cuban people did not exist, and the white slave, like the black slave, had no more than one right and one obligation: the right to degrade himself and the obligation to adulate his oppressors. Journals were subject to distrustful, despicable, and ignorant censorship[15] in the most trivial of matters, which is what they generally reported, since political subjects were strictly forbidden. Even the title of a given article had to be such that it did not cast even the slightest suspicion on the proconsul's distrustful spirits.[16]

It was not necessary, then, for Thrasher's Havana journal to publish "Monografía de la sonrisa" to make General Concha decide to suspend the *Faro*. There was nothing disrespectful in this literary article, which the censor had passed; but what people took notice of, yes, was the journal's silence about General Enna's death. Moreover, pressure from conformists, who favored colonialism and were terrified by the conspirator's aggressive stance, grew more intense. It is unsurprising, then, that Captain-general Concha gave in to this popular pressure, terminating the *Faro* much like he had executed Narciso López's fifty expeditioners lined up on the walls of Atarés castle.

> In a certain way, the *Faro*'s existence was convenient for Spain's politics; here was a *Cuban* journal, directed by Thrasher, whom people considered, for good reason, to be in favor of Cuba's annexation to the US, and for this journal wrote Carlos del Castillo, Bachiller, Costales, and other Cubans.[17]

The *Faro Industrial*'s publication, then, gave the impression that there was a free Cuban press, but the reality was quite different. The Captain-general had Havana's *Faro* in his pocket, as he had the rest of the island's journals, which were, frankly, dependents, accomplices, and abettors. Below is anecdotal evidence for this.

> The Spanish general had intercepted the correspondence of individuals whom he considered suspects. One day, there arrived a letter from Gaspar Betancourt to one of Thrasher's associates. Concha opened it, called a writer in and gave him a letter, in

which *El Lugareño* solicited the help of his friend with the revolutionary work. Although there was nothing in the letter that could have compromised the Havana writer, this embarrassed him; he swore he was innocent and that he was willing to take arms to defend the Spanish cause. "Writers," the dictator told him, "defend the motherland with their pen: the day before yesterday was the anniversary of the invasion of Cárdenas; write an article for *El Faro*." The writer wrote the article and closed it in the following manner: "It is not redundant to write here a remembrance of those who spilled their blood in the defense of the throne and the integrity of our lands. Tomorrow, it will have been a year ago: those who died on the path down which their duty, their honor, and their limitless loyalty led them, receive the votes of a grateful people and the rightful regard of a generous queen; those who survived to tell of their deeds received from their country the compensation that they deserved and are held up as glorious examples for their brothers in arms."[18]

Those shameless coercions were the natural outcome of an absolutist regime that tried to silence the civic protests of a people, who could not demand of all their children the courage of heroism.

"At the end of the final page of the government article, General Concha wrote the following words: Havana, May 17, 1851. Publish this article in the *Faro* tomorrow, the 18th *Concha*."[19]

Needless to say, the article was published in *El Faro* on Concha's appointed day: coincidently, a Cuban journal came out condemning General López's venture and the henchmen of annexation. The strategy was crude and transparent to the public, but it is an old complaint of tyrants that, lacking honorable support and sympathy for their violations, they have to contend themselves with appearances. Then, in 1851, the people of the *Faro* wanted to repeat the sly maneuver of 1850 by publishing a pamphlet about what happened to Narciso López's invaders.

John S. Thrasher published a piece entitled "List of prisoners brought to Havana from the late Cuban Expedition under the command of Genl. Narciso López, and final disposition of them as knows [sic]" (Havana, September 11, 1851, 4 pages). After the list on the third page, with Thrasher's own signature, there is a long passage in English, in which he explains what happened to the expeditioners who had been taken prisoner by the Spanish and what he and the consuls had done to help them.[20]

The suppression of *Faro* deprived General Concha, in his role as Cuban dictator, of an instrument of deception. But this did not suffice, and Thrasher had to appear before the Military Commission that had been chaired, for some time, by none other than the rebellious General Narciso López and whose role in Cuba was to deal with pending judgments against those who disturbed the public order, including those who spoke out publicly in favor of abolishing slavery and of the more far-reaching business of national and civic liberty.

General Concha lamented his fate:

> It was only reasons of humanity and what, to my mind, was most fitting for the best representation of the magnanimousness of our sovereignty, that dictated our response to the conduct observed among the pirates, who were spared the ultimate punishment. Shortly thereafter followed the trial of a person, who was reputed to be one of the most active correspondents of the annexationist papers of the United States and a most effective agent of *the piratical expeditions*. Mr Thrasher, the individual to whom I am referring, was an American citizen domiciled on the Island, with which he had become amply familiar in his trade, and having taken charge of the direction of the journal entitled *Faro Industrial*, he worked with determination to support those who favored the cause that he appeared to serve.[21]

99

Further on, Concha explained his own behavior:

And because one can see from which point on I gave importance to prior censorship, I will comment here on my conduct with respect to a journal that was published in Havana under the title of *El Faro Industrial*. The news I had received until then about the thinking that had presided over the creation of this paper, and the not particularly veiled ideas of its proprietor, Mr Thrasher, a citizen of the United States domiciled on the island; the no less evident tendencies of the regular editors, and finally the articles and poems that frequently escaped the wisdom or vigilance of the censor, and which contained phrases and concepts with a double meaning, on which the authors then commented in their own circles – all this suggested to me more than once that it would be appropriate to close this periodical. But what would have given the government, in the midst of general tranquility, a similar means of making a clear statement about censorship's ineffectiveness? I preferred, then, to let the journal keep its miserable life, bereft of subscribers, until a better opportunity presented itself; and its conduct, in the midst of the general grief about the death of the valorous General Enna, promptly presented me with such an opportunity. Already from the time of the arrival of the López expedition on the Island, *El Faro Industrial* had used practices that were generally disagreeable. After announcing with a few lines, *taken from another paper*, the news of that general's death, it printed a sequel to an article entitled "La sonrisa." All of Havana looked upon this publication with contempt, and no one could believe that the government would take steps to shut it down. I gave the order, then, to suspend the publication of *El Faro*.[22]

Not satisfied with the disappearance of the *Faro Industrial*, given how useful an instrument it had been in his hands, Captain-general Concha ordered Thrasher to be brought before a court by labeling him "the most effective agent of *the piratical expeditions*." A pretext was easy to find: "It did not take long," General Concha wrote in his Memoirs, "to surprise him with his correspondence." Consequently, the North American journalist Thrasher was arrested in Havana on October 16, and, after staying in jail for some days, he was locked up in the Punta castle. Sentenced to a prison term of eight years, he was sent to fulfill his sentence in the penitentiary fortress of Ceuta, in Africa, and he was shipped there. In mid-December, Thrasher arrived at Vigo and, from there, he was sent to Cádiz and on to the infamous North African prison.[23]

The writings of Julio Esteban Chassagne provide a good account of the adventures of Thrasher and his fellow prisoners in Cádiz and Ceuta.[24]

The intrepid journalist must have had a good deal of standing among his fellow prisoners, because they organized a group of political expatriates in the famous Ceuta citadel of El Hacho, and Thrasher was elected president of this group.[25]

Another prisoner wrote the following:

Thrasher suggested the idea of establishing a set of rules that would serve as internal governance, with the goal of making our conduct conform to regulations that would free us from the intervention of the prison warden in our private lives. The leader served as a judge to direct or resolve the questions or misfortunes that happened among us.[26]

Mr Barringer, who was the minister of the United States in Madrid at the time, insured that the Spanish government looked with favor upon his countryman Thrasher, including him in a general pardon that the queen had been willing to grant the prisoners of Narciso López's last expedition, who had been shipped to the Peninsula. Conveying the pardon to the minister plenipotentiary of the United States, the Marquis of Miraflores, in a dispatch from January 11, 1852, stated that in granting Mr Thrasher the benefits of a general pardon, with which we were singularly pleased, considering that this resolution would have been very agreeable and satisfactory to the government of the United States, Her Majesty's government has done so under the express condition that the abovementioned individual would not return to Spain's overseas provinces in the future and that, in case that he were to be found in any of them, he would be subject to fulfilling his sentence as if he had never been pardoned.[27]

When freed on January 26, according to Chassagne's *diary*, Thrasher sailed from Gibraltar to Madrid on the 30th, and then on to the United States.

When Thrasher left the Ceuta prison, he set out to free the Hungarian captain Ludwig Schlessinger, General Narciso López's adjutant, preparing his escape with the help of a boat that Thrasher dispatched from Cádiz. Nothing more was known in El Hacho about Thrasher's plans.[28]

Once far from Ceuta, the audacious journalist wrote from Madrid to Cuba's Captain-general to protest the bad treatment and the injustices.[29] In May of 1853, Thrasher presented to the Secretary of State of his country an account of what had happened to him since August 1850, when he had been entrusted with *El Faro*, to base upon his account a diplomatic claim in the amount of $350,000 against the Spanish government for damages and prejudices that it had caused. It would be interesting to read this account, and to read carefully between the lines. General Concha, in his turn, in the *Memoirs* that he published that same year, considered it a great disgrace that the American journalist would have been "pardoned after such a short time."

In the United States, the government in Washington persisted in the 1848 plan to purchase Cuba as an international *object*, and *literature* was put out to prepare public opinion for this plan. Politicians in the US South, where slavery was the basis of the economy, insisted that Cuba be attached federatively, as a new slave state, which would strengthen the southern slavers in the anticipated conflict between the South and the North. At the time of this political agitation, the separatist conspiracy continued in Cuba, with real and simulated tendencies toward annexation, and exiles, imprisonments, and executions intensified the bitterness toward Spain. At the end of this year, Thrasher returned to New Orleans, where he pursued close contact with annexationist Cubans, who continued their conspiracy there.

According to Herminio Portell Vilá,[30] the tenacious Thrasher proceeded to publish in New Orleans the journal *The Beacon of Cuba* (*El Faro de Cuba*), without either economic support or prospects for continuing the journal. Thrasher hoped to hand it over to Villaverde, who had begun the publication of *El Independiente*.

Cirilo Villaverde's unpublished *Diary* contains curious items about Thrasher and his relations with the Cuban patriots, which show clearly Thrasher's attitude, at times not so complacent, towards these Cubans.[31]

The relations that Thrasher had with Villaverde and the Cuban conspirators in the warm land of Louisiana were not always cordial. A note from Cirilo Villaverde harshly accuses Thrasher with the following words:

Sunday, December 26, 1852. (In New Orleans) Last night, after being at Sánchez's house,[32] where J.M. Hernández spoke endlessly and Pérez talked at length about his meeting with Thrasher at Castellón's bar, we went there to meet up with a group of Cubans, most of them his supporters. About 30 of them confirmed Sánchez' power, among them 9 members of "Young Cuba." It is likely that they had to leave, because it was said that they had taken an oath not to support any liberation project by anyone, who was not a member of their group. Thrasher, who saw the occasion as an opportunity to place himself at the head of all the Cubans who were not part of the *Junta de Nueva York*, proceeded to sow discord, saying that we, the friends of Sánchez, were creating disunity and dissension among the Cubans. Reason: because Pérez had told Thrasher that, instead of being called the conciliator, he should be called the *divider of the Cubans*, which was all the worse because Thrasher was a foreigner. . . .

But in 1854, we still find Thrasher, along with *El Lugareño* and others, keeping alive a conspiracy that was already on the decline. On September 1, Thrasher and Gaspar Betancourt Cisneros each made many speeches commemorating Cuba's martyrs.

In prose filled with revolutionary fervor and rhetorical pomp, Thrasher highlighted the alliance, or better, the *union* of Cubans and North Americans, anointed by the blood of those who had been shot to death for the cause of Cuban freedom, and he rejected the idea, "typical of absolutist minds and supporters of the divine right of kings," that any collaboration between Saxons and Iberians in the shared endeavor of progress were impossible. "The union of the martyrs is the union of the races," exclaimed the annexationist Thrasher in a laudable gesture of brotherhood.[33] But the orator himself was also proslavery; it seems that his principles vacillated, since slavery precluded making blacks part of this union, however pure and consecrated they were through their martyrdom. The antinomian Thrasher no doubt forgot that in Cuba, all the races burned together in the same holocaust of freedom. In fact, the first two Cubans killed by absolutism had been of a different color and ethnicity.

When Thrasher, once free of Ceuta, had returned to his country, those in favor of Cuba's incorporation into the United States had not yet abandoned their efforts. A stern supporter of slavery, Thrasher no doubt believed that one of the most effective ways in which he could contribute to the project of annexing Cuba was by spreading among the American people the knowledge that he had gained during his long stay on the island, and that, to get his propaganda out there, he could find no better vehicle than the English translation of Alexander von Humboldt's *Political Essay on the Island of Cuba*. But Thrasher committed the inexcusable mistake of suppressing the very part of the book that contradicted his own racial and political biases, along with everything in it that went against his arguments in favor of maintaining slavery.

Nevertheless, Thrasher's translation appeared in 1856, when annexationism had already suffered further setbacks with the death, in 1855, of the Catalan Ramón Pintó, with the behavior of General Quitman, and with the dissolution of the *Junta Cubana*.

The events that followed changed the course of the annexationist ideal. Even in 1859, Senator J. Slidell delivered before the Congress in Washington a great tribute to Cuba's virtues; Cuba was "capable of playing a brilliant role in the high councils of the American nation." And even in 1860, President Buchanan of the United States insisted in the annexationist proposition; but its time had already come and gone.

It is evident that, in the mid-nineteenth century, many North Americans wanted Cuba's annexation, or at least trusted that the island would be acquired in the future, which, according to them, would benefit their interests. As Jenks reaffirms, repeating J.L. Rodríguez, only the US Civil War prevented the annexation from being carried out.[34]

In April 1861, the Civil War broke out between the North and the South; it ended in 1865 with the liberal triumph over slavery, followed by a time filled with the unrest and worries typical of any postwar period. Europe, which was not afraid of the Monroevists then, with France intervening militarily in Mexico and Spain retaking Santo Domingo, occupied the Chinche Islands[35] and bombed Valparaíso.

Uncle Sam was frail then, and Monroe had few defenders. Yankee territorial expansion was unthinkable.

Many years later, an autonomist weekly commented sourly on the behavior of the pro-slavery advocate Thrasher:

> Thrasher's *Preliminary Essay* and his *Notes* enhance the interest of Humboldt's Political Essay, and there would be nothing to complain about had the translator contented himself with saying that the annexation of Cuba to the United States Republic was not a local question but of great national interest, or that the emancipation of slaves would wipe out Cuba and its entire production – then so important to the trade of all the civilized nations –, the roster of wealth-producing societies, omitting the political and economic mistakes that Cuba committed. But he dared to mutilate the German sage's *Political Essay*, suppressing the thoughtful and far-sighted observations that the Baron von Humboldt made about black slavery, observations that the Spanish translator respected, making of them the chapter VII of that version.[36]

What the translator Thrasher did with Humboldt could not possibly have been any more disloyal, since he mutilated those important observations without the author's permission and without even apologizing in the short preface where, on the contrary, he gives the impression that the translation is complete. Let me stress this traitorous sin not just by evoking the worn phrase *traduttore, traditore*, although there is an element to it that is very important for understanding the meaning of Thrasher's *Preliminary Essay* and the twisted spirit of those times, during which the most inhumane despotisms paraded as legal institutions in this part of the world.

The mutilations of Humboldt's text are neither few nor insignificant.

I unwittingly acquired from a Leipzig bookseller a copy of the English translation of Humboldt, which had previously been owned by that distinguished author, and on one of its pages, there are some handwritten lines, in French, by Alexander von Humboldt himself. In these lines, in the tremulous handwriting of his 87 years, Humboldt noted the changes that Thrasher had made to the Spanish text of J.B. and V. y M. [José López de Bustamante], an edition that the translator himself claimed in his preface, with evident mendacity, to have followed.

In these brief handwritten notes, Humboldt wrote that the faithless translator had made these changes "no doubt for political reasons."

He went on to say that, on page 336 of the New York edition, Thrasher ended the *Political Essay*, leaving out the entire section that the Spanish version called "Esclavos" [Slaves] (Paris, 1827, Ch. VII, pp. 261–87). And the wise author made, also in his own hand, a few brief comparisons between the two editions, putting next to each other the pages, where there were alterations.

Thrasher really falsified Humboldt's work, not only suppressing paragraphs and ideas but also radically changing the order of his materials. Here, we can see that Thrasher made up the following chapters, different from Humboldt's original chapters. Let us compare the titles from Thrasher chapters with those in the Spanish edition:

Chapters according to Thrasher

Chapter I: General Views
Chapter II: Physical Aspects
Chapter III: Climate
Chapter IV: Geography
Chapter V: Population
Chapter VI: Slavery
Chapter VII: Races
Chapter VIII: Sugar Cultivation
Chapter IX: Agriculture
Chapter X: Commerce
Chapter XI: Internal Communications
Chapter XII: Revenue
Chapter XIII: A Trip to Trinidad

Chapters according to Humboldt

Capítulo I: Consideraciones generales acerca de la posición y del aspecto físico de la Isla de Cuba – Observaciones astronómicas
Capítulo II: Extensión. – Clima. – Estado de las costas. – División territorial
Capítulo III: Población
Capítulo IV: Agricultura
Capítulo V: Comercio
Capítulo VI: Hacienda
Capítulo VII: Esclavitud
Capítulo VIII: Viaje al Valle de los Güines, etc.

This change in the text must have been malicious, for its purpose was to conceal the information in the anti-slavery paragraphs.

The misfortune and outrageous defacement of the *Political Essay on the Island of Cuba* by the proslavery advocate Thrasher gave Humboldt a felicitous opportunity to stick up for freedom at a time when, in the United States' election campaign, the pro-slavery factions, with Buchanan as their presidential candidate, battled against the abolitionists, with Fremont as theirs.

Thrasher's "political reasons" were not, however, enough of a mitigating factor for Humboldt's unyielding moral integrity; Humboldt could not abide such defiling of his ideas. He expressed his surprise and outrage in an article that he published in the *Spenersche Zeitung*, from which I quote the following paragraphs:

> Under the title of *Essai politique sur l'île de Cuba*, published in Paris in 1826, I collected together all that the large edition of my *Voyage aux regions equinoxiales du Nouveau Continent* contained upon the state of agriculture and slavery in the Antilles. There appeared at the same time an English and a Spanish translation of this work,[37] the latter entitled *Ensayo político sobre la isla de Cuba*, neither of which omitted any of the frank and open remarks which feelings of humanity had inspired. But there appears just now, strangely enough, translated from the Spanish translation, and not from the French original, and published by Derby & Jackson in New York, an octavo volume of 400 pages under the title *The Island of Cuba, by Alexander Humboldt; with notes and a preliminary essay, by J.S. Thrasher.*

That translator, who has lived a long time on that beautiful island, has enriched my work with more recent data on the subject of the numerical standing of the population, of the cultivation of the soil, and the state of trade, and, generally speaking, exhibited a charitable moderation in his discussion of conflicting opinions. I owe it, however, to a moral feeling that is now as lively in me as it was in 1826, publicly to complain that in a work which bears my name the entire seventh chapter of the Spanish translation, with which my *Essai politique* ended, has been arbitrarily omitted. To this very portion of my work I attach greater importance than to my astronomical observations, experiments of magnetic intensity, or statistical statements.

I have examined with frankness (I repeat here the words I used 30 years ago) only what pertained to the organization of human societies in the colonies; the unequal distribution of rights and life's enjoyment, and the threats and dangers that legislators' wisdom and voluntary moderation of free men can avert – whatever the form of government. It befits the traveler, who saw up close what torments or degrades human nature, to bring the laments of the wretched to the ears of those who have the power to assuage them. I have recalled in this exposé the extent to which the old Spanish slave laws are less inhumane and less atrocious than those of the slave States in continental America north and south of the equator.

A steady advocate as I am for the most unfettered expression of opinion in speech or in writing, I should never have thought of complaining if I had been attacked on account of my statements; but I do think I am entitled to demand that in the Free States of the continent of America, people should be allowed to read what has [been] permitted to circulate from the first year of its appearance in a Spanish translation. Alexander von Humboldt, Berlin, July, 1856.[38]

This severe protest was reprinted in the New York *Daily Times*; and the journalist Thrasher was left in a bad public position. Nonetheless, he tried to justify himself with the following letter:

New York, August 17, 1856. To the editor of the New York *Daily Times*:

Dear Sir: I have noticed in your journal an article which has been published by Baron Humbolt in the *Spenersche Zeitung*, in relation to my translation of his essay on the Island of Cuba, published by Derby & Jackson. As your readers may be led to infer that I have willfully mutilated a work of that great writer, I request you will publish the following explanation.

Being desirous of placing in the hands of the American readers such information in relation to the Island of Cuba as my studies had enabled me to obtain, I made the translation referred to, as being the best work I have ever seen on the subject. I undertaking this labor, I was not aware that any English version of the work had ever been made, and I used the Spanish edition for text, simply because, being ignorant of the French language, I could not translate the essay from that tongue.

As it was written thirty years ago, during which time the material development of Cuba had been very great, a continuance of Baron Humboldt's remarks became necessary, in order to bring the subject matter up to the present time, and this labor I have inserted in notes. In carrying out the design of a work on Cuba, I deemed that I could not take up the subject at a more appropriate point than that where the illustrious author had left it in 1825.

The chapter complained of as having been omitted is a distinct essay, "On Slavery," and is so entitled in the volume where it is published. Cuba is only incidentally alluded to in it, while it begins with this express declaration: "I here close the *Examen*, or Political Essay on Cuba, in which I have presented the state of this important Spanish possession as it at present exists." Baron Humboldt's complain is not that I have mutilated his essay on Cuba, but that I have not published all the matter contained in the volume from which I have translated his work on that important island. I would add that no one entertains a higher or more sincere regard than I do for the great and venerable name of Baron Von Humboldt.

I would ask those journals that may have alluded to or published the article in question to publish also this letter. Very respectfully, yours, J.S. Thrasher.

As Manuel Villanova has rightly pointed-out, Thrasher's letter likely made matters worse: "Thrasher was unwilling to acknowledge the mistake he had made: he made it worse by claiming that the seventh chapter of the Spanish version is a distinct essay *about slavery*, because it is not even the last chapter."[39]

Humboldt no doubt understood the motives that blinded Thrasher, and he set out to battle them, because, as Villanova remarked:

> The opinions that Humboldt expressed in 1826 about the state of the black slaves of the Spanish colonies in America at the beginning of the nineteenth century was neither as impassioned nor as emphatic as what he said in the article he published in Berlin in July of 1856 upon finding out about Thrasher's omissions in his version of the *Political Essay*.[40]

That Cuban liberal thought it fitting, even in 1887, to scold Humboldt for the blandness of his *Political Essay* with respect to this topic:

> The learned German lacked at that time the keen sense that typically shines through his work. His opinions about the laws and customs that influenced the fate of the blacks in the Spanish colonies, suffers, on the one hand, from a very limited view of the ideas and the customs, and, on the other, from having been seduced by the language used in the instructions and regulations that were then passed to set the conditions and treatment of slaves.

> The famous traveler deduced what the fate of the Cuban slaves would be like from the humane way in which some families in the capital treated their domestic blacks. Humboldt himself remarked on how different the circumstances of those slaves were.[41]

Slavery in rural areas was, indeed, much worse. But, in any event, I do not consider it fair to reduce Humboldt's glory because he did not condemn black slavery in Cuba as vehemently as might be natural for a Cuban pen, aching and dipped in the ink of that slavery.

Humboldt was right when, in the personal autobiographical notes that we now have in our possession, he affirmed his disloyal translator's political aims, since Thrasher's Preliminary Essay was published by proslavery advocates in New York papers, precisely in order to counteract the effect that Humboldt's writings about Cuban slavery had had among abolitionists when they were reprinted in the *New York Herald* and the *Courier*. All this caused great excitement in the United States, as the Prussian Ambassador Von Gerolt wrote in a confidential letter to Humboldt in 1856.[42]

In personal letters, Humboldt described the unscrupulous Thrasher harshly and said about him that he was one more piece of evidence that North American proslavery elements wanted to annex Cuba. Humboldt was on the right track, since, as we have seen, Buchanan, the presidential candidate of the proslavers, was decidedly in favor of the absorption of the Pearl of the Antilles, and Thrasher was a stubborn annexationist and defender of blacks' personal servitude.

The republican politicians attributed great value to Humboldt's letter, criticizing Thrasher for suppressing Humboldt's ideas in favor of emancipation. Fremont, their presidential candidate, wrote to the learned leader that he had helped their cause in this way from Berlin: "In your history and your opinions," he wrote to Humboldt, "we find ample reasons for believing that the struggle in which the friends of liberal progress are engaged will carry the power of your name."

We need not recount Thrasher's misdeeds. His behavior is cut from the same cloth as that of the Council of Havana, which, years earlier, had banned the *Political Essay* because of its attacks on the slavers, and as that of the Cuban separatists who, although they were typically liberals, were not all supporters of the slaves. Although, to escape Spanish absolutism, they were even willing to side with the devil, who is a character to beware of and who, thanks to the propaganda that the reactionaries usually make for him, enjoys the well-deserved and enviable fame of a hardened liberal.

To be sure, this is not to exculpate Thrasher but, rather, a way of explaining the climate of those times, when the ignominy of the slave trade and of slavery fed debaucheries and passions very much rooted in the dawn of humanity, and humanity, slow and careful in its advance, only believed it necessary to abolish black slavery in the Americas in times of a liberalism preached in the eighteenth century, or better, at the turn of the nineteen century. When a nation lacks the liberties necessary for the fullness of life, the people search for them through shortcuts and detours that are very tortuous, cheerless, and perilous. It is like love, another essential quality of life, which people always pursue, even through nefarious detours, when it is maliciously prevented from naturally expanding its noble rule.

I end here my narrative of how the North American edition of the *Political Essay on the Island of Cuba*, by the Baron Alexander von Humboldt, threw new light on his person, indirectly connecting the eminent cosmographer with one of the most important periods during which Cubans sustained a long, interminable, and bloody battle for the fundamental and integral freedoms of their nation.

Havana, Martí Day, 1930 [January 28, 1853]

Acknowledgements

The author is grateful to Giorleny D. Altamirano Rayo for her help with the translation. [Trans.]

Notes

1. This essay was first published as part of Fernando Ortiz's Libros Cubanos edition of Alexander von Humboldt's *Ensayo político sobre la isla de Cuba* in 1930. It was reprinted without changes in subsequent editions of that text in 1959 and 1998. I have checked, updated, and added to Ortiz's references as necessary; all changes are placed in [square brackets].
2. The book was published in New York by Derby & Jackson, 199 Nassau Street. It has 397 pages in 12° and includes a map of Cuba.
3. Vidal Morales [y Morales], *Iniciadores* [*y primeros mártires* (Havana, 1931)], 226.
4. Carlos de Sedano, *Cuba desde 1850 a 1873, Colección de informes, memorias, etc. sobre el gobierno de la isla de Cuba.* Madrid, 1873, 8.
5. Morales, *Iniciadores*, 186.
6. [Ibid., 186–7.]
7. Ibid., *Iniciadores*, 194.

8. Ibid., *Iniciadores*, 227.
9. [Ibid., *Iniciadores*, 226.]
10. [Villanova, "Humboldt y Thrasher," Part III,] *La Semana*. [*Periódico Autonomista de los Lunes* (Havana) 1.3 (September 19, 1887), p. 6]. [Although he does not always quote from Villanova, Ortiz takes much of what follows here almost verbatim from Villanova's articles in the first five issues of *La Semana*.]
11. *Cyclopedia of American Biography* (paper on *James Wilkinson*), New York, 1889.
12. Manuel Villanova, ["Humboldt y Thrasher," Part II,] *La Semana* [I.2] [September 12, 1887), [9].
13. I must acknowledge here my gratitude to the young Cuban historian Herminio Portell Vilá for providing me with interesting information about the role Thrasher played in the conspiracies and invasions by Narciso López, which Vilá has studied with unsurpassed acuity and persistence.
14. [Villanova adds here that this article purported to have been a translation – "con la indicación de ser traducido." "Humboldt y Thrasher," Part II, 9.]
15. A governor of Puerto Príncipe took a red pencil to the word "republic" that Manuel de Monteverde had used. Monteverde was one of the writers who were most hostile to all ideas that tended to subvert Spanish domination and damage the influence of Catholicism (Villanova).
16. Villanova, ["Humboldt y Thrasher," Part II, 8.]
17. [Villanova, "Humboldt y Thrasher," Part II, 9.]
18. [Villanova, "Humboldt y Thrasher," Part II, 9.]
19. [Villanova, "Humboldt y Thrasher," Part II, 9.]
20. Some of the incidents of those times can be read in the text of Thrasher's speech in New Orleans, which appears in a file of the famous "Comisión militar. Segunda pieza de la causa seguida en averiguación del los autores del periódico *La Voz del Pueblo Cubano*." *Boletín del Archivo Nacional* (Havana), XIX. 4–6 (July–December, 1920), 217–26.
21. *Memorias sobre el estado político, Gobierno y Administración de la Isla de Cuba, por el teniente general don José de la Concha*. Madrid, 1853, 226.
22. Ibid., 282.
23. [This paragraph is taken from Villanova, "Thrasher y Humboldt," Part III, *La Semana* 1.3 (September 19, 1887), 6.]
24. Julio Esteban Chassagne, *Mi primer paso al mundo, o sea mis prisiones, Hacho, Ceuta*, January 12, 1852. The author was the only Cuban who had been involved with López in Vuelta Abajo during his invasion. In his diary, he wrote: "*In Cádiz. January 10 (1852)*. At 2 p.m., they took us, together with those from the brig *Ripa*, whom we met there, to the war steamer *Lepanto*, and at 11 at night, 24 convicts were transferred from the steamship *Caledonia* to the *Lepanto*, among them some from the movement in Puerto Príncipe and also *John Thrasher*, and we sailed to Ceuta at around 12 in the morning."
25. *Diario del Julio Esteban Chassagne. 17 January 1852.*
26. Juan O' Bourke, *Relación de su fuga de Ceuta*, in Vidal Morales, *Iniciadores*, 327.
27. Villanova ['Humboldt y Thrasher"].
28. [Vidal Morales, *Iniciadores*, 327.]
29. Letter from Mr John S. Thrasher to the governor and Captain-general of the island of Cuba, Don José Gutiérrez de la Concha. Madrid, March 22, 1852, refuting the Captain-general's claims that he had been treated and judged leniently. *Boletín del Archivo Nacional* (Havana), XIX, 4–6 (July–December 1920), 207–17.
30. Generously conveyed to the author by Portell Vilá from his work-in-press, *Narciso López y su época* [Havana: 1930–1958, 3 vols].
31. *Diario de Cirilo Villaverde: New York, Saturday, May 29, 1852.* "... meeting with Macías, who tells me that Perico Velazco, the General's little mulatto [mulatico] had come with *Thrasher* from the Ceuta prison." *Monday, July 26, 1852*: "... I saw Thrasher and left him the translation of his writings,* which I had done for him; he didn't like it. I was resistant to the idea of publishing a paragraph in which he seems to condemn the politics and the conduct of General López ... I did not like *Thrasher*'s translation of López's words, and I corrected it and then gave it to the press." *Tuesday, July 27, 1852*: "... On my return, I passed by *Thrasher*'s inn and found him in the company of Schlessinger with whom I had

a heated discussion about the translation and publication of the article, the result of which was that I refused to publish it and that Thrasher was to send for his manuscript. He wants to publish everything exactly as the terrible translator had done it, and I refused." *Wednesday, July 28, 1852*: "It seems that Thrasher is going to see Betancourt to complain about my refusal; the latter came to see me today at the very time, when I was getting ready to move. Betancourt tells me that he has the piece that Thrasher (or Pancho de Armas) translated and that he would read and correct it, because it should be published, since it was a good piece and publishing it would please its author."
*Was this the article that appeared in the *Boletín del Archivo Nacional* XX? Perhaps, because this piece was delivered in New Orleans at a banquet in Thrasher's honor.

32. José María Sánchez Iznaga.
33. *Addresses delivered at the celebration of the third anniversary in honor of the Martir [sic] for Cuban Freedom*, by Gaspar Betancourt Cisneros, president of the revolutionary junta, and J. S. Thrasher, at the Mechanics' Institute Hall, New Orleans, September 1, 1854.
34. [Leland Hamilton Jenks,] *Our Cuban Colony. [A Study in Sugar.]* New York, 1928.
35. [The Islas Chinches of what is today Peru and Ecuador were an important source of guano exported to Europe.]
36. Manuel Villanova, ["Humboldt y Thrasher,"] *La Semana*, Havana, September 5, 1887, [6] and subsequent issues.
37. I do not know this other English translation to which Humboldt refers here.
38. [Ortiz likely took this letter from Villanova, "Humboldt y Thrasher," *La Semana* (September 5, 1887), 6. The basis for my translation here is Humboldt's original German letter. For Thrasher's letter, I have used the English version from the New York *Daily Times*.]
39. ["Humboldt y Thrasher,"] *La Semana*, Havana, September 5, 1887 [7].
40. [Villanova, "Humboldt y Thrasher," Part III, *La Semana*, Havana, September 26, 1887, 5.]
41. [Villanova, III, 6.]
42. *Lettres [americaines]*, 251. [*Letters of Alexander von Humboldt to Varnhagen von Ense. From 1827 to 1858*. With Extracts from Varnhagen's Diaries and Letters of Varnhagen and others to Humboldt. Transl. from the 2nd German ed. By Friedrich Kapp. New York: Rudd and Carleton, 1860, 326.]

Translations of Cuba: Fernando Ortiz, Alexander von Humboldt, and the curious case of John Sidney Thrasher

Vera M. Kutzinski

This essay combines a critical assessment of Fernando Ortiz's writings on Alexander von Humboldt with an inquiry into the challenges of carrying Humboldt's writing and thinking into another idiom. My focus is on how Humboldt's *Essai politique sur l'île de Cuba* (1826), a text that was banned in Cuba because of its anti-slavery sentiments, has fared at the hands of different translators since the early nineteenth-century. I follow Ortiz's lead in scrutinizing John Thrasher's infamous defacement of Humboldt's writing in *The Island of Cuba* (1856), situating Thrasher's version in relation to other English, Spanish, and German translations of this text. I argue that Thrasher's case, while no doubt extreme, represents a difference in degree but not in kind when compared to how other translators have handled Humboldt to make him more "readable."

These days, Alexander von Humboldt's popular images are mainly those of a traveling adventurer and a collector of all sorts of scientific data. Clearly, he was both – but he was also much more: Humboldt's writings on the Americas show him to be a first-rate empirical scientist, a remarkable imaginative thinker, and a subtle narrator. It is for good reason that the venerated Cuban anthropologist Fernando Ortiz, in his introduction to the 1930 edition of the *Essai politique sur l'île de Cuba* [*Political Essay on the Island of Cuba*], emphasized that Humboldt's various honorary epithets – Simón Bolívar had called him the "re-discoverer of America," the Cuban philosopher José de la Luz y Caballero the "second discoverer of Cuba" – do not really do justice to the renowned German scientist and scholar.[1] Ortiz, in fact, portrayed Alexander von Humboldt as a "bold inventor" of the island of Cuba and of the Spanish Americas as a whole, as someone who recognized both the uniqueness of that part of the western hemisphere and its growing importance to the rest of the world. Ortiz was also well aware that many aspects of Humboldt's *Voyage aux régions équinoxiales du Nouveau Continent* [*Voyage to the Equinoctial Regions of the New Continent*] (1805–1834) had long remained underappreciated. Most notably among them were Humboldt's keen and vociferous criticisms of New World slavery in his *Political Essay on the Island of Cuba*, a part of his 30-volume *Voyage* that was also published as a free-standing two-volume set in 1826.

Alexander von Humboldt visited the island of Cuba twice during his American journey (1799–1804), in 1800 and 1804. More than twenty years later, in 1825 and 1826, Humboldt finally published his *Political Essay on the Island of Cuba*. It is this work that, for Ortiz and others, made Humboldt an honorary Cuban, despite the fact that the first Spanish translation of the *Essai*, following hard on the heels of the original French publication in 1827, was promptly banned by the Havana City Council "on account of the observations that [this book] made about slavery." Few Cubans had actually read Humboldt's *Political Essay on the Island of Cuba* until 1930, when Fernando Ortiz reprinted the suppressed Spanish translation of the *Essai politique sur l'île de Cuba* in his prestigious Libros Cubanos series. However, 1959 and 1960 were the years that saw the most dramatic revival of Cuban (and Latin American) intellectuals' interest in Humboldt. In short succession, three editions of Humboldt's *Ensayo* were prepared in Havana, honoring the centenary of the Prussian's death on the eve of the new, revolutionary Cuba: one by the journal *Revista Bimestre Cubana*, the official publication of the influential Sociedad Económica de Amigos del País [Economic Society of the Friends of the Country], edited by Ortiz; another by Emilio Roig de Leuchsenring, then Historian of the City of Havana; and a third one by Jorge Quintana Rodríguez, Director of the Cuban National Archive. These editions were effectively reprints of Ortiz's 1930 edition of Humboldt's book with new prefaces; all included Ortiz's extensive introduction and his afterword, entitled "El traductor de Humboldt en la historia de Cuba" [Humboldt's translator in the context of Cuban history].[2] The afterword is of special interest because it shows how Humboldt's writings on Cuba have been distorted in translation, which is the larger subject of my essay.

Humboldt's translator, to whom Ortiz so tellingly denies titular recognition, is John Sidney Thrasher, who published an English version of Humboldt's text in New York in 1856 and whose case is at the center of this essay. I want to preface my analytical probing of Thrasher's translation with a critical look at Ortiz's two essays to draw attention to his cautionary tale about the politics of translation in the context of not-so-neighborly US–Cuban relations, both in 1930 and in 1959–1960. I will then trace the career of Thrasher's translation and situate it in relation to other translations of Humboldt's *Essai politique sur l'île de Cuba* – into English, Spanish, and German – arguing that Thrasher's case, though indeed curious, may represent a difference in degree but not necessarily in kind when compared to how Humboldt's other translators have treated this text. Despite its centrality within literary studies, translation "often remains under-analyzed and under-theorized."[3] This is, in part at least, the result of the fact that the subject of translation tends to invite a host of critical commonplaces – fidelity, accuracy, reliable, and readability are the most popular – which impede, rather than facilitate, rigorous studies of translation. I will be attentive throughout to the often misleading assumptions behind these terms.

I

Ortiz's titles his introduction to the *Ensayo politico sobre la isla de Cuba* "Introducción bibliográfica," and while it does provide significant bibliographical information about Humboldt's writings on Cuba and the Americas, Ortiz's 136-page essay (in the Libros Cubanos edition) has a different purpose. Above all, Ortiz is interested in showing how intimately intertwined Alexander von Humboldt's work is with the history of Cuba's culture and national consciousness. He opens his introduction by adapting the remarks that the German ambassador Karl Bunz made at the dedication of the commemorative statue of Humboldt in Mexico City in 1910, substituting Cuba for Mexico: "El autor de la obra *Cosmos* pertenece al mundo;

el ilustre sabio pertenece a Alemania; el autor del *Ensayo político sobre la Isla de Cuba* a esta patria cubana pertenece" [The author of *Kosmos* belongs to the world; the famous scholar belongs to Germany; and the author of the *Political Essay on the Island of Cuba* belongs to this our Cuban nation] (VIII). Thus claiming Humboldt for Cuba, Ortiz strategically frames his essay with references to the various ways in which Humboldt had been publicly honored elsewhere in the Americas – in Mexico, in Venezuela, and even in the United States – admonishing his fellow countrymen for "no [haber] rendido todavía al sabio germano el tributo de reconocimiento que le debe" [still not having given the learned German the recognition they owe him] (CXLIII). Ortiz's conclusion follows logically: "Alentemos la esperanza de que algún día, ¿por qué no pronto?, tenga una recordación plástica en nuestros paseos el ínclito Humboldt, y cerca de él [Francisco] Arango y Parreño, [José Antonio] Saco, [José María] Heredia y tantos otros que a la nación y a la cultura de Cuba dieron conciencia" [Let us foster the hope that some day – and why not soon? – our public promenades will have monuments that remember the eminent Humboldt, and next to him those that recall Francisco Arango y Parreño, José Antonio Saco, José María Heredia, and so many others who gave consciousness to the nation and the culture of Cuba"] (CXLIV). Ortiz, no doubt, would have been happier had the colossal Humboldt statue that the Cuban government presented, in 1939, to the Humboldt University in what was to become East Germany a few years later had been placed in Havana instead. The commemorative Humboldt stamp that Cuba issued in 1969, the year of Ortiz's death, would likely have struck him as a poor substitute. Ortiz's purpose, then, is quite clear: his edition of the *Ensayo político* is not just to honor a legacy of anti-dogmatic and heterodox thinking; it is to monumentalize the man whose name, rendered in Spanish, should be *Alejandro de Humboldt y Colón* (his mother's maiden name was Colomb).[4]

What accounts for Fernando Ortiz's interest in Humboldt in 1929 was, at least in part, the fact that the Machado regime could not have been any further from the principles of what Ortiz calls "el liberalismo humboldtiano" [Humboldtian liberalism] (XCVIII). Emphasizing that Humboldt, in the words of the poet John Whittier whom Ortiz quotes, "aborreció toda esclavitud, la mental y la espiritual como la física ... Sólo fué intolerante con la intolerancia" [abhorred slavery in all of its forms, the intellectual and spiritual as much as the physical ... He was intolerant only of intolerance itself] (XCV), helps Ortiz draw implicit comparisons between the Cuba of the late 1920s, characterized by government censorship and on the brink of an economic depression, and a Cuba that had chafed under colonial domination a hundred years earlier. To Ortiz, the banning of Humboldt's *Ensayo político* exemplifies the same spirit of intellectual intolerance that he sees in his own day: "Esta persecución colonial de la obra de Humboldt nos hace pensar que si hubiera podido preverse lo que el sabio iba a escribir en 1827 sobre la sociedad cubana de 1800 a 1804, ni el rey de España habría consentido entonces su viaje, ni los aristócratas de la Habana lo habrían tratado con la simpatía con que lo hicieron" [The colonial persecution of Humboldt's work makes me think that if the King of Spain had been able to foresee, in 1800 to 1804, what Humboldt was going to write about Cuban society in 1827, he would not have consented to Humboldt's voyage; nor would the Havana aristocrats have treated Humboldt with the kindness with which they did] (CXXIX). Ortiz is, of course, alluding to Humboldt's famous pronouncement that "slavery is possibly the greatest evil ever to have afflicted humanity,"[5] written at a time when even the Delmonte group, the mainstay of early Cuban abolitionism, was still very much in its infancy. At the same time, Ortiz was also fully aware of Humboldt's abiding respect for Arango y Parreño, whom Ortiz portrays as an enlightened reformer, despite the fact that Arango was also a prominent slaveholder, who had been, in no small measure, responsible for convincing the Spanish Cortes not to abolish the transatlantic slave trade in 1811. Arango had been one of Humboldt's gracious Cuban hosts, and he directly engaged with Humboldt's anti-slavery arguments in his detailed critical annotations of the *Essai politique sur l'île de Cuba* in 1827.[6] (Ortiz's edition includes Arango's notes along with Thrasher's.) That Ortiz himself regarded Arango not just as a premier statesman, as Humboldt himself did, but as a national hero, whose bust should be right next to Humboldt's, shows that slavery is not really the main issue here. Even more important to Ortiz, in 1930 and especially in 1959, is the issue of Cuba's political independence, historically from Spain, and, at those later moments, from the US. Even if Humboldt had not openly advocated Cuban sovereignty, according to Ortiz, "que Humboldt simpatizó con la libertad de Cuba, no cabe dudarlo; toda su historia lo abona" [there is no doubt that Humboldt was sympathetic to Cuban freedom; his entire history points in that direction] (CXXV). As evidence for this, Ortiz cites Humboldt's support for other Latin America independence movements, but Humboldt's support came after the fact. By the time that Humboldt wrote the *Essai politique sur l'île de Cuba* in the mid-1820s, political independence had already become a reality in all of Spain's continental possessions. Only Cuba, Puerto Rico, and the Philippines remained under metropolitan rule.

Ortiz's focus on Cuban independence also explains why he felt compelled to write about John Thrasher to recount an "interesting," but largely forgotten, episode in Cuban history: the mid-nineteenth century plan, or plot, to annex Cuba to the US Ortiz's essay on Thrasher is the other part of the frame for Humboldt's *Political Essay on the Island of Cuba*: if Ortiz's goal in the introduction was to monumentalize Humboldt by claiming his work as part of Cuba's intellectual and cultural legacy, his aim in the afterword is to vilify Thrasher as the person who tried to sully that legacy. Ortiz's second piece prefaces the first and only Spanish translation of the lengthy "Preliminary Essay" Thrasher wrote for his Humboldt translation. Ortiz includes it in his edition, emphasizing its "valor documental positivo para apreciar los puntos de vista que acerca de los temas cubanos eran sostenidos en aquellos negros tiempos por un escritor norteamericano que intervino personalmente en los episodios que se desarrollan en nuestra tierra" [documentary value for being able to show in detail the views that a North American writer, who personally intervened in affairs that unfolded on our soil, held about Cuban affairs in those dark times] (II.184). Nevertheless, as we shall see, historical documentation, though a significant part of Ortiz's essay, is neither his only nor his most important concern; his tone is far too strident for an historical piece.

Let us turn our attention, then, to the subject of Ortiz's disparagement. Who was John Sidney Thrasher anyway? According to Ortiz, Thrasher "fué un periodista americano que vino a Cuba para aprovechar el río revuelto de las agitaciones contra el absolutismo español y encauzarlas hacia el anexionismo del lucero de Cuba a la constelación federativo de los Estados Unidos de América, como una estrella más" [was an American journalist, who came to Cuba to take advantage of the waters churning with Cuban agitations against Spanish rule and to channel these waters toward the annexation of Cuba's bright star to the federated constellation of the United States of America, as one more star among many] (II.186). Thrasher spent a number of years in Cuba, and Ortiz gives us a detailed account of the career of this "intrépido journalista" [intrepid journalist]. In 1850, Thrasher became the unofficial editor-in-chief of *El Faro Industrial de la Habana* [The Industrialist Beacon of Havana], which, its name notwithstanding functioned as a literary journal that presumably steered clear of politics, which of course it did not. Publishing a few pieces to throw the Cuban authorities off his political scent, Thrasher turned *El Faro* into a vehicle for anti-Spanish mockery. This worked for as long as the journal helped Cuba's Captain-general José Gutiérres de la Concha – Ortiz tellingly calls him "Cuba's dictator" – to uphold the appearance of a free Cuban press. Gutiérres de la Concha, who is the other villain in this story, was laying in wait for an opportune moment to close the journal down, and Thrasher promptly delivered when the journal failed to print a proper obituary for the Spanish General Enna, who died in 1851 in a battle with Narciso López's pro-annexation filibusters. López himself, on whose exploits *El Faro* had reported in detail, would die a few months later, and his co-conspirators were executed. Thrasher's pro-annexation views were well known on the island, and he was rightly suspected of collaborating with López under the code-name "El Yankee." Yielding to the increasingly negative popular opinion that was building against *El Faro*, Concha decided to make an example of Thrasher, whom he labeled "el más eficáz de los agents de las *expediciones piráticas*" [the most effective agent of *the piratical expeditions* of Narciso López] (II.203). Concha not only closed down *El Faro*; he also made sure that Thrasher ended up with an eight-year jail sentence. Without delay, Thrasher was shipped off to the infamous North African prison of Ceuta. A year later, however, he was released under a general pardon as a result of US diplomatic intervention, much to the Concha's disappointment and disgust. Thrasher's release carried with it the condition that he would not return to Spain's overseas colonies and that "en el caso de que se le encontrasen en alguna de ellas, se consideraría sujeto a cumplir su sentencia" [if he were ever found in any of them, he would be subject to serving his full sentence] (II.205–6).

Being thus barred from returning to Cuba, the "tenaz Thrasher" shifted his base of operations to New Orleans, where he founded the journal *The Beacon of Cuba* (*El Faro de Cuba*) and sought out the company of exiled anti-loyalist Cubans, most of whom, according to Ortiz, were wary of him. In New Orleans, Thrasher continued to fan the flames of pro-US-annexation. Although annexationism was losing ground among Cubans by the mid-1850s, many North Americans, writes Ortiz, "deseaban las anexión de Cuba, o cuando menos, confiaban su adquisición al porvenir … solo la guerra civil de los Estados Unidos impidió que la anexión fuese llevada a cabo" [wanted Cuba's annexation, or at least trusted that it would be acquired in the future … only the US Civil War prevented the annexation from becoming a reality] (II.210). At the core of the annexation debate was, of course, slavery – or more precisely, the economics of slavery. In fact, one of the sentiments that fueled separatist (that is, pro-annexation) fires in Cuba was the fear, on the part of Cuba's economic elite, that Spain would not be able to withstand the increasing pressure from Britain to abolish slavery, which, they argued, would spell ruin for Cuba's sugar economy. This fear proved unfounded; slavery would not be abolished in Cuba until 1886, and meanwhile, the sugar industry boomed. Some believed that the best chance of maintaining an economy founded on slave labor was to join the US as another slave state, and US politicians, especially from the South, were strongly supportive of such a plan, especially since Cuba was already a major trade partner for the US. By contrast, Humboldt had actually argued quite convincingly, in the *Political Essayon the Island of Cuba*, that such economically-based arguments for maintaining slavery were unfounded, but few Cubans, outside of Arango's Sociedad Económica de Amigos del País, were familiar with his arguments. It is hardly a coincidence that the Society's journal, the *Revista Bimestre Cubana*, would reissue this very text more than a century later. For Ortiz, the journal's editor-in-chief at the time, publishing Humboldt's *Political Essay on the Island of Cuba* was also a way of honoring the Arango's intellectual and political legacy.

Thrasher's own politics were unequivocally proslavery, and, seeing his political fortunes wane by the mid-1850s, he resorted to a different strategy: he decided to bolster his political credibility by translating into English Alexander von Humboldt's *Political Essay on the Island of Cuba*. On the one hand, this was a curious choice because the Spanish translation of this text had been banned in Cuba. On the other hand, precisely the fact that it had been banned also ensured that hardly anyone would be able to challenge Thrasher's version. Ortiz writes:

> Como convencido esclavista, él [Thrasher] sin duda creyó que una de las maneras más eficaces de contribuir a aquella empresa había ser difundiendo en el pueblo americano los conocimientos que él había adquirido durante su larga residencia en la isla, y para realizar esa propaganda no encontró libro mejor que la traducción al inglés del *Ensayo político sobre la Isla de Cuba*, de Alejandro de Humboldt; pero cometió la inexcusable falta de suprimir la parte de esta obra que había de estar en contradicción con sus prejuicios raciales y políticos, y todo lo que en ella combatía su criterio a favor del mantenimiento de la exclavitud. (II.209–10)

> [As an advocate of slavery, Thrasher no doubt believed that one of the most effective ways in which he could contribute to the project of annexing Cuba was by disseminating among the American people the knowledge that he had gained during his long stay on the island, and, to get his propaganda out there, he could find no better vehicle than the English translation of Alexander von Humboldt's *Political Essay on the Island of Cuba*. But he committed the inexcusable mistake of suppressing the very part of the book that contradicted his own racial and political biases and everything in it that went against his arguments in favor of maintaining slavery.]

What Thrasher had not taken into account, however, was Humboldt himself. Ortiz's indictment of Thrasher, then, follows Humboldt's lead. Ortiz owned Humboldt's copy of Thrasher's book, and that very copy, which is now at the Biblioteca Nacional José Martí, had Humboldt's own handwritten annotations in it (see Figure 1).[7] Ortiz explains:

> En una de sus páginas constan unas líneas manuscritas en francés por el proprio Alejandro de Humboldt, en las cuales, con su letra ya temblona a sus 87 años, señala las variaciones que Thrasher hace del texto castellano de J. B. de V. y M. que el mismo traductor en su prefacio dijo haber seguido con manifiesta mentira. Humboldt ... dice que el infiel traductor debió hacer les supresiones "sin duba por razones políticas." Dice, además, que ... Thrasher termina el *Ensayo político* suprimiendo todo el artículo que la edición española llama "Esclavos". (II.121–23)

> [On one of the pages, there were handwritten lines in French by Alexander von Humboldt himself, in which Humboldt, with the trembling hand of his 87 years, pointed to the changes Thrasher had made to the Spanish text by J. B. de V. y M., which that same translator, in his preface, had indicated that he had followed – clearly a lie.

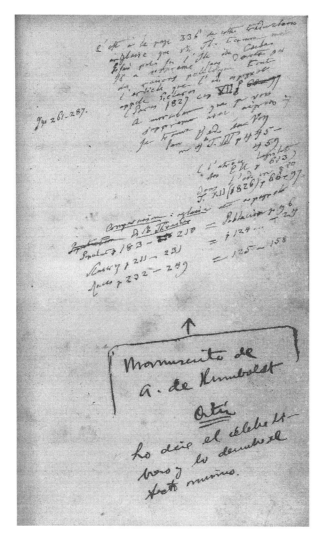

Figure 1.   Page of Humboldt's notes on Thrasher's text, courtesy of the Biblioteca Nacional José Martí in Havana. Photograph by Tobias Kraft.

> Humboldt said ... that the unfaithful translation must have made these changes "no doubt for political reasons." He said further that... Thrasher ends the *Political Essay*, suppressing the entire article that the Spanish version called "Slaves"].

Humboldt's notes became the basis for the open letter he wrote in 1856 for publication in the *Spenersche Zeitung* in Germany.[8] An English version of the letter was printed in the New York *Daily Times* and in several other papers in the same year, making Humboldt a celebrity in US abolitionist circles.[9] Ortiz includes both Humboldt's letter and Thrasher's unrepentant reply in his essay.[10]

Ortiz does not mince his words. Thrasher, he writes, "no pudo ser más desleal" [could not have been any more disloyal] to Humboldt in committing the "pecado traicionero" [traitorous sin] of turning Humboldt, of all people, into a pro-slavery advocate like himself (II.212). He calls Thrasher's mutilations "outrageous" and "ill-intentioned," specifying that the translation "no sólo [suprimió] párrafos y conceptos, sino alterando radicalmente el orden de sus materiales" [not only suppressed paragraphs and ideas but also radically changed the order of Humboldt's materials] (II.213). To illustrate his points, Ortiz juxtaposes the chapter breakdown in Thrasher's version to the order of the chapters in his source text, which was not, as one might have expected, Humboldt's own French text but the 1827 Spanish translation. As he admitted in his unapologetic response to Humboldt's public rebuke, Thrasher did not read French.[11]

Chapters according to Thrasher
Chap. I: General Views
    II: Physical Aspects
    III: Climate
    IV: Geography
    V: Population
    VI: Slavery
    VII: Races
    VIII: Sugar Culture
    IX: Agriculture
    X: Commerce
    XI: Internal Communications
    XII: Revenue
    XIII: A Trip to Trinidad

Capítulo según Humboldt
Cap. I: Consideraciones generales acerca de la posición y del aspecto físico de la Isla de Cuba – Observaciones astronómicas
    II: Extensión. – Clima. – Estado de las costas. – División territorial.
    III: Población.
    IV: Agricultura
    V: Comercio
    VI: Hacienda
    VII: Viaje al Valle de los Güines, etc. (II.213–14)[12]

What is remarkable here is that Ortiz himself appears not to have consulted the French text either; nor was he aware, as he tells us in a footnote,[13] that there had been an earlier English version of Humboldt's *Political Essay* by the British poet Helen Maria Williams, which was published as Chapter 28 in Volume VII of the *Personal Narrative of a Voyage to the Equinoctial Regions of the New Continent* in 1829. Had Ortiz checked either the French text or even Williams's translation, he would have realized that what he called "chapters according to Humboldt" were, in fact, add-ons by the translator (presumably José López de Bustamante, of whom we know next to nothing). Humboldt himself did not divide the *Essai politique sur l'île de Cuba* into chapters, neither in the 1825 nor the 1826 version; he used only a handful of titled subsections in both editions.[14]

Although Thrasher follows the Spanish translators' decision to divide Humboldt's *Essai* into numbered and titled chapters, his own chapter divisions are quite different. Most conspicuous, but only if one knows where to look, is Thrasher's omission of Humboldt's offending section on slavery, which was based on observations that Humboldt made during his visits to three sugar plantations in the vicinity of Havana (one of them, *La Ninfa*, was owned by Arango). Surprisingly, in Ortiz's "Capítulo[s] según Humboldt," the slavery chapter is also missing. It would have to be chapter VII; "Viaje al Valle de Güines" [Trip to the Valley of Güines] is actually chapter VIII in the Spanish version. While this is clearly an unintended error, it is also not without irony that Ortiz's list of Humboldt's supposed chapters omits the very section for whose suppression he takes Thrasher to task. To clarify: Thrasher's chapter VI, which is also entitled "Slavery," is *not* the Spanish edition's chapter VII but part of Humboldt's discussion of Cuba's population. When Thrasher responded to Humboldt's accusations, he claimed that he had not included the section on slavery because it was a "distinct essay" that "only incidentally alluded, to [Cuba]." According to his own argument, then, Thrasher should have ended his translation at the very point where Humboldt himself indicated that the *Political Essay* ends. He did not but, instead, continued on after cutting out about 30 pages.

Thrasher's textual manipulations do not end there. For one, he retitles the book, something that Humboldt disliked intensely. In Thrasher's hands, the *Ensayo político sobre la isla de Cuba* becomes simply *The Island of Cuba* (see Figure 2); inside the book, Humboldt's text is further reduced to "Humboldt's Cuba."

For another, Thrasher excised not only the sentences and paragraphs in which Humboldt criticized slavery; he also cut numerous lengthy passages in which Humboldt expounds on the work of others and on his scientific collaborations with them, and he left out many of Humboldt's footnotes, replacing them with his own. In addition, there is also an abundance of subtler modifications that are not as easily noticeable. Thrasher frequently alters Humboldt's numbers, among other things, to make the population of slaves and free blacks seem smaller than it actually was. There are no interpretive moves that, for instance, could increase "three-fifths" of Cuba's free population to "three-fourths."[15] There are also seemingly unobtrusive changes in paragraphing, which attempt to stem the flow of Humboldt's narrative. So intent was Thrasher on reconfiguring this narrative that he rarely kept any of Humboldt's own paragraph breaks, and the new paragraphs he introduces are notably shorter, breaking up the text into more easily digestible (or "readable") pieces. This is evident from the inventory with which each of Thrasher's "chapters" opens, which includes his own additions, in square brackets, in a way that makes them virtually indistinguishable from Humboldt's writing (see Figure 3).

Thrasher's "notes" at the end of each "chapter," which take the place of Humboldt's own prose, insure that the "chapters" close on commentaries that further Thrasher's political agenda.

In his Chapter I, for example, Thrasher replaces Humboldt's detailed discussion of the difficulty of fixing Havana's exact geographical position with remarks on ship building, and he inserts a lengthy table of all ships built in Havana between 1723 and 1796.[16] Where Humboldt ends this section with a scientific question (in this case about variations in magnetic inclination), Thrasher directs his readers' attention to the conflicts between Spain and colonial Cuba, where, during the mid-nineteenth century, he informs us, Spain no longer allowed ships to be built but only to be repaired. "The reason assigned for this," says Thrasher, "is that ship-building in Cuba deprives the labor of the mother country of employment"[17] – the unspoken implication being that Cuba would be far better off economically if it separated from

HUMBOLDT'S IMPORTANT WORK ON CUBA.
NOW READY:
THE ISLAND OF CUBA.
BY ALEXANDER HUMBOLDT.
TRANSLATED FROM THE SPANISH, WITH NOTES AND A PRELIMINARY ESSAY.
BY J. S. THRASHER.
BRINGING DOWN THE HISTORY TO THE PRESENT TIME.
With a Map. 12mo; price $1 25.

It is believed this work, by the eminent Humboldt, now first presented to the public, under the auspices of a gentleman whose facilities have rendered his position invaluable for such a purpose, will be read with interest by the Public. An accurate and minute Map, from the latest Spanish authorities, accompanies the book.

CONTENTS.

Preliminary Essay—Comprising a complete View of the Territorial, Political, Industrial and Social Relations of the Island.
General Views.
Physical Aspect.
Climate.
Geography.
Population.
Slavery.
Races.
Sugar Culture.
Agriculture.
Commerce.
Internal Communications.
Revenue.
A Trip to Trinidad.

From the New-Orleans Courier.

This excellent work has never been presented in English, and will be welcomed with pleasure by many thousands who will lose no time in availing themselves of it as a source of information on a subject of growing interest and importance. It will be enriched by considerable additions, written by the translator, which will put the reader in possession of a knowledge of the present social, financial and political condition of the Cubans. The knowledge which Mr. Thrasher has of Cuba from a long residence there, and from his having devoted many years to a study of its condition and its relation to the mother country and the United States, eminently qualifies him for the preparation of such a work. Of the merits of the original no doubt can be entertained. Wherever science is cultivated the name of Humboldt is justly honored. We shall await the appearance of this work to make more extended comments.

DERBY & JACKSON, Publishers, New-York.
Can be ordered through any bookseller.

Figure 2. Advertisement for Thrasher book from the *New York Daily Times* (1856).

HUMBOLDT'S CUBA.

CHAPTER I

GENERAL VIEWS.

Political importance of the island of Cuba and port of Havana
—Their relations to contiguous countries—Increase of public
wealth and revenue—Description of Bay and City of Havana—
Public buildings—Streets—Public walks and grounds—Ashes
of Columbus—Palms—Vicinity of Havana—Suburbs—Projected
moat—Defences of Havana—Population—Increase—Marriages,
births, and deaths—Hospitals—Health—Markets—Hospitality—
[NOTE.—Establishment of Navy yard at Havana—Don Augustin
de Arriola—List of ships built at Havana—Abandonment of the
Navy-yard.]

THE political importance of the island of Cuba
does not arise solely from its great extent, though it
is one half larger than Haiti, nor from the admirable
fertility of its soil, nor from its great naval resources,[1]
nor from the nature of its population, three-fourths
of which are freemen; but it derives a far greater

[1] See Note at the end of the chapter.

5

Figure 3.   Page from Helen Maria Williams's translation of Humboldt's *Relation historique*.

Spain and became attached to the US. A review of *The Island of Cuba* from 1856 even went so far as to call Cuba the island of "manifest destiny."[18]

The overall effect of Thrasher's adjustments is to straighten out the narrative line of a discourse that always, as is so characteristic of Humboldt, meanders, doubles back onto itself, and wanders off in several directions at once. In Thrasher's translation, there is none of the breathlessness and even disorientation that comes with reading Humboldt's long paragraphs. Nor is there any sense of the dense texture of Humboldt's prose, which abounds in seemingly capricious and random capitalizations, italics, variations in spelling, and frequent words and phrases in Spanish and other languages. Intent on showing local variations and different cultural perspectives, he refuses to standardize much of anything, including units of measure. Reading Humboldt means moving through an ever-changing maze of toises, feet, and millimeters, piasters, francs, and sols, hogsheads and hundred-weights, barrels and kilos, Centigrade, Fahrenheit, even Réaumur, not to mention different kinds of square leagues. Humboldt is a bit like Jorge Luis Borges' eponymous Funés the Memorious, who fundamentally lacks any ability to categorize what he sees around him – which, in the end, drives him mad. In Humboldt's case, however, it is not madness that ensues but what Ottmar Ette has called "an openness of the processes of understanding"[19] – both Humboldt's and our own.

There is no attempt at representing these dynamic processes of understanding in Thrasher's text, which standardizes everything: temperature measurements are changed to Fahrenheit, toises to feet, and piasters and francs to dollars (often without currency conversion). Such standardization works together with the omissions to make Humboldt's voice indistinguishable from Thrasher's own. The often awkward formalities of Humboldt's Franco-German prose yield to the smoother colloquial cadences of Thrasher's US American idiom. The radically shortened paragraphs, the lack of seeming digressions, and the familiar cadences may well be why Thrasher's translation "reads well today," as Markus Wiener, the publisher of the 2001 reprint of Thrasher's *The Island of Cuba*, asserts.[20] In the same stroke, Wiener dismisses Helen Maria Williams' translation of the Cuba essay as a "literal translation ... which is written in a nineteenth-century German academic style. The style is very old-fashioned and for today's reader nearly unreadable." The main reason why Williams, a British poet, would have written according to the then prevalent stylistic conventions of German academia is because Humboldt himself did. The broader (and tacit) implication here is that Humboldt himself is unreadable.[21]

In his 1856 public letter, Humboldt himself actually endorsed Williams' and López de Bustamante's translations for not "omit[ting] any of the frank and open remarks which feelings of humanity had inspired." He continued: "Steady advocate that I am for the most unfettered expression of opinion in speech or in writing, I should never have thought of complaining if I had been attacked on account of my statements; but I do think I am entitled to demand that in the Free States of the continent of America, people should be allowed to read what has been permitted to circulate from the first year of its appearance in a Spanish translation."[22] What had been permitted to circulate, though not in Cuba, included what Humboldt now calls the "very portion of my work to which I attach greater importance than to my astronomical observations, experiments of magnetic intensity, or statistical statements." This remark has led one historian to suggest that

> el juicio que Humboldt emitió en 1826 sobre el estado en que encontraban al comenzar del siglo XIX los negros esclavos de las colonias españolas en América, no fue ni tan expresivo no tan enfático come el que dio en el artículo que publicó en Berlin en julio de 1856 al conocer la supresión llevada a cabo por Thrasher en la versión del *Ensayo Político*. (II.381)

> [the opinion Humboldt expressed in 1826 about the state of the black slaves of the Spanish colonies in America at the beginning of the nineteenth century was neither as impassioned nor as emphatic as what he said in the article he published in Berlin in July of 1856 upon finding out about Thrasher's excisions in his version of the *Political Essay*].

Manuel Villanova, whose remarks from 1887 Ortiz quotes in this passage, is only one in a long line of historians who would later criticize Humboldt for not being more passionate about his loathing of slavery.[23] Villanova even provides a reason beyond Humboldt's oft-cited limited lack of exposure to the real horrors of Cuban slavery:

> Fáltole esta vez al sabio alemán el sagaz criterio que generalmente brilla en sus obras. Su juicio sobre la legislación y las costumbres, en cuantos influían en la suerte de los negros

en las colonias españolas, se resiente... de haberse dejado seducir por el lenguaje empleado en las instrucciones y reglamentos dictados para fijar la condición y el trato de los esclavos. (II.216)

[The German scholar lacked at that time the good sense that typically shines through his work. His opinions about the laws and customs that influenced the fate of the blacks in the Spanish colonies, suffers ... from having been seduced by the language used in the instructions and regulations that were then announced to ameliorate those conditions and the slave trade].[24]

Clearly a veiled stab at Arango y Parreño and other Cuban reformers,[25] Villanova's criticisms are quite puzzling in light of Humboldt's following sentences from his *Essai politique sur l'île de Cuba*, with which he must have been familiar.

It is in vain that wily writers have invented phrases such as *black peasants of the Antilles, black vassalage,* and *patriarchal protection* in order to veil the institutionalized barbarity in ingenious linguistic fictions. It is a profanation of the noble arts of the spirit and the imagination to use illusory compromises and misleading sophistries to excuse the excesses that afflict humanity and bring about violent upheavals.[26]

As this passage demonstrates, Alexander von Humboldt was far too alert to the discourses on slavery in his day to be seduced by their "linguistic fictions." The remarks in his letter notwithstanding, he was also, both in 1826 and in 1856, well aware that the significance of his *Essai politique sur l'île de Cuba* went beyond his tirades against slavery. As Ortiz points out, Humboldt quite literally put Cuba on the map by fixing, for the first time, the geographical positions of its towns and cities, by conducting detailed geological and mineralogical research, collecting new plant species, and writing in detail about the island's population. Humboldt also provided valuable details about sugar production and trade, comparing Cuba to the rest of the Antilles, to Spain's and Portugal's continental colonies, to European countries, and to the United States. Humboldt *Political Essay* on *the Island of Cuba* as whole delivers a complex scientific, cultural, and philosophical analysis of the Cuban economics, which included the legal and illegal slave trade and slavery itself. Ortiz knows that the full significance of Humboldt's analysis cannot be measured by a handful of passionate outcries against slavery, as heartfelt as those were, and he ends his essay by noting, almost a bit sheepishly, that

no creemos justo mermar la gloria de Humboldt porque éste no dió a sus condenaciones de la esclavitud negra en Cuba toda la vehemencia que era natural en una pluma cubana, doliente y mojada en aquella misma negrura. (II.219)

[it would not be fair to reduce Humboldt's glory just because he did not denounce black slavery in Cuba as vehemently as might be natural for a Cuban whose pen had been dipped in the ink of that slavery].

My point is that Humboldt's *Political Essay on the Island of Cuba* is a not a dogmatic text, with respect to abolitionism or anything else. Not even Thrasher's distortions could make it entirely that, which is why he needed to add his Notes and his extensive "Preliminary Essay" – and Humboldt himself granted that this essay did "enrich" his own text by updating earlier information about Cuba. Such "enrichment" notwithstanding, what Thrasher produced as a translation was nothing less than a fraudulent text, which is little different, in tenor and intent, from the slave narratives that were ghost-written by proslavery southerners in the US at the time[27] and published in some of the same journals that reprinted Thrasher's

"Preliminary Essay."[28] It is rather astonishing, then, at least to this writer, that Thrasher's Humboldt translation would have been reprinted in the US as recently as 2001, because "it reads well today," and that another, much more scrupulous, English translation would be so easily discredited because it does *not*. Luis Martínez Fernández' edition of Thrasher's text, published by Markus Wiener (whom I quoted earlier) under the title *The Island of Cuba. A Political Essay*, mentions briefly but does not correct any of Thrasher's countless manipulations, although the editor does make other changes in Thrasher's text, all of them unacknowledged. Martínez Fernández leaves us with the impression, much like Ortiz does, that Thrasher's major offense was to have omitted a single "chapter." The Wiener edition restores this section in the appendix, in a new translation not from the French but from an unspecified German translation. In short, this entire edition is based on translations (and reprints) of other translations – which is, troublingly, quite in Thrasher's spirit.

I do not wish to exonerate Thrasher by pointing out that many of his translational moves, if we can call them that, are remarkably consistent with the ways in which translations of Humboldt's work have been prepared and have circulated since the early nineteenth century: that is, in often radically abridged versions that do not even indicate what is missing.[29] One translational tradition extends from the first Spanish version of the Cuba essay all the way to the present. All Spanish editions of the *Political Essay on the Island of Cuba*, including the most recent editions from 1998 and 2004, by Miguel Angel Puig Samper and Irene Prüfer-Leske, respectively, use modernized versions of the first Spanish translation, even when they claim to be "new." One can track this tradition by the systematizing apparatus that the later editions adopt from the first Spanish edition. This practice has even spilled over into some recent German translations of the *Essai politique sur l'île de Cuba*.[30] This is not even to mention the fact that the two-volume 1826 edition of the *Essai* has never been translated in its entirety – into any language. It is almost as if it no longer matters what Humboldt himself actually wrote, and especially how he wrote it.

What we lose in almost all existing Humboldt translations – I cannot speak to the ones in languages such as Hungarian – and only most dramatically in Thrasher's, is the radical openness of Humboldt's narrative structure, which reflects the unorthodox nature of his ideas. Humboldt's *Essai politique sur l'île de Cuba*, like his other writings, jumps back and forth between anecdotes, sociological, historical, political, and philosophical commentary, and detailed scientific observations, including many statistical tables and copious footnotes. The text moves rapidly between close-ups and broad, at times startling comparisons and contrasts, drawing readers in by offering them a plethora of specifics about nearly everything that Humboldt saw around him. In this way, he challenges readers to take in phenomena and events in what he called their "total effect" and as parts of a far-flung web of hemispheric and global interrelations. A Humboldt text, such as the Cuba essay, might either be a called a *Gesamtkunstwerk avant la lettre* or, with Friedrich Cramer, a representation of a "fundamentally complex system" in which the whole is always greater than the sum of the parts.[31]

Creating a "total effect" that is not totalizing is the intellectual principle behind the networks of scientific collaborations that Humboldt's *Essai politique sur l'île de Cuba* represent, and these networks often included people with whom he had strong political disagreements (Arango y Parreño is only one of many examples).

"Total effect" is the aesthetic principle that Humboldt follows in all of his writings, and it is, I believe, what any translation of his work must respect the most. The problem is that the majority of those who have translated the *Essai politique sur l'île de Cuba* into English, Spanish, and German during the nineteenth, twentieth, and twenty-first centuries have treated whichever source text they preferred[32] as a (social-) scientific text, disregarding entirely its literary aspects as a carefully structured and textured narrative.

There is a dire need for a more literary approach to translating Humboldt. Even the *Essai politique sur l'île de Cuba*, which is hardly the stuff of a riveting adventure tale, has distinctive rhythms, at the level of the narrative as a whole, of the paragraph, and even the sentence. An important part of being true to Humboldt's writing in an English translation is not just to insure the historical and structural integrity of his French texts at the narrative level (this, we should be able to take for granted), but also to attempt to render the cadences of his prose by imagining how he might sound writing in formal English today, with a command of that language as strong as his command was of French and of Spanish. Doing so involves keeping intact Humboldt's long paragraphs, his quirky inconsistencies, and the text's multi-lingual surface, but not necessarily the structure of his sentences. The goal should not be to mimic Humboldt but to convey to readers a strong sense that the kind of thinking and writing that privileges complex, multi-perspectival understanding over system-atization and totalization is still alive today.

II

There has, of course, been one attempt at a literary translation of Humboldt's writings: Helen Maria Williams's much-maligned *Personal Narrative of a Voyage to the Equinoxial Regions of the New Continent* (1814–1829), which includes the earliest version of the *Essai politique sur l'île de Cuba*.[33] The problem is that this version is now 180 years old and that English usage has changed considerably during that time, far more so, in fact, than has French, which partly accounts for the difficulty of Williams's "old-fashioned" style for today's readers; but we should not simply conflate difficult with unreadable. In today's translation studies parlance, one might say that Williams did not sufficiently "domesticate" Humboldt's texts to make them more easily readable – or more consumable – in English. Instead, her literal approach to translation, not unusual for its time, seems to "foreignize" Humboldt's writing to English readers, which, in Lawrence Venuti's estimation, might make her an ideal translator, at least in the ideological terms he elaborates.[34] Readability, however, need not be a function of translational "domestication." If we imagine readability, rather too narrowly I think, as the effect of a text, whose surface remains entirely untroubled by anything that would go against the grain of the linguistic (and representational) conventions of a particular time, then we would have to regard Humboldt's multi-lingual texts with their underlying Franco-German syntax as essentially unreadable. By that definition, any text that bears unassimilated traces of another language would have to be deemed unreadable, which is patently absurd. The problem with Williams's translations of Humboldt, however, is rather different. Her prose has what one might call a "quality of abusive fidelity."[35] What tends to make Williams's style ungainly is her decision to retain Humboldt's impersonal passive constructions, which work far better in French and German than they do in

English. The main element of unreadability comes with Williams's use of seeming Latinate cognates, which, though they are not, strictly speaking, incorrect in most cases, often produce a great deal of puzzlement. At times, they border on actual malapropisms, whose effect can be rather comical. For instance, Williams translates "Indiens, sobres, sans appétit pour la chair des animaux"[36] as "Indians, sober, without taste for animal food,"[37] meaning, actually, "Indians who neither drink alcohol nor eat meat." The problem here arises from Williams's attempt to imitate Humboldt's syntax in English, which is evident throughout her translation. The following passage from the beginning section of the *Political Essay on the Island of Cuba*, which I first quote in Humboldt's French version, is representative of her approach. (I have underlined trouble spots for translators in all of the following citations.)

> Près du *Campo de Marte* se trouve le jardin botanique, bien digne de fixer l'attention du gouvernement, et un autre objet, dont l'aspect afflige et révolte à la fois les baraques devant lesquelles sont exposés en vente les malheureux esclaves. C'est dans la *promenade extra muros* qu'on a placé, depuis mon retour en Europe, une statue en marbre du Roi Charles III. Ce lieu avoit d'abord été destiné à un monument de Christophe Colomb, dont on a porté les cendres, après la cession de la partie espagnole de Saint-Domingue, à l'île de Cuba. Les cendres de Fernand Cortez ayant été transférées, la même année, à Mexico, d'une église à une autre, on a vu donner de nouveau la sépulture, à une même époque, à la fin du dix-huitième siècle, aux deux plus grands hommes qui ont illustré la conquête de l'Amérique.[38]

> Near the *Campo de Marte* is the Botanical Garden, well worthy to fix the attention of government, and another object, fitted to excite at once pity and indignation, the barracks before which the wretched slaves are exposed to sale. A statue in marble of Charles III. has been placed since my return to Europe in this *Extra muros* walk. This spot was at first destined for a monument to Christopher Columbus, whose ashes, after the cession of the Spanish part of Saint Domingo, were brought to the island of Cuba. The same year the ashes of Fernand Cortez were transferred in Mexico from one church to another: thus at the same time, at the end of the 18th century, the two greatest men who promoted the conquest of America, received new sepulchres.[39]

Williams follows Humboldt's sentences precisely, even to the point of producing needless hyperbatons (as in the second sentence). She keeps Latinate nouns such as "cession" and "sepulchre" (sépulture), while rendering the italicized French "promenade" as "walk" (without italics). Although typically diligent about retaining Humboldt's italics, Williams does so only for Spanish words and phrases, some of which she capitalizes for no good reason. While this might be one way of rendering Humboldt's own inconsistent use of capitalization and lower case, I doubt that this was Williams's intent. "Saint-Domingue" becomes the oddly hybridized "Saint Domingo," which is strangely appropriate – and arresting – given the island's colonial history of Spanish and French rule. That Humboldt approved of Williams's translation is unsurprising, because he could easily hear his own cadences in her prose. But Humboldt also knew what he meant to write and would thus have been a highly unreliable judge of whether a text that so closely resembled his own, at the level of the word and the sentence, actually signified in the same way in a structurally different language. The notion that Humboldt "authorized" Williams's translation with what might also have been an ironically polite remark, therefore, should be held in suspicion.[40]

Other interesting translational issues come into view when we add John Thrasher's version of this passage into the picture. His version begins with a new paragraph (inserted) and ends with a lengthy footnote on Columbus' and Cortés' respective re-burials, which consists of quotations from William Prescott's *History of the Conquest of Mexico*. Only those who know that Prescott's history was not published until 1843 would realize that this is not Humboldt's own footnote.

> The botanical garden, near *Campo Marte,* is worthy of the attention of the government. Since my return to Europe a marble statue of Carlos III has been erected in the extra-mural *paseo.* Its site had been first selected for a monument to Columbus, whose ashes were brought to Havana on the cession of the Spanish part of St Domingo to the French: The remains of Hernan [sic] Cortés having been carried during the same year (1796) from one church in Mexico to another, there occurred the coincidence of a re-interment at the same time, near the close of the eighteenth century, of the two greatest of the men who were made illustrious by the discovery and conquest of America.[41]

Several adjustments and errors are worthy of note here (I have underlined them). Unlike Williams, Thrasher varies Humboldt's diction (changing "ashes" to "remains" in the second iteration) and tends to steer clear of cognates ("sepulture" becomes "interment"). His use of the words "Carlos" and "paseo" (promenade) makes clear that he is working from the Spanish translation, which does not retain Humboldt's italics of the phrase "*promenade extra muros*" and where the fact that Humboldt used a Spanish phrase would thus have been invisible. The unmarked addition of the date, though informative, alters Humboldt's text, as does the substitution of "Havana" for Humboldt's less specific "the island of Cuba." Both Thrasher and Williams erroneously translate Humboldt's Mexico ("Méjico" in the Spanish version) as Mexico rather than Mexico *City*, which is what "Mexico," rather than "Méxique," would have signified in French text at the time.[42] Thrasher's last sentence contains a clearer translation error, the result of rendering as a passive construction what is actually not one in Humboldt's text. In this way, Thrasher oddly deprives the conquest of human agency in a way that would be atypical for Humboldt, in the same way that he eliminates Humboldt's reference to his own travels.

By far most remarkable here is the brevity of Thrasher's version, due to his omission of what is the most jarring clause in this passage: the unexpected appearance of the *barracones* right next to Havana's Botanical Garden. Williams translates this grammatically curious clause, which is almost a fragment, as "another object, fitted to excite at once pity and indignation, the barracks before which the wretched slaves are exposed to sale." If one follows Humboldt's grammar, however, one would notice that "autre objet" here does not refer to the "barracks" but to the spectacle in front of them, and that this spectacle, the sale of the slaves, who are locked up in the notorious and very Cuban *barracones,* is what at once saddens and outrages the location. It is as if the building itself existed in a state of sadness and outrage, which is then transferred onto the viewer (Humboldt and the reader). Taking French grammar into account might result in "something else altogether, whose appearance at once aggrieves and appalls: the barracks [barracones] in front of which the pitiable slaves are exposed for sale." Here, the colon has been added to make the sentence more readable, as it were, in English, while still retaining a trace of the sentence's original – one might say, "othering" – structure. This clause signals the intrusion of the discourse of slavery into an otherwise tranquil observational setting, and the grammatical scaffolding appropriately supports its disruptive effect, which extends from the sudden sensual intrusion of the foul smell of poorly cured meat a few sentences earlier. This meat, called *tasajo*, was a staple in the diet of the African slaves, and it was as pervasive in Havana as slavery was in Cuba – certainly as much part of the landscape as the lush vegetation. The references to Columbus and Hernán Cortés, which follow in the very next sentence as a seeming *non sequitur*, add to these impressions and observations the discourse of discovery and conquest, even as they allude to the more recent revolution in what was to become Haiti in 1804. From this far-flung context of global history, the narrative shifts just as abruptly to a detailed botanical *excursus* on palm trees to draw us into Humboldt's ever-present discourse on the marvels of the tropics.[43] Unlike traditional travel narratives, then, Humboldt's text does not have a linear structure. Instead, his writing generates an interplay of scientific details (the physical dimensions of the harbor), sensual impressions (the stench of *tasajo*), multi-layered historical references (the conquest, the Haitian Revolution, and Humboldt's own trip), and future projections (the possible abolition of slavery).

Where the texture of Humboldt's travel narrative is most condensed, as is the case in the above passage, we can see quite clearly how different discourses interrupt and transect each other, producing a narrative shape that is decidedly jagged and fragmented. On a larger scale, the *Political Essay on the Island of Cuba* is itself a fragment. It is a part of Humboldt's actual travel narrative, the so-called *Relation historique* or *Personal Narrative*, which began to appear in Paris in 1814 and which would not be complete until 1831. This three-volume travelogue covers merely one-third of Humboldt's entire voyage to and in the New World, up to April 1801, that is, just after Humboldt had departed Cuba for the Andes region. Although Humboldt had planned a final volume for years, he never actually wrote it, and many of the missing portions of the *Relation historique* have been reconstructed from his travel diaries.[44] The *Relation historique*, then, is a fragment, in which the movement of travel ceases with the *Political Essay on the Island of Cuba* in volume three; it is also a fragment of the 30 volumes of the *Voyage to the Equinoctial Regions of the New Continent*. My diagram (see Figure 4) offers a radically abbreviated view of the 30 volumes that comprise Humboldt's *Voyage* and also shows how both the existing and forthcoming English translations of the *Essai politique sur l'île de Cuba* fit into this collection of fragments.[45]

The *Voyage*, which remains incomplete even with its 30 volumes, was published over the course of more than 30 years by a number of different publishers, several of whom went bankrupt in the process.[46] In fact, Humboldt rarely ever completed a book. Like the *Relation historique*, the *Examen critique* (1834–1838), *Asie Centrale* (1843), and *Kosmos* (1845–1858 and 1862) all remained incomplete, and quite intentionally so. Alexander von Humboldt regarded the individual volumes of his writing as parts of a larger work-in-progress, which included not only his own work but also that of the many other scientists and scholars, with whom he collaborated during his lifetime. Prospectively, it also included his translators and those, like ourselves, who would read and write about his work in the future. Together, all these elements and dimensions make Humboldtian writing a "living discourse,"[47] whose dynamic multi-directional movement not even a translation such as Thrasher's can fully arrest. But whatever the shortfalls of the translations of Alexander von Humboldt's *Essai politique sur l'île de Cuba* – and we have seen that

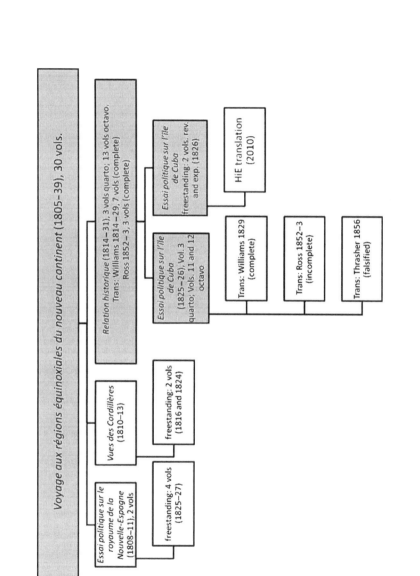

Figure 4.

they are considerable at times – they still do extend the life of the text, even if it is by indirectly issuing a call for another translation.

Notes

1. Barnet and Quesada cement the link between Humboldt and Ortiz (and Columbus) by calling Ortiz the "third discoverer of Cuba" (Barnet and Quesada, "Alejandro," 75). All translations in this article are mine unless otherwise marked.
2. My page references to Ortiz's essays are to the two-volume 1930 edition of Humboldt's *Ensayo político sobre la Isla de Cuba* (see Humboldt, *Ensayo político*). Ortiz's "Introducción" was reprinted to honor the bicentennial of Humboldt's birth, the same year in which Ortiz died (that is, 1859 and 1959).
3. Ungar, "Writing in Tongues," 127.
4. See Humboldt, *Ensayo político,* CIX.
5. Humboldt, *Essai politique*, I.310.
6. A note by Manuel Villanova, who apparently compiled Arango's writings for the 1888 edition, informs us that "the 1827 "Observaciones" refer to the first volume of 1826 *Essai politique sur l'île de Cuba.* A copy of this edition is lodged in the Biblioteca de la Sociedad Económica de Amigos del País de la Habana." See Arango, "Observaciones."
7. The author should like to thank Tobias Kraft for sending her his digitized copy of Humboldt's notes on Thrasher.
8. For a transcription of this letter, see Schwarz and Knobloch, *Alexander von Humboldt,* 382.
9. The Prussian Minister to the US, Friedrich von Gerold, wrote to Humboldt on August 25, 1856: "I hasten to comply with your wish by sending you two extracts from papers published here (the 'New York Herald' and the 'Courrier des Etats Unis'), containing your publication on the subject of slavery in Cuba, as well as the excuse published by Mr Thrasher, which is, it must be confessed, exceedingly lame. The affair has excited great attention here, and could not but be welcome to the opponents of slavery, who have made Fremont their candidate. Some days ago, his German supporters, many thousands in number, held a mass meeting in his support, and honored him with a splendid torch-light procession in the evening. The slavery question is becoming more alarming from day to day. While the House of Representatives refuse to appropriate moneys for the support of the army, news is daily coming in from Kansas of bloody conflicts between the free-soilers and the slaveholders. It is hoped, however, that after the presidential election (in November), domestic peace will be restored" (Kapp, *Letters*, 326). Humboldt, wryly noting that Van Buren won the election, sent this letter on to Varnhagen von Ense, "knowing the warm interest you take, my dear friend, in the slavery question" (324). Varnhagen replied on September 18, 1856: "The great influence of the name of your Excellency in the United States, & in America in general, is a gratifying sign of the improvement of those countries in civilization..." (327).
10. Ortiz likely took both from Villanova. See Villanova, "Humboldt y Thrasher I," 6–7.
11. Thrasher, "Baron Humboldt"; see also II.217.
12. See also Humboldt, *Ensayo político* (1827), 380.

13. "Desconocemos esta otra traducción inglesa a que se refiere Humboldt" (II.215n1). Humboldt claims in his letter that this translation came out in 1826, at the same time as his *Essai politique sur l'île de Cuba*; he gets the year wrong. That Ortiz was unaware of the third English translation of Humboldt's *Personal Narrative*, which Thomasina Ross prepared in 1852–53 for Longman, Hurst, and Orme in London, is unsurprising, because that translation includes only a severely abridged version of the *Political Essay on the Island of Cuba* (Humboldt, *Personal Narrative,* trans. Ross). For an even more abridged version of the *Political Essay on the Island of Cuba* see Wilson, *Personal Narratives.*
14. *Political Essay on the Island of Cuba. – The Havannah. – Hills of Guanavacoa, considered in their geognostical relations. – Valley of Los Guines. – Batabano, and Port of Trinidad. – The King and Queen's Gardens* (Humboldt, *Personal Narrative,* trans. Williams, XII.1).
15. Humboldt, *Essai politique,* I.1; *The Island of Cuba,* 1.
16. Humboldt, *The Island of Cuba* (1856), 118–23.
17. Humboldt, *The Island of Cuba,* 123.
18. *New York Daily Times,* "Review," 3.
19. Ette, "Alexander von Humboldt und das Projekt der Moderne," 16.
20. Humboldt, *The Island of Cuba* (2001), vii.
21. Markus Wiener's dismissal of Williams recalls Irene Prüfer-Leske's comment that Hanno Beck's German translation includes too much untranslated Spanish and is therefore nearly inaccessible to readers who have no Spanish (Prüfer Leske, "Übersetzungen," 224).
22. Humboldt, "Baron von Humboldt," 2.
23. See Zeuske, "Comparing or Interlinking?"
24. As evidence for Humboldt's alleged lack of good sense in 1826, Villanova cites the addition of the following sentence, in his 1856 letter, to what might otherwise seem like a direct quotation from the *Essai politique sur l'île de Cuba*: "J'ai rapellé dans cet exposé combien ancienne législation espagnole de l'esclavage est moins inhumaine et moins atroce que celle des États à esclaves dans l'Amérique continentale au nord et au sud de l'équateur" [I recalled in this work how the old Spanish slave laws are less inhumane and less cruel than these of the slave states in continental America north and south of the equator] (Schwarz and Knobloch, *Alexander von Humboldt,* 383). See Villanova, "Humboldt y Thrasher IV," 5–6. But it is incorrect that such language does not already exist in the *Essai politique sur l'île de Cuba* (see Humboldt, *Essai politique,* I.327n1).
25. Villanova seems to have been completing his edition of Arango's writings at the same time that he was publishing his "Humboldt y Thrasher" series in *La Semana.*
26. Humboldt, *Essai politique,* I.307.
27. Overzealous US abolitionists were also known to commission fraudulent slave narratives from free blacks who had never been slaves.
28. It was apparently not the only factitious text that Thrasher published during his journalistic career (II.195).
29. Abridgment and changes in narrative order also puts some translations in close proximity to the popularized accounts of Humboldt's travels that have appeared in English and other languages since the nineteenth century. For the most recent example in English, see Helferich, *Humboldt's Cosmos.*
30. See Humboldt, *Politischer Essay.* See also Humboldt, *Ensayo político* (1998, 2004).
31. See Cramer, *Chaos and Order.*
32. It is well worth asking what *accuracy* and *reliability* might mean in a Humboldt text, given that Humboldt revised and amended his writings almost obsessively and that his texts were issued by different publishers in different editions, often simultaneously, and over a period of almost more than 30 years. The Cuba essay alone appeared in three different editions: first, in 1825, as part of the quarto and octavo editions of the *Relation historique*; then, in 1826, in a revised and expanded two-volume edition (see Figure 4). Contrary to what Beck, Prüfer-Leske, and Fiedler and Leitner claim, these editions are by no means identical. Prüfer-Leske, following Beck, claims that the octave edition and the two-volume edition "enthalten keine Korrekturen Humboldts und überliefern den Text schlechter als das [so-called] Original selbst" [do not contain any revisions by Humboldt and bring the text across less well than the original does] (Prüfer-Leske, "Übersetzungen," 200–21). There is no support for Beck's opinion that the basis for any translation "could only be the

original in the third volume of the 'Relation Historique'" (Humboldt, *Cuba-Werk*, 234). A complete inventory of the textual differences between all three editions can be found at http://www.press.uchicago.edu/hie, the web site that will be launched in 2010 in connection with the publication of the first translation of Humboldt's two-volume *Essai politique sur l'île de Cuba*, the first volume in the *Alexander von Humboldt in English* (HiE) series (see Humboldt, *Alexander von Humboldt's Political Essay*).

33. This is the only complete English version of Humboldt's actual travel narrative, the so-called *Relation historique*. Williams also translated other parts of his *Voyage,* notably *Vues des Cordillères et monumens des peuples indigènes de l'Amérique* (see Humboldt, *Researches*).

34. One of the shortcomings of Venuti's popular theory is that, for him, "domestication" is typically only an issue when a text is translated *into* English, not from English. Against this background of translating into English, Venuti recodes fidelity as "foreignizing" and readability as "domestication" into another language (Venuti, *The Scandals of Translation*).

35. Ungar, "Writing in Tongues," 129.

36. Humboldt, *Essai politique*, I.151.

37. Humboldt, *Personal Narrative* (1814–1829), VII.131.

38. Humboldt *Essai politique*, I.13.

39. Humboldt, *Personal Narrative* (1814–1829), VII.10.

40. See Fiedler and Leitner, *Alexander von Humboldts Schriften*, 103–4.

41. Humboldt, *The Island of Cuba*, 108. "Near the *Campo de Marte* is the botanical garden, an object worthy of the government's attention, and something else altogether, whose appearance at once aggrieves and appalls: the barracks [barracones] in front of which the pitiable slaves are exposed for sale. Since my return to Europe, a marble statue of King Charles III has been installed on the *extra muros promenade* in a place that had initially been designated for a monument to Christopher Columbus. Columbus's ashes were brought to the island of Cuba after the end of Spanish rule in Saint-Domingue. Since Fernando Cortés' ashes were transferred from one church to another in Mexico City in the same year [1796], the two men who embodied the conquest of America both received new tombs in the same period at the end of the eighteenth century" (Humboldt, *Alexander von Humboldt's Political Essay*).

42. The author thanks Ryan Poynter for alerting her to this difference.

43. See Ette, *Alexander von Humboldt und die Globalisierung*, 169–212.

44. See Holl, "Geschichtsschreiber der Kolonien," 52–3.

45. Both *Vues des Cordillères* and the *Essai politique sur le royaume de la Nouvelle-Espagne*, the two other publications represented in this diagram, were also part of Humboldt's writings on the Americas (the *Voyage*); but they are not part of his actual travel narrative (the *Relation historique,* or *Personal Narrative*).

46. The publication dates printed in the volumes are not necessarily any precise indiction of when a particular work actually appeared (see Fiedler and Leitner, *Alexander von Humboldts Schriften*).

47. Holl, "Geschichtsschreiber der Kolonien," 69.

References

Arango y Parreño, Franciso de. "Observaciones al 'Ensayo político sobrela isla de Cuba' escritas en 1827." In *Obras del Excelentísimo Señor D. Francisco de Arango y Parreño,* ed. Manuel Villanova, 2 vols, 533–46. Havana: Howson y Heinen, 1888.

Barnet, Miguel, and Alberto Quesada. "Alejandro de Humboldt (1769–1859) y don Fernando Ortiz (1881–1969): dos sabios descubridores de Cuba." In *Alejandro de Humboldt en Cuba,* ed. Frank Holl, 75–82. Havana, Cuba: Oficina del Historiador de la Ciudad de La Habana, 1997.

Cramer, Friedrich. *Chaos and Order. The Complex Structure of Living Systems.* Trans. D. I. Loewus. Weinheim: VHC, 1993.

Ette, Ottmar. "Alexander von Humboldt und das Projekt der Moderne." In *Ansichten Amerikas. Neuere Studien zu Alexander von Humboldt*, ed. Ottmar Ette and Walther L. Bernecker, 9–17. Frankfurt am Main: Vervuert Verlag, 2001.

Ette, Ottmar. *Alexander von Humboldt und die Globalisierung. Das Mobile des Wissens.* Frankfurt am Main and Leipzig: Insel Verlag, 2009.

Fielder, Horst, and Ulrike Leitner. *Alexander von Humboldts Schriften. Bibliographie der selbständig erschienenen Werke.* Berlin: Akademie Verlag, 2000.

Helferich, Gerard. *Humboldt's Cosmos: Alexander von Humboldt and the Latin American Journey that Changed the Way We See the World.* New York: Penguin USA, 2005.

Holl, Frank. "Alexander von Humboldt – 'Geschichtsschreiber der Kolonien'." In *Ansichten Amerikas. Neue Studien zu Alexander von Humboldt,* ed. Ottmar Ette and Walther L. Bernecker, 51–78. Frankfurt am Main: Vervuert Verlag, 2001.

Humboldt, Alexander von. *Voyage aux régions équinoxiales du Nouveau Continent fait en 1799, 1800, 1802, 1803, et 1804, par Al. de Humboldt et A. Bonpland.* Paris: F. Schoell, 1805–1834.

Humboldt, Alexander von. *Personal Narrative of Travels to the Equinoctial Regions of the New Continent during the years 1799–1804 by Alexandre de Humboldt and Aimé Bonpland.* Trans. Helen Maria Williams. 7 vols. London: Longman, Rees, Brown, and Greene, 1814–1829.

Humboldt, Alexander von. *Researches, Concerning the Institutions & Monuments of the Ancient Inhabitants of America, with Descriptions and Views of some of the most Striking Scenes in the Cordilleras.* Trans. Helen Maria Willliams. 2 vols. London: Longman, Hurst, Rees, Orme & Brown, 1814.

Humboldt, Alexander von. *Essai politique sur l'île de Cuba.* 2 vols. Paris: Gide Fils, 1826.

Humboldt, Alexander von. *Ensayo político sobre la isla de Cuba.* Trans. D. J. B. e V. Y. M. Paris: Paul Renouard, 1827.

Humboldt, Alexander von. *Ensayo político sobre la Isla de Cuba.* Ed. Miguel Angel Puig-Samper, Consuelo Naranjo Orovio, and Armando García González. Aranjuez, Madrid: Ediciones Doce Calles, 1998.

Humboldt, Alexander von. *Personal Narrative of Travels to the Equinoctial Regions of America, During the Years 1799–1804.* Abridged. Trans. Thomasina Ross. 3 vols. London: Henry G. Bohn, 1852–53.

Humboldt, Alexander von. *The Island of Cuba by Alexander Humboldt.* Trans. J. S. Thrasher. Cincinnati: Derby & Jackson, 1856.

Humboldt, Alexander von. "Baron Von Humboldt's Political Essay on Cuba – Letter from the Author on the Omission of a Chapter by the Translator." *The New York Daily Times.* August 12, 1856, 2.

Humboldt, Alexander von. *Ensayo político sobre la isla de Cuba.* Colección de Libros Cubanos XVII. 2 vols. Havana: Cultural, S.A., 1930.

Humboldt, Alexander von. "Homenaje al Segundo Descubridor de Cuba, Alejandro de Humboldt." *Revista Bimestre Cubana* LXXVI (1959).

Humboldt, Alexander von. *Ensayo político sobre la isla de Cuba.* Havana: Oficina del Historiador de la Ciudad de la Habana, 1959.

Humboldt, Alexander von. *Ensayo político sobre la Isla de Cuba.* Nota preliminar por José Quintana Rodríguez y introducción por Fernando Ortiz. Havana: Archivo Nacional de Cuba, 1960.

Humboldt, Alexander von. *Cuba-Werk.* ed. Hanno Beck. Studienausgabe, Vol. 3. Darmstadt: Wissenschaftliche Buchgesellschaft, 1992.

Humboldt, Alexander von. *Ensayo político sobre la Isla de Cuba.* Ed. Miguel Angel Puig-Samper, Consuelo Naranjo Orovio, and Armando García González. Vedado, Havana: Fundación Fernando Ortiz, 1998.

Humboldt, Alexander von. *The Island of Cuba. A Political Essay by Alexander von Humboldt.* ed. Luis Martínez-Fernandez. Princeton and Kingston: Markus Wiener and Ian Randle Publishers, 2001.

Humboldt, Alexander von. *Politischer Essay über die Insel Kuba.* Trans. Irene Prüfer-Leske. San Vicente: Alicante, ECU, 2002.

Humboldt, Alexander von. *Ensayo político sobre la isla de Cuba (1826).* Ed. María Rosario Martí Marco, and Irene Prüfer Leske. Alicante, Spain: Universidad de Alicante, 2004.

Humboldt, Alexander von. *Alexander von Humboldt's Political Essay on the Island of Cuba.* Ed. Vera M. Kutzinski and Ottmar Ette. Trans. J. Bradford Anderson, Anja Becker, and Vera M. Kutzinski. Annotations by Tobias Kraft, Anja Becker, and Giorleny D. Altamirano Rayo. Chicago: University of Chicago Press, forthcoming.

Kapp, Friedrich, ed. *Letters of Alexander von Humboldt to Varnhagen von Ense. From 1827 to 1858. With extracts from Varnhagen's Diaries and Letters of Varnhagen and others to Humboldt*. Trans. Friedrich Kapp. New York: Rudd & Carleton, 1860.

New York Daily Times. "Review of *The Island of Cuba*." June 20, 1856, 3.

Ortiz, Fernando. *Introducción bibliográfica al libro "Ensayo político sobre la isla de Cuba" de Alejandro de Humboldt: bicentenario de Humboldt*. Prólogo por Julio LeRiverend Brusone. Havana. Serie histórica//Academia de Ciencias de Cuba, Nr. 7, 1969.

Prüfer Leske, Irene. "Übersetzungen, Manipulationen und Neuübersetzungen des *Essai politique sur líle de Cuba* Alexander von Humboldts." In *Ansichten Amerikas. Neuere Studien zu Alexander von Humboldt*, ed. Ottmar Ette and Walther L. Bernecker, 219–30. Frankfurt am Main: Vervuert Verlag, 2001.

Schwarz, Ingo, and Eberhard Knobloch, eds. *Alexander von Humboldt/Samuel Heinrich Spiker Briefwechsel*. Berlin: Akademie Verlag, 2007.

Thrasher, John Sidney. "Baron Humboldt and Mr. Thrasher." *New York Daily Times*. August 17, 1856. Reprinted in Humboldt 2001.

Ungar, Steven. "Writing in Tongues: Thoughts on the Work of Translation." In *Comparative Literature in an Age of Globalizaton,* ed. Haun Saussy, 127–38. Baltimore: John Hopkins University Press, 2006.

Venuti, Lawrence. *The Scandals of Translation. Towards an Ethics of Difference*. London and New York: Routledge, 1998.

Villanova, Manuel. "Humboldt y Thrasher, I." *La Semana*. September 5, 1887, 6–7.

Villanova, Manuel. "Humboldt y Thrasher, II." *La Semana*. September 12, 1887, 8–9.

Villanova, Manuel. "Humboldt y Thrasher, III." *La Semana*. September 19, 1887, 6.

Villanova, Manuel. "Humboldt y Thrasher, IV." *La Semana*. September 24, 1887, 5–6.

Villanova, Manuel. "Humboldt y Thrasher, V." *La Semana*. October 3, 1887, 6–7.

Wilson, Jason. *Personal Narrative of a Journey to the Equinoctial Regions of the New Continent*. Abridged. London: Penguin, 1995.

Zeuske, Michael. "Comparing or Interlinking? Economic Comparison of early nineteenth-century Slave Systems in the Americas in Historical Perspective." In *Slave Systems: Ancient and Modern*, ed. Enrico Dal Lago and Constantina Katsari, 148–83. Cambridge: Cambridge University Press, 2008.

About an attempt to climb to the top of Chimborazo

By Alexander von Humboldt
Translated by Vera M. Kutzinski

> Alexander von Humboldt wrote the final version of "Über einen Versuch den
> Gipfel des Chimborazo zu ersteigen" [About an Attempt to Climb to the Top of
> Chimborazo] almost 50 years after his return from the Americas. He published it
> in his *Kleinere Schriften* [*Shorter Writings*] in 1853, a scan of which is available
> from Google Books. As Humboldt himself mentions, he based a good part of this
> essay on his travel diary from 23 June 1802.[1] Although he followed his diary fairly
> closely, Humboldt, as was his wont, updated the essay to include recent
> information. The earlier version from 1838 lacks the later, revised essay's copious
> endnotes.

[133][2] The highest peaks on two continents: on the Old Continent, Kinchinjunga
[Kangchenjunga], Dhawalagiri [Dhaulagiri] (white mountain), and Jawahir [Djawa-
hir]; on the new one, Aconcagua and Sajama;[3] their summits have not yet been
reached by humans. The highest point that anyone has ever reached on either
continent is in South America, on the south-east slope of Chimborazo. There,
travelers ascended to almost 18,500 pieds de Paris, once in June 1802 (to 3016 toises)
and a second time in December 1831 (to 3080 toises) above sea level. In the Andes,
then, barometric measurements were made at elevations 3720 feet higher than the
summit of Mont Blanc. The height of Mont Blanc is rather negligible when
compared to that of the Cordilleras, where many well-traveled paths (passes) are at
higher elevations; indeed, the summit of Mont Blanc surpasses the upper part of the
large city of Potosi by only 323 toises. I have found it necessary to open with this
smattering of numerical data to give the imagination certain points of reference for
the hypsometric and (as it were) plastic contemplation of the earth's surface.

Reaching great heights is of little scientific interest when those elevations are well
above the snow [134] line and can be visited for only a few hours. Direct
measurement of elevation by way of the barometer has the advantage of quick
results; but the peaks are often surrounded by high plateaus in their immediate
vicinity, which are suitable for trigonometric calculations, and on which all the
components of a measurement can be checked repeatedly. A single barometric
reading, by contrast, creates considerable errors in the overall results due to rising
and falling air masses at the edge of a mountain range and the variations they cause
in temperature decreases. The perpetual snows make it almost entirely impossible to
carry out geognostic observations of the composition of the rock; only single ridges

with very eroded strata protrude. There is virtually no organic life in these lofty wastelands of the earth. Even the mountain vultures (condor) and flying insects rarely find their way up into these thin layers of air, the latter being propelled up involuntarily by the air currents. Nowadays, there is hardly any scientific interest in the efforts of traveling physicists who try to reach the earth's highest peaks; but curiosity about them has remained very much alive in the popular imagination. What appears unreachable exerts a mysterious pull; one wants to know that everything is at least being tried, even if it does not lead to success. Chimborazo has been the tedious subject of all questions that were posed to me when I first returned to Europe. The exploration of the most important laws of nature; the most vivid description of the plant zones and the climatic differences that affect agriculture [135] – those issues were hardly ever able to steer attention away from the snow-capped mountain that, in those days – before [Robert] Fitzroy's measurements on the southern coast of Chile and [Joseph Barclay] Pentland's voyage to Bolivia – was deemed the absolute pinnacle of the span of the Andes chain.

I shall borrow here the plain description of a mountain voyage from the as yet unpublished portions of my diaries. All the details of the trigonometric measurements that I carried out on the plateau of Tapia near the new Riobamba were published soon after my return in the introduction to the first volume of my astronomical observations.[4] I have attempted to represent visually, in a tableau included in my geographical and physical atlas of South America, the geography of plants on the slopes of Chimborazo and the mountain close to it, following [Carl Sigismund] Kunth's superb identifications of the alpine flora of the Cordilleras that Bonpland and I had collected. The tables included in this tableau are the result of copious observations; they illustrate the law of temperature decreases in relation to elevation.

The story of the ascent itself, which is of little dramatic interest, had been reserved for the fourth and final volume of my travels to the equinoctial regions of the New Continent. My long-time friend, Mr [Jean-Baptiste] Boussingault, now a member of the Paris Academy of Sciences and one of the most talented and well-read travelers of these modern times, has recently, at my request, recounted his own endeavors, which rather resemble my own, in the *Annales de* [136] *Chimie et de Physique* [110, no. 2 (1835): 193–219]. Because our narratives complement each other, the unadorned fragment of a diary that I am offering here may well be received with greater indulgence. For the time being, then, I will eschew more elaborate geognostic and physical discussions.

On 22 June 1799, I had been on the top of the crater of the Peak of Tenerife [Mount Teide]; three years later, almost to the day (23 June 1802), I went 6700 feet higher, almost to the top of the summit of Chimborazo. After a long stay in the highlands of Quito, one of the most wonderful and picturesque regions in the world, we made a trip to the China forests of Lora, the upper part of the Amazonas River, west of the famous cataracts (Pongo de Manseriche), and across the sandy desert along the Peruvian coast of the South Sea to Lima, to observe there the transit of Mercury across the disc of the sun (on 9 November 1802). For several days, in the clearest weather, which was favorable for trigonometric measurements, we enjoyed a marvelous view of the bell- or dome-shaped summit of Chimborazo from the pumice-covered plain on which people were beginning to build the new city of Riobamba (after the terrible earthquake of 4 February 1797). We observed the snow blanket of the mountain, which was still 15,700 toises in the distance, through a large telescope, and we discovered several rocky ridges without any vegetation.[5] These ridges, sticking out of the snow like thin, black stripes, ran toward the summit and gave us some hope that one might find a foothold on them in the snowy zone. Riobamba Nuevo [137] lies below and in view of the gigantic, now cleft mountain range of Capac-Urcu, which the old Spaniards called El Altari; according to native legend, Capac-Urcu had once been taller than Chimborazo and collapsed after having spewed lava for many years. This fearsome natural event occurred at the time shortly before the Inca Tupac Yupanqui conquered Quito. Riobamba Nuevo should not be confused with the old Riobamba from the large map by La Condamine and Don Pedro Maldonado. That city was completely destroyed by the horrible catastrophe of 4 February 1797, which killed 30,000 people within a few minutes. According to my chronometric determinations, the new Riobamba is situated 42 time seconds more to the east than the old Riobamba but at almost the same latitude (1° 41′ 46″ south).

We were in the plains of Tapia, from which, on 22 June, we set out on our expedition to Chimborazo; we were already 8898 pieds de Paris (1483 toises)[6] above the level of the South Sea. We followed the gradual incline of this high plateau, which is part of the valley bottom between the eastern and western chain of the Andes – the chain of the active volcanoes Cotopaxi and Tungurahua, and that of the extinct volcanoes Iliniza and Chimborazo – to the foot of Chimborazo where we were to spend the night in the Indian village of Calpi. This plateau has a sparse cover of cacti trunks and Schinus molle, which resembles a weeping willow. Herds of thousands of multicolored llamas were foraging there for their meager nourishment. At such a great altitude, the strong nightly heat radiation of the ground, under clear skies, is detrimental to agriculture because of the cooling of the air and the freezing of the ripening [138] seed. Before arriving in Calpi, we visited Licán: Licán is now also a village, but prior to the conquest of the land by the first Inca (the same Tupac Yupanqui whose well-preserved corpse Garcilaso de la Vega could still see in the family grave in 1559), it had been quite a considerable city and the residence of the Conchocando, or sovereign, of the Puruay [Puruhuayes]. The natives believed that the small number of wild llamas that one finds on the western slope of Chimborazo only returned to the wild and are descended from the herds that scattered and escaped after the destruction of the old Licán.

In the arid high plains close to Calpi, to the north-west of Licán, rises a lone small hill, the black mountain, or Yanaurcu, whose name the French academicians did not mention but which deserves much attention from a geognostic perspective. The hill lies south-south-west of Chimborazo at a distance of less than three miles (15 to 1°), and is separated from that colossus only by the high plains of Luisa. Although people have been disinclined to regard this hill as a side eruption of the colossus, it is nonetheless certain that this eruption cone originated with sub-terranean forces below Chimborazo which, for millennia, had in vain sought an outlet. The hill is of a later origin than the large, bell-shaped mountain. Together with the hill Raguangachi to the north, Yanaurcu forms a continuous rise that is shaped like a horseshoe; the arc (more than half a circle) is open toward the east. It is likely that in the middle of the horseshoe lies the opening from which black lava spewed forth, which is now [139] spread all around. There, we found a funnel-shaped hollow about 120 feet deep, in the interior of which was a small, round hill whose elevation did not reach the surrounding rim. Yanaurcu is actually the name of the southern culmination point of the edge of the old crater, which is at most 400 feet above the plains of Calpi. Raguangachi is the name of the northern slope. The whole rise recalls – through its horseshoe shape, though not through the type of its rock – the slightly higher hill Yavirac (El Panecillo de Quito) which rises up in isolation at the foot of the volcano Pichincha in the plains of Turubamba, and which the maps of La Condamine (or better, Morainville [who traveled with Pedro Vicente Maldonado]) erroneously represented as a perfect cone. According to native legend, and to the purportedly ancient manuscripts that the cacique (or apu) of Licán, a descendent of the old ruler of the land (Conchocandi), boasted of owning, the volcanic eruption of the Yanaurcu happened right after the death of the Inca Tupac Yupanqui, thus probably in the middle of the fifteenth century. Tradition has it that a fireball or even a star fell from the skies and set the mountain ablaze. Such myths, which associate aeroliths with conflagrations, are also widespread among the Mexica peoples.[7]

The rock of Yanaurcu is a porous, dark, clove-brown slag, which is often entirely black; one could mistake it for porous basalt. But it is entirely lacking in olivine. The white crystals sparsely embedded in it are tiny and are probably labradorite. Here and there, I saw bits of iron pyrite [fool's gold]. This rock [140] is probably black augite porphyry, as is the whole formation of Chimborazo; we will speak of it below, and I would like to call it trachyte because, like our trachyte in the Siebengebirge near Bonn, it does not contain feldspar (with a bit of albite). Although the slag-like masses of Yanaurcu, transformed by active fire, are very light, real pumice has not been ejected there. The eruption broke through a gray, irregularly layered mass of dolerite, which forms the high plateau here and resembles the rock of Penipe (at the foot of the volcano Tungurahua), where syenite and granitic mica are shot through with it. On the eastern slope of Yanaurcu, or, rather, at the foot of the hill that lies in the direction of Licán, the natives led us to a protruding rock on which there was an opening that resembled the mouth of a decaying gallery. Here, and already at a distance of 10 feet, one hears a loud subterranean roar, which is accompanied by an air current or subterranean wind. The air current is far too weak to be the sole origin of all this noise, which clearly originates from an underground stream that crashes down into a deep cavern, and whose plunge agitates the air. A long time ago, a monk who was a priest in Calpi had had the same idea and had begun to build the gallery in an open chasm to procure water for his village. The hardness of the black augite had likely stalled the project.

Despite the incredibly large glaciers, the brooks that flow down from Chimborazo to the high plains have so little water that one can suppose that most of it [141] flows through the fissures into the mountain's interior. Even in the village of Calpi itself, one could once hear a loud roar below the buildings without cellars. Before the terrible earthquake of 4 February 1797, a stream suddenly appeared at one of the deeper points in the south-west part of the village. Many of the Indians thought that this stream was part of the waters that flow below Yanaurcu. Since the great earthquake, however, this brook has once again disappeared.

After a night in Calpi, at 9720 feet (1620 toises) above sea level (according to my barometric measurements), we set out on our actual expedition to Chimborazo on the morning of the 23rd. We tried to ascend the mountain from the south-south-eastern side; and the Indians who were to serve as our guides, but few of whom made it any further than the eternal snow line, also preferred this direction. We found that

Chimborazo was surrounded by large plateaus that are layered like steps, one above the other. First, we crossed the Llanos de Luisa; then, after a fairly gradual ascent of scarcely 5000 feet, we reached the high plateau (llano) of Sisgun. The first plateau step is 10,200 feet high, the second one 11,700. These grass-covered high plateaus thus reach an altitude comparable, in one case, to that of the highest peak of the Pyrenees (Pico de Aneto) and, in the other case, to the summit of the volcano of Tenerife. The complete flatness (horizontality) of these high plains suggests the long presence of standing water. One has the impression that one beholds the bottom of an ocean. On the slopes of the Swiss Alps, one also notices at times this phenomenon of step-like stacked plains that, like [142] the emptied-out basins of the alpine lakes, are now connected through narrow, open passes. At Chimborazo, like everywhere around the high peaks of the Andes chain, the extensive grassland (los pajonales) is very monotonous; the family of grasses – species of Paspalum, Andropogon, Bromus, Dejeuxia, Stipa – is hardly ever disturbed by herbs that belong to the dicotyledonous plants. This grassland is almost like the kind of steppe that I saw in the parched parts of northern Asia. Chimborazo's flora generally seemed to us much less rich and varied than that of the other snow-capped mountains around the city of Quito. In the highlands of Sisgun, only a few calceolarias, composites (*Bidens*, *Eupatorium*, *Dumerilia paniculata*, *Werneria nubigena*) and gentians, among them the beautiful *Gentiana cernua* abloom with crimson blossoms, rise above the social grasses, most of which belong to northern European families. The air temperature typical for this region of alpine grasses (at an elevation of 1600 to 2000 toises) fluctuates between 4 and 16 °C during the daytime, and between 0 and 10 °C at night. According to my observations near the equator at an elevation of 10,800 feet, the mean temperature across the entire year seems to be approximately 9 °C. In the flat land of the temperate zone, this is equivalent to the mean temperature of northern Germany, for instance, Lüneburg (latitude 53° 15'); but there, the distribution of heat across the individual months (which is the most important factor in determining the character of the vegetation in a region) is so uneven that the mean temperature in February is -1.8 °C and in June +18 °C.

[143] I had planned to conduct trigonometric operations on the beautiful, completely level grass plateau of Sisgun. I had prepared myself to measure a position line there. The elevation angles would have turned out very considerable because of the proximity to the summit of Chimborazo. I could only determine a vertical height of less than 8400 feet (an elevation like that of the Canigou in the Pyrenees). It is unfortunately the case that, given the immense mass of the individual mountains in this range, any calculation of the elevation above sea level is necessarily a composite of barometric and trigonometric measurements. I had brought along the sextant and other instruments to no avail: the summit of Chimborazo remained shrouded in dense fog. It is a fairly steep climb from the high plains of Sisgun to a small alpine lake (Laguna de Yanacocha). Until then, I had stayed on my mule, dismounting only from time to time to join my travel companion, Mr Bonpland, in collecting plants. Yanacocha does not merit the name of a lake. It is a small, circular basin barely 130 feet in diameter. The sky became more and more overcast, but scattered between and above the layers of fog, one could clearly make out single cloud clusters. The summit of Chimborazo appeared for a few brief moments. Since a lot of snow had fallen the night before, I left the mule where we found the low line of this freshly fallen snow: a line that one must not confuse with the eternal snow line. The barometer showed that

we had only reached an altitude of 13,500 feet. On other mountains, also near the equator, I have seen it snow at up to 11,200 feet but [144] not below that. My companions, Bonpland and Carlos Montúfar, rode up to the perpetual snow line, that is, up to the elevation of Mont Blanc, which, it is known, would not always be covered with snow below this latitude (1° 27' southern). We left our mules and horses there to await our return.

At 900 feet above the small water basin of Yanacocha, we finally saw a bare rock head. Until then, the grassy ground had made a geognostic examination impossible. Large rock faces, directed from north-east to south-west and at times split into shapeless columns, rose up from the cover of eternal snow; they were brown-black augite, shiny like pitchstone porphyry. The columns were very slender, probably 30 to 60 feet high, almost like the trachyte columns of Tablahuma near the volcano Pichincha. One group of them stood by themselves and at a distance almost recalled ships' masts and tree trunks. The steep rock faces led us through the snowfields to a small rim leading toward the summit, a rocky ridge without which we would not have been able to proceed, since the snow was so soft that one almost dared not set foot on it. The ridge consisted of very weathered, crumbly rock. It was often vesicular, like basaltic mandelstone.

The path became ever narrower and steeper. All of the natives except one abandoned us at the elevation of 15,600 feet. All pleas and threats were in vain. The Indians claimed to suffer more severely from shortness of breath than we did. We were left by ourselves: Bonpland; our agreeable friend, the younger son of the Marquis [145] de Selva-Alegre, Carlos Montúfar, who was later shot to death in the struggle for independence (on the order of General Morillo); one Mestizo from the nearby village of San Juan; and I. It was with great effort and patience that we managed to get up higher than we had hoped, since we were shrouded in fog most of the time. The ridge – in Spanish very appropriately called *cuchilla*, that is, knife edge – was often only eight to ten inches wide. To the left, the drop was covered with snow, the surface of which the frost had made like glass. This mirror-like surface had a slant of about 30°. To the right, our view fell eerily on an abyss 800 or 1000 feet deep, from which bare rock faces rose up vertically. We always leaned our bodies more toward that side; for the drop on the left seemed even more dangerous, because there was no chance there to grab on to the jagged rock jutting out, and because the thin icy crust did not protect one against sinking down into the loose snow. On that ice crust, we could roll down only very light, porous pieces of dolerite. The slanted snow face extended so far that we lost sight of those pieces before they even came to rest.

The lack of snow both on the ridge that guided us and on the rock face to our right (to the east) can be attributed less to the steepness of the rock face and the wind gusts than to the gaping clefts that breathe out the warm air of the earth's deeper strata. Soon, we found it more difficult to climb on because the rock was getting ever crumblier. There were some very steep stretches where one had to use hands and feet [146] at the same time, which is quite typical for alpine hiking. Because the rock had very sharp edges, we ended up with painful cuts, especially on our hands. Leopold Buch and I suffered from such injuries to an even greater extent near the crater of the Pico of Tenerife, where there was an abundance of obsidian. In addition – if a traveler may be permitted to mention such trivial details – I had had a sore on my foot for several weeks, which, caused by the accumulation of niguas [chiggers][8] (*Pulex penetrans*) and aggravated by the fine pumice dust (during my measurements on the

Llano de Tapia), had become increasingly worse. The looseness of the rocks on the ridge made greater caution necessary, because many masses that we had thought sturdy and attached were, in fact, lying loose in the sand. We walked in single file and even more slowly for it, because one had to test the places that seemed unsafe. Fortunately, the attempt at reaching the summit of Chimborazo came at the end of our mountain travels in South America, so that our earlier experiences could guide us and give us greater confidence in our endurance. It is a peculiar aspect of all excursions in the Andes that, above the eternal snow line, whites always find themselves in tricky situations without a guide, indeed without any knowledge of the localities. Here, one is the first everywhere.

We could not see the summit anymore now, not even glimpse it briefly, and we were thus doubly curious to know how much farther we still had to go. At one point, where the narrowness of the ridge made it possible for two people to stand next [147] to each other in some comfort, we unpacked the [Torricelli] mercury barometer. We were only at 17,300 feet, that is, barely 200 feet higher than we had been three months earlier on Antisana, when we had climbed up a similar ridge. Measuring altitude during mountain climbing is the same as taking the air temperature on a hot summer day: one always finds, with some frustration, that the thermometer reading is not as high, and the barometer reading not as low, as one had expected. Since the air, despite the altitude, was saturated with water, we found the loose rocks and the sand that filled the cracks between them to be soaking wet. The air was still 2.8 °C above freezing. Shortly before, we had found a dry spot where we had been able to stick the thermometer three inches deep into the soil. It stayed at $+5.8°$. The result of these observations at an altitude of about 17,160 feet (2860 toises) is quite remarkable: already 2400 feet lower, at the eternal snow line, the mean temperature of the atmosphere is only $+1.6°$, according to data that Boussingault and I had carefully collected. The temperature of $+5.8°$, therefore, has to be attributed to the subterranean heat of the dolerite mountain, not (I say) of the entire mountain but of the air currents that rise from its interior.

After an hour of cautious climbing, the ridge became less steep, but unfortunately (!) the fog was just as thick as before. Now, all of us, one after the other, began to suffer from serious nausea. The urge to vomit was combined with some dizziness, which was more annoying than the difficulty in breathing. A person of color, a Mestizo from San Juan, had refused to leave us, out of sheer kindness without the least of [148] self-serving motives. He was a strong, poor farmer who suffered more than we did. We bled from our gums and our lips. The conjunctiva (tunica conjunctiva) of our eyes was also bloodshot. These symptoms of extravasation in the eyes, of bleeding gums and lips did not worry us, since we had become familiar with them from earlier experiences. In Europe, Mr [Joseph] Zumstein had already begun bleeding at far lower altitudes on Monte Rosa. During the conquest of the equinoctial regions of America (the Conquista), Spanish soldiers were unable to cross the lower limits of the eternal snow line, that is, they could not go any higher than Mont Blanc; and yet, already Acosta, in his *Historia natural de las Indias*, a sort of physical description of the earth which one might call a masterwork of the sixteenth century, writes awkwardly about "nauseations and stomach cramping" as the painful symptoms of altitude sickness, which resembles sea sickness. On the volcano of Pichincha, I once experienced, without bleeding, such a strong nausea accompanied by dizziness that I was found lying on the ground, unconscious, after I had momentarily separated from my companions on a rock wall above the chasm of Verde-Cuchu to conduct some electrometric experiments in a clearing. The altitude was low, below 13,800 feet. But on Antisana, at the considerable height of 17,022 feet, our young travel companion, Don Carlos Montúfar, suffered heavy bleeding from his lips.

All these symptoms vary considerably [149] according to age, constitution, the softness of the skin, and the prior exertion of the muscles; but for single individuals, they are a sort of measure of the thinning of the air and the absolute altitude that one has reached. According to my observations in the Cordilleras, whites begin to display these symptoms when the barometer is between 14 inches and 15 inches plus 10 lines. It is known that the heights that air balloon pilots claim to have reached usually deserve little credence; and when a reliable and extremely precise observer, Mr Gay-Lussac, on 16 September 1804, went up to the immense height of 21,600 feet (that is, between the elevation of Chimborazo and that of Aconcagua in Chile) without any bleeding, that fact may be attributed to the lack of muscular exertion. According to the current state of knowledge in eudiometry, the air in those upper regions appears to be as oxygenated as it is in the lower ones; but since in thinner air, at half the barometric pressure that we typically experience in the plains, each breath delivers a smaller amount of oxygen to the blood, it is understandable how this may result in a general feeling of weakness. The reason for this asthenia – how dizziness, worse yet, nausea and [thin] air lead to vomiting – is not a subject to be discussed here; any more than it is to prove that the sweating out of blood (the bleeding from the lips, gums, and eyes), which indeed not everyone experiences at such high altitudes, is by no means satisfactorily explained by the cancellation of a "mechanical counter-pressure." Rather, one should study the probability [150] of how the greatly lowered air pressure results in a tiring of the legs when one exerts oneself in regions with very thin air; according to the memorable discovery by two clever explorers, Wilhelm and Eduard Weber,[9] the lifted leg, which is attached to the torso, is held up and supported by the air only through atmospheric pressure.

Despite the complete lull, the layers of fog that prevented us from seeing distant objects seemed suddenly to break up, perhaps because of electrical processes. Once again, we beheld the dome-shaped summit of Chimborazo and now very close to us. It was a grave, magnificent sight. The hope that we might reach this longed-for peak after all reinvigorated our strength. The ridge, which was only spotted with a thin layer of snow here and there, widened a bit; we hurried onward with secure footing when suddenly a sort of ravine about 400 feet deep and 60 feet in diameter presented our endeavor with an insurmountable obstacle. We could clearly see that our ridge continued on in the same direction on the other side of the ravine; but I doubt that this ridge extended all the way to the summit itself. There was no way around the chasm. It had been the case that on Antisana, Mr Bonpland was able to traverse the solid, packed-down snow for a considerable distance after a very cold night. Here, one could not risk such an attempt given how loose the snow was; also, the shape of the cliff made it impossible to climb down. It was one o'clock in the afternoon. We very carefully set up the barometer; it showed 13 inches and 11 2/10 lines. The air temperature was now 1.6° below freezing; after having spent several years [151] in the hottest regions of the tropics, we found even such little cold paralyzing. It did not help that our boots were completely soaked with water from the snow, since the sand that covered the ridge was mixed with old snow. According to Laplace's barometric formula, we had reached an altitude of 3016 toises or, more specifically, 18,096 pieds de Paris. Assuming that La Condamine's information about Chimborazo's elevation is correct – it has been preserved on a stone tablet at the Jesuit Colegio in Quito – we still had 1224 feet to go, vertically, to the summit, which is equivalent to three times the height of the dome of St Peter's in Rome.

La Condamine and Bouguer state explicitly that they climbed Chimborazo up to an elevation of 14,400 feet; but they boasted that they saw the barometer at 15 inches 10 lines on Corazón, one of the most picturesque of the snow-capped mountains (Nevados) near Quito. They claim that this was "the lowest reading that anyone had seen up to now." At the point on Chimborazo described above, the air pressure was almost two inches lower than that; lower also than on the highest point that Captain Gerard reached on the Tashigang in the Himalayas 16 years later. In England, I was exposed to an air pressure of 45 inches inside a diving bell for almost a whole hour. The flexibility of the human organism is thus able to withstand 31-inch changes in barometric pressure. The physical constitution of the human species might well change gradually, if great cosmic causes made permanent such extremes in air thinning or air density.

[152] We stayed only for a short time in this sad wasteland, which was soon once again wrapped in fog. The humid air was completely still at the time. The denser mist did not offer any clues about a particular [wind] direction; I therefore cannot say if at this elevation, as is so often the case on the peak of Tenerife, the west wind blows, its direction counter to that of the tropical Passat winds. We could no longer see the summit of Chimborazo, nor any of the neighboring snow-capped mountains; and even less so the highlands of Quito. It was as if we were trapped inside an air balloon. Only a few rock lichen had followed us across the eternal snow line. The last cryptogamic plants that I had collected were *Lecida atrovirens* (*Lichen geographicas*, Web[er]) and a gyrophora of Acharius, a new species (*Gyrophora rugosa*), at about 16,920 feet elevation. The last moss, *Grimmia longirostris*, greened 2500 feet lower. Mr Bonpland had caught a butterfly (sphinx) at 15,000 feet, and we saw a fly even 1600 feet higher than that. The following fact offers the most conspicuous proof that these animals had been carried into this upper region of the atmosphere involuntarily by the air current that rises above the heated plains. When Boussingault climbed the Silla de Caracas in order to repeat my measurement of the mountain, he saw, at 8000 feet around noon time when the west wind blew there, whitish objects streaking through the air; he initially took them for ascending birds whose white feathers reflected the sunlight. These objects rose up from the valley of Caracas with great speed, and they rose above the summit of the Silla by turning to the north-east where they [153] probably reached the ocean. Some dropped down earlier on the southern slope of the Silla; they turned out to be leaves of grass made luminous by the sun. Boussingault included some of them, still with ears intact, in a letter he sent to me in Paris, where my friend and colleague Kunth immediately recognized them as *Wilsa tenacissima*, which grow in the valley of Caracas and which he had just described in our work *Nova genera et species plantarum Americae aequinoctialis*. I have to add that we did not see a single condor on Chimborazo; those strong vultures, which are quite common on Antisana and Pichincha, have no familiarity with humans and behave rather brazenly. The condor loves clear air, so that it can more easily espy its prey or food (since it prefers cadavers) from up high.

Since the skies were getting increasingly dimmer, we hurried down on the same ridge that had facilitated our ascent. Now, even greater caution than during the ascent was in order because of unsure footing. We delayed only as long as we needed to collect rock fragments. We anticipated that people in Europe would often ask us for "a small piece of Chimborazo." In those days, not a single type of rock from any part of South America had been identified; the rock of all of the high mountains in the Andes was simply called granite. When we had reached about 17,400 feet, strong hail began to fall. These were opaque, milky-white hailstones with concentric rings. Some seemed to have been significantly flattened through their rotation. Twenty minutes before we reached the lower border of the eternal snow line, [154] the hail turned to snow. The flakes were so large that many inches of snow quickly accumulated on the ridge. Had the snow surprised us at 18,000 feet, we would have certainly been in grave danger. A few minutes after two o'clock, we reached the point where we had left our mules. The Indians, who had also stayed there, had been worried about us more than was necessary.

The part of our expedition that was above the eternal snows lasted for only three and a half hours, during which time we never once sat down to rest, despite the thinner air. At the snow line, that is, at an elevation of 2460 toises, the thickness of the dome-shaped peak still had a diameter of 3437 toises and, near the highest summit (almost 150 toises below it) a diameter of 672 toises. The latter number is also the diameter of the upper part of the dome or bell; the former figure expresses the breadth at which the eye beholds the snow field of Chimborazo from Riobamba Nuevo; this glacier can be seen, together with its two mountain tops, on the sixteenth and twenty-fifth plate of engravings in my *Vues des Cordillères* [see Figures 1 and 2]. Using the sextant, I carefully measured the individual parts of the outline as it rises up from the plains of Tapia on a clear day, in glorious contrast against the deep blue of the tropical sky. The purpose of such measurements is to calculate the volume of the colossus, to the extent that it exceeds the area in which Bouguer had conducted his experiments concerning the magnetic attraction of the mountain in relation to the pendulum. A superb geognost, [155] Mr Pentland, to whom we owe the geognostic knowledge of the highlands of Titicaca and who, equipped with many proper astronomical and physical instruments, twice visited upper Peru (Bolivia), assured

Figure 1. *Vue du Chimborazo et du Carguairazo* (22.1 x 37.2 cm). Plate XVI in *Vues des Cordillères et Monumens des Peuples de l'Amérique.* Paris: F. Schoell, 1810. Drawn by Wilhelm Friedrich Gmelin (1760–1820) in Rome on the basis of Humboldt's sketch and engraved by Friedrich Arnold (d.1809) from Berlin. Courtesy of The Library of Congress.

Figure 2. *Le Chimborazo vu depuis le Plateau di Tapia* (50.8 x 68.5 cm). Plate XXV in *Vues des Cordillères et Monumens des Peuples indigènes de l'Amérique.* Paris: F. Schoell, 1810. Drawn by Jean-Thomas Thibault (1757–1826) on the basis of Humboldt's sketch and engraved by Louis Bouquet (1765–1814). Courtesy of The Library of Congress.

me that my drawing of Chimborazo is duplicated, as it were, in the Nevado de Chuquibamba, a trachyte mountain in the western cordillera north of Arequipa which rises to an elevation of 19,680 feet (3280 toises). Due to its many tall peaks and their sheer size, this region between the fifteenth and eighteenth degree southern latitude has, next to the Himalayas, the highest elevations of the earth's known surface, that is, insofar as these swellings in the ground were caused not by the original form of the rotating planet but by the rise of mountain chains and single domes of dolerite, trachyte, and albite rock.

Because of the newly fallen snow, we found, on our way down Chimborazo, that the lower part of the eternal snow line momentarily overlapped the lower, sporadic snow patches on the bare, lichen-covered rock and the grassy plains (pajonal); it was, however, always easy to make out the actual perpetual snow line (then at 14,820 feet, or 2470 toises) through the thickness of the layer and its peculiar character. I have demonstrated elsewhere – in a treatise on the causes of the curvature of the isothermal lines, included in the third part of *Asie centrale* – that, according to the sum total [156] of my measurements, the differences in how high the eternal snow line is on the various nevados in the province of Quito fluctuate by a mere 38 toises, or 228 feet;[10] that its mean height itself should be set at 14,850 feet, or 2475 toises; and that its border, in the region 16 to 18 degrees south of the equator (in Bolivia), is at an elevation of a full 2670 toises. The reasons for this are the relationship of the mean annual temperature to the mean temperature of the hottest months; the mass, extent, and greater elevation of the surrounding heat-radiating plateaus; the dryness of the atmosphere; and the total lack of any snowfall between March and September.[11] It is an exception, then, that the lower edge of the perpetual snow line, which by no means coincides with the isothermal curve of $0°$, rises rather than falls as one goes farther away from the equator. On the northern, Tibetan, slope of the Himalayas, the snow line is at 2600 toises in the regions between $30\ 3/4°$ and $31°$ northern latitude, for quite similar reasons concerning heat radiation on the nearby plateaus; by contrast, this edge reaches up to only 1950 toises on the southern, Indian slope. Because of this peculiar influence of the shape of the earth's surface, a considerable part of inner Asia outside of the tropics is inhabited by peoples of advanced civilizations, who still practice agriculture and are ruled by monks, whereas in South America, below the equator, geographically comparable regions are covered by eternal ice.[12]

On our return trip to the village of Calpi, we took a somewhat more northerly route than the Llanos de Sisgun, through the Páramo de Pungupala with its abundant plant life. We had already returned to the amicable priest of Calpi by five o'clock in the afternoon. As usual, the foggy day of our expedition was followed by clear weather. On 25 June, Chimborazo revealed itself [157] to us in Riobamba Nuevo in its full splendor – I want to say, in the quiet magnitude and majesty that define the character of nature in a tropical landscape. A second attempt on the ridge split by the crevasse would surely have turned out to be as fruitless at the first one, plus, I was already occupied with the trigonometric measuring of the volcano Tungurahua.

On 16 December 1831, Boussingault, together with his friend, the British Colonel Hall, who would soon after be murdered in Quito, made another attempt at reaching the summit of Chimborazo, first from Mocha and Chillapullu, then from Arenal, that is, by a different route to the one Bonpland, Don Carlos Montúfar, and I had taken. He had to break off the climb when his barometer was at 13 inches 8 1/2 lines and showed a temperature reading of +7.8° in the warm air. In other words, he saw the uncorrected mercury column at almost three lines lower, and, at 3080 toises, was 64 toises higher than I had been. Here are the words of this traveler, who knew the Andes so well, and who was the first to have the daring to carry chemical apparatuses up to the edges and into the craters of volcanoes! "The path," writes Boussingault, "that we made through the snow during the last part of our expedition allowed us only very slow progress; to the right, we could grab on to a rock face; to the left, there was a frightful abyss. We could already feel the effect of the thinning air and had to sit down every two to three steps. But as soon as we had sat down, we rose again; for our suffering lasted only as long as we were moving. The snow, on which we had to tread, was [158] very soft and only three to four inches deep on top of a smooth, hard crust of ice. We had to cut steps into it. A black man went first in order to perform this labor, which soon exhausted his strength. When I tried to pass him and to relieve him, I slipped and, fortunately, Colonel Hall and the black man himself grabbed me." "For a moment," Mr Boussingault adds, "all three of us were in serious danger. Farther on, the snow was more favorable; and at 3.45 in the afternoon, we were finally standing on the long-anticipated ridge which was a few feet wide but surrounded by chasms. Here, we convinced ourselves that it was impossible to proceed. We were at the foot of a rocky prism whose upper area, covered with a mound of snow, forms Chimborazo's real summit. To get an accurate picture of the topography of the entire mountain, one should imagine a vast, snow-covered mass of rock that looks as if it were supported by buttresses on all sides. Those buttresses are the ridges that lean up against the mountain and protrude from the eternal snows." The loss of a physicist like Boussingault would have been extraordinarily costly compared to the small benefits that endeavors of this sort can contribute to the sciences.

As passionately as I had wished 30 years ago that the height of Chimborazo be carefully measured trigonometrically, the absolute result would still be beset with some uncertainty. Using different combinations [159] of these same factors, or at least relying on measurements that were all collective, Don Jorge Juan and the French academicians offer heights of 3380 and 3217 toises – heights that differ by 978 feet, that is, by one-twentieth. The result of my own trigonometric measurements (3350 toises) lies between these two, but it approaches the Spanish result by one-one-hundred-and-twelfth. Bouguer's lower figure is based, at least in part, on the elevation of the city of Quito, which he underestimates by 30 to 40 toises. Using old barometric formulas without correcting for the heat, he finds 1462 toises, instead of the 1507 and 1492 toises on which Boussingault and I very surprisingly agreed. The elevation I assigned the plains of Tapia, where I measured a base line of 873 toises,[13] seems similarly to be free of mistakes. I found 1482 for that height; and Boussingault found 1471 toises at a very different time of the year, that is, with a different heat decrease in the stacked layers of air. Bouguer's calculation, by contrast, was very complicated because he was forced to figure out the elevation of the plains of the eastern and western Andes chain by using the very small elevation angles of the trachyte pyramid of Iliniza, measured in the lower coastal region of Nigua. The only large mountain on earth for which measurements now agree up to one-two-hundred-and-forty-sixth is Mont Blanc. Monte Rosa was measured with four different rows of triangles by an excellent observer, the astronomer [Francesco] Carlini, which yielded 2319, 2343, 2357, and 2374 toises; [Barnaba] Oriani found 2374 toises, also through triangulation; these are differences of one-thirty-fourth. I find the oldest detailed mention of Chimborazo in the work of the intelligent, but rather satirical, Italian traveler [160] Girolamo Benzoni, whose writings were printed in 1565. He states that the *Montagna di Chimbo*, supposedly 40 *Miglia* high, appeared to him boldly *come una visione*. The indigenous peoples of Quito had known long before the arrival of the French measurers that Chimborazo is the highest of all the snow-capped mountains in their region. They saw that it mostly rose above the eternal snow line. Precisely that observation made them think of the now collapsed Capac-Urcu[14] as higher than Chimborazo.

About the geognostic composition of Chimborazo[15] I want to add here only the general remark that, if – according to the important result that Leopold von Buch published in his last classical treatise on "Erhebungskrater" [craters created by layers that rise uniformly] and volcanoes (Poggendorf's *Annalen [der Physik]*, vol. 37, pp. 188–90) – the name *trachyte* should be applied only to rock masses that contain feldspar, and *andesite* to those than contain albite, then the rock of Chimborazo by no means merits both names. More than 20 years ago, when I had asked this same able geognost to do an oryctognostic examination of the rocks of the Andes chain which I had brought home with me, he noticed that augite replaces hornblende in the case of Chimborazo. This fact is mentioned several times in my 1823 *Essai géognostique dur le gisement des roches dans les deux hémisphères*. In addition, my Siberian travel companion, Gustav Rose, who has opened new paths for geognostic study through his remarkable work on fossils related to feldspar and their association with augite and hornblende, found neither albite nor feldspar in any of the rock samples I had collected [161] of Chimborazo. The entire formation of this famous peak of the Andes consists of labradorite and augite; both fossils are recognizable in clear crystallization. According to Gustav Rose's nomenclature, Chimborazo is augite-porphyry, a type of dolerite; it is also lacking in obsidian and pumice. Only two samples contained any hornblende, and only in very small amounts. According to findings by Leopold von Buch and Elie de Beaumont, Chimborazo is similar to the rock type of Etna. Next to the ruins of the old city of Riobamba, three miles east of Chimborazo, one has found true diorite porphyry, a mixture of black hornblende (without augite) and white, glassy albite – a rock that recalls the beautiful rock face of Pisoje near Popayán, which is split into columns, and the Mexican volcano of Toluca, which I also climbed.

Some of the pieces of augite porphyry which I found on Chimborazo at an elevation of 18,000 feet on the ridge leading to the summit, mostly in loose pieces 12 to 14 inches in diameter, have small vesicles and are porous and of a red color. These pieces have shiny vesicles. The blackest of them are sometimes light like pumice and look like they have just been transformed by fire. They did not, however, flow in streams, as lava does, but were likely pushed out of fissures in the cliff of the mountain that had risen up earlier. I have always regarded the entire high plateau of the province of Quito as one single large volcanic hearth. Tungurahua, Cotopaxi, and Pichincha [162] with their craters are simply different outlets of the same source. If volcanism in the broadest sense of the word names all phenomena that depended on the reaction of the interior of a planet with its oxidized surface, then this part of the highland, more than any other in the tropical regions of South America, is subject to the effects of volcanism. The volcanic forces rage even below the bell-shaped augite porphyries that, like Chimborazo, have no crater. Three days after our expedition, we heard in the new Riobamba, at one o'clock in the morning, a furious subterranean crash (*bramido*), which was not accompanied by any quake. A serious quake followed only three hours later, without having been announced by any prior noise. Similar *bramidos* – all of them believed to have come from Chimborazo – had been heard in Calpi a few days earlier. They occur most frequently in the village of San Juan, which is even closer to the colossus. Such a racket below ground attracts the natives' attention no more than distant thunder in a heavily clouded sky does in our Nordic zone.

These are some of my observations from the ascent of Chimborazo, which I have simply reported here from my unpublished travel journal. Where nature is so powerful and so expansive, and where our efforts are purely scientific, no embellishment is needed.

Notes

1. Humboldt described his ascent of Chimborazo in a lecture he delivered to the Association of Naturalists in Jena, Germany, on 26 September 1838. The earlier version, entitled "Über zwei Versuche den Chimborazo zu besteigen" [About Two Attempts to Ascend Chimborazo], was published in Heinrich Christian Schumacher's *Jahrbuch für 1837* (Stuttgart: Cotta, 1837), 176–206. A French version followed in 1838: "Notice sur deux tentatives d'ascension du Chimborazo" in *Annales de Chimie et de Physique* 69 (1838): 401–34. The 1837 essay was first translated by Dr Martin Barry, a member of the Royal College of Surgeons of Edinburgh who had studied in Heidelberg and resided in Paris in 1827, in "Jameson's Journal" – the *Edinburgh New Philosophical Journal*, edited by Robert Jameson – and reprinted in four installments in the section "The Contemporary Traveller" in the *Mirror of Literature, Amusement and Instruction* 31 (1838): 92–8, 134–6, 163–5, 181–4. This London weekly was devoted to "select extracts from new and expensive works." The French text of Humboldt's diary is available in Margot Faak's *Reise auf dem Río Magdalena, durch die Anden und Mexico*, part 1 (Berlin: Akademie Verlag, 1986), 215–25. For a Spanish translation, see Segundo E. Moreno Yánez, *Diarios de viaje en la audiencia de Quito* (Quito: Oxy, 2005), 189–204. [Trans.]

2. The bracketed page numbers refer to the pagination of Humboldt's German text in *Kleinere Schriften* (Vol. 1. Stuttgart: Cotta, 1853), 133–73; any words and phrases in other languages, notably Spanish, French, and Latin, have not been translated unless Humboldt himself also rendered them in German. Parenthetical page numbers at the beginning of each note are Humboldt's references to the pages of his essay. Occasional math errors have been tacitly corrected. One pied de Paris = 324.8406 millimeters. [Trans.]

3. [163] (P. 133) This is the place to bring together the numbers that, according to the current state of our hypsometric knowledge (Spring 1850), express the culmination points of the mountain chains on both continents. Since, in addition to fluctuating opinions, careless reductions of measurements have become the reason for such very different information in books and maps, I offer here the most important altitudes in British feet, toises, and meters.

The highest peaks of India were identified more than 70 to 80 years later than those of the American Cordilleras. Not until the years 1819 to 1825 did people figure out, by way of combining famous works by British travelers ([Brian Houghton] Hodgson, Webb, Herbert, William Lloyd, the brothers Gerard [Alexander and James]), that in the part of the Himalaya chain that stretches from east to west, one had to recognize Dhawalagiri (white mountain) and Jawahir as the tallest peaks. To Dhawalagiri (lat. 28° 40′, long. 80° 59′ east of Paris) were attributed 26,345 pieds de Paris = 4391 toises = 8558 meters = 28,977 British feet; to Jawahir (lat. 30° 22′, long. 77° 37′) 24,160 pieds de Paris = 4027 toises = 7848 meters = 25,749 British feet. The measurement of Dhawalagiri, which the Tyrolean Jesuit [Joseph] Tieffenthaler had already marked on his map of the Himalayas in 1766 under the name *Montes Albi quis Indis, nive obsiti*, is less certain and erroneously explained in letters from Colebrooke to me (see *Asie Centrale*, vol. 1, pp. 281–90, and *Kosmos*, vol. 1, p. 41). Letters that I received from my friend Dr Joseph Hooker, the knowledgeable botanist of the last expedition to the South Pole, from Darjeeling in Sikkim-Himalaya (summer 1848), informed me that in the meridian of Sikkim between Dhawalagiri and [Gunung] Samalari, between Bhutan and Nepal, Colonel Baugh, director of the Trigonometric Survey of India, had measured a mountain, Kinchinjunga or Kintschin-Dschunga, with great precision, a mountain whose western snow peak was at 26,439 pieds de Paris = 4406 toises = 8588 meters = 28,278 British feet above sea [164] level. The eastern snow-capped peak is 25,356 pieds de Paris = 4226 toises = 8236 meters = 27,826 British feet high (compare *Journal of the Asiatic Society of Bengal*, Nov. 1848, vol. 17, part 2, p. 577). The notable colossus Kinchinjunga is shown on the title engraving of the magnificent work by Joseph Hooker, *The Rhododendrons of Sikkim-Himalaya*, 1849. This mountain is 379 toises higher than Jawahir, and it has been measured with such diligence that the seven results of Mr [Andrew] Waugh's trigonometric calculation from different points only fluctuated between 28,125.7 and 28,212.8. The base line that was measured in the plains was 36,685 British feet long. Later measuring of Dhawalagiri caused the *Rhododendra* monograph to declare Kinchinjunga as the higher of the two mountains. It appears, however, that there is such a small difference between these two and a third gigantic peak, Deodangha, that one is uncertain whether that difference may not be the result of an erroneous measurement. All three mountains are surely a little above 28,000 feet (above 26,272 pieds de Paris). "Mr Waugh concludes," Dr Joseph Hooker wrote to me from Darjeeling on 26 April 1849, "that there can be but little difference between Dhawalagiri, Kinchinjinga [*sic*] and Deodangha, that no other peaks approach these."

For 18 years, from 1830 to 1848, the following were regarded as the highest points of the cordilleras of the New Continent: Nevado de Sorata, the southern peak of this snow-capped mountain, a bit south of the village of Sorata (or Esquibel) in the eastern chain of Bolivia; and Nevado de Illimani, west of the mission of Yrupana, also in the eastern chain of Bolivia, the one that is most distant from the coast. In those days, the following elevations were attributed to the two mountains: Sorata (south lat. 15° 51′ and longitude west of Paris 70° 54′) 23,692 pieds de Paris = 3940 toises = 7696 meters = 25,250 British feet; Illimani (lat. 16° 39′, longitude 70° 9′) 22,519 pieds de Paris = 3753 toises = 7315 meters = 23,999 British feet. Pentland, who had long been the political representative of the British government in the free state of Bolivia, had made these hypsometric observations in 1827 and sent them to Mr Arago to publish them in the *Annuaire du Bureau des Longitudes pour 1830* (p. 323). Since then, they have unfortunately been disseminated in all sorts of languages, in all writings on mountain elevations, and in many hypsometric mountain profiles. Since the appearance of the large, beautiful map of the basin of the Laguna de Titicaca, however, which Mr Pentland published in London in June 1848 (title: *La Laguna de Titicaca and the Valleys* [165] *of Yucay, Collao and Desagüadero in Peru and Bolivia*), we have learned that the above information about the heights of Sorata and Illimani are inflated by 3716 and 2675 pieds de Paris. The map grants Sorata 21,286 and Illimani 21,149 British feet, that is, only 19,972 and 19,843 pieds de Paris (3328 and 3307 toises), respectively. Mr Pentland gathered these results during a second stay in Bolivia, when he recalculated the trigonometric measurements from 1838. Therefore, for 18 years, from 1829 to 1848, it was erroneously claimed that Chimborazo, for which I had found 20,100 pieds de Paris = 3350 toises = 6530 meters = 21,422 British feet, was a full 3592 pieds de Paris (or 3827 British feet) lower than Sorata; even that the latter had only 2653 pieds de Paris (or 2828 British feet) less than Dhawalagiri, the highest peak of Himalayas. I myself have contributed much to the dissemination of these faulty opinions. We know now that Sorata is 126 feet lower than Chimborazo, and 6371 pieds de Paris (or 6791 British feet) lower than Dhawalagiri. Of the two trigonometric measurements of the Peak of Tenerife, which [Jean-Charles] Borda had made during the two expeditions of 1771 and 1776 (the first one with [Alexandre-Guy] Pingré, the second with Chastenet de Puységur), the first one was also in error by 1224 pieds de Paris. An angle had been accidentally recorded as 33' rather than 53'. After their research on the island in 1742, Borda and Pingré, surmising information from elevation angles at an assumed distance, gave the Peak of Tenerife a mere 1701 toises above sea level. The excellent trigonometric operation of 1776 yielded 1905 toises, while the barometric measurement that was recalculated according to [Pierre Simon, Marquis de] Laplace's formula, produced 1976 toises. Borda's earlier error was thus 1200 1/9 feet of the whole calculation, while, in the case of Sorata, the error was 3700 1/5 feet of the elevation only (compare my *Voyage aux régions équinoxiales*, vol. 1, pp. 277–83, where I first published fragments of an unpublished manuscript by Borda, which is preserved in the Dépôt de la Marine in Paris).

But even though Sorata and Illimani are lower than Chimborazo, it probably remains impossible to declare the latter the highest point on the entire New Continent. In August 1835, the officers of the *Expedition* and the *Beagle*, led by Captain [Robert] Fitzroy, measured Nevado de Aconcagua (lat. 32° 39') in the north-east of Valparaiso by using elevation angles, and they determined that it was between 23,000 and 23,400 British feet high. If one estimates this Nevado's elevation at 23,200 feet (or 21,767 pieds de Paris), [166] it would be 1667 pieds de Paris higher than Chimborazo (*Narrative of the Voyages of the Adventure* and *Beagle*, vol. 2, 1839; *Proceedings of the Second Expedition, under the Command of Capt. Fitzroy*, p. 481; Darwin, *Journal of Researches*, 1845, pp. 253 and 291). According to newer calculations of the same angles by Pentland, Aconcagua is supposed to have a height of 23,010 British feet = 22,434 pieds de Paris = 3739 toises (Mary Somerville, *Physical Geography*, 1849, vol. 2, p. 425). The mountain would thus be 2334 pieds de Paris higher than Chimborazo. Pentland's beautiful map shows four other peaks in that same western cordillera of Bolivia, east of Arica, between lat. 18° 7' and 18° 25', all of which exceed the height of Chimborazo. Those mountains are Sajama, Parinacota, Gualateiri, and Pomarape. The tallest of them (Sajama) supposedly has 20,971, the lowest (Pomarape) 20,360 pieds de Paris. Sajama would be 1463 pieds de Paris lower than Nevado de Aconcagua, but 871 feet higher than Chimborazo. I do not find it unimportant periodically to articulate in numbers what we know or believe about the form of the surface of our planet. Regrettably, I think, the highest points of the massive rises are isolated phenomena, even if they, like the fruitless climbs of high snow-capped mountains, fascinate people no end.

4. (P. 135) My trigonometric measurements of the elevation of Chimborazo above the level of the South Sea occurred in June of 1803 on the pumice-covered high plains of Tapia not far from the new city of Riobamba, between the church of La Merced and the monastery of St Augustine. The base line was 1702.40 = 874 toises long. The third segment of this line was measured three times. The distance from the endpoint A of the base line to the

mountain's summit turned out to be 30,662.73; the horizontal distance, 30,437.40; in segments of the circle 16′ 27.65″. The elevation angle, freed from refraction and measured with the sextant on the artificial horizon, was A 6° 48′ 58.20″; the resulting elevation of the summit of Chimborazo above the plain of the base line was 3639.35 = 1867.25 toises. According to my barometric readings, then, the high plateau of Tapia is 2891.2 = 1482.8 toises above sea level (Boussingault found it to be 11 toises less in a different season, when the heat decrease of the stacked air layers was different). Consequently, the entire elevation of Chimborazo is 6530.5 = 3350 toises, or 20,100 pieds de Paris.

According to Laplace's refraction formula from his [167] *Mécanique céleste*, Chimborazo would be at 3637.75 (with the effect of refraction) and 3645.32 (without refraction). In order for the result of the total elevation to shift by 21.4 meters, the error of the base line would have to be 10 meters. If the elevation angle were off by 10″, that would impact the total height calculation by only 1.5 meters (for details on the individual parts of the entire calculation, compare Oltmanns in my *Recueil d'observations astronomiques*, introduction, vol. 1, pp. lxxii–lxxiv). My conclusions about the elevation of Chimborazo fall between the determinations of La Condamine and Don Jorge Juan; it approaches the latter's by 30 toises. If one considers the complications that conclusions about elevation confronted at a time when temperature corrections were applied to barometric measurements either not at all or with the completely wrong methods – and yet it was necessary to reduce geodetic operations from a height of 1350 to 1500 toises to sea level, as in the case of the measured base line between Caraburu and Oyambaro or Quito – one can explain the great differences in the results that derived from the same observations by both the French and the Spanish astronomer. Other combinations led to different hypsometric determinations. Bouguer and La Condamine give Chimborazo 3220 toises; Don Jorge Juan and his colleagues 3380 toises. The elevation of Quito, which, however, La Condamine and Bouguer had already underestimated by 32 toises – even Boussingault himself by 36 toises (216 feet) – does not directly affect these differences, because the elevation of the snow-capped mountains does not depend on it. Rather, it depends on the reduction to sea level of the measured base line, between Caraburu and Oyambaro in the plains of Yaruqui, by way of a series of triangles whose position points are mostly between 1800 and 2200 toises high. Don Jorge Juan himself delivers conspicuous proof of the unreliability of such complicated combinations, when, on the basis of various hypotheses, he reports the length of the base line of Caraburu at 1155, 1214, 1268, and 1283 toises (differences of 678 feet). Elevation angles of the summit of Chimborazo were taken from four surveying stations, nearest the mountain and yet only at 4° 19′ 55″ in Mulmul; but Mulmul itself could only be connected with the base line in Yaruqui (at a distance of 22 geographical miles) through triangles and the requisite series of signals. We have only a very imperfect notion of how the reduction to sea level, of this base line and of all the signals, occurs in order simultaneously to determine Chimborazo's absolute elevation. One only learns in general terms [168] that what was used for that reduction was the *Cacumen lapideum* of Pichincha and the two pyramids of Nevado de Iliniza, which are visible far toward the coastline; I reproduced the pyramids in *Vues des Cordillères*, Plate XXXV. The French academicians already assumed, however, that the Rucu-Pichincha was 2491 to 2432.69 toises (414 feet) too low. "Je ne pouvois partager, en août 1740, avec M. Bouguer," writes La Condamine, "les fatigues d'une course pénible et laborieuse de près de deux mois, dans la Province d'Esmeraldas, pour déterminer, dans un lieu *dont la hauteur au dessus de la mer fût connue*, celle de quelques-unes de nos montagnes, afin de pouvoir réduire au niveau de la surface de la mer la valeur du degré que nous avions mesuré sur le haut de la Cordelière. L'observatoire de M. Bouguer (le point d'où il pouvoit voir Iliniça) étoit établi dans l'Isle de l'Inca sur la rivière d'Esmeraldas. – En mars 1741 j'étois occupé d'un travail peu agréable sur la hauteur absolue des montagnes. J'étois bien sûr que le travail de M. Bouguer a l'Isle de l'Inca et les angles observes a Papa-ourcou près du Cotopaxi comme au Quinche, où nous avions opéré ensemble, n'avoit pas besoin de vérification, et d'autant moins, que cent toises d'erreur sur la hauteur des montagnes n'auroient pas change de deux toises la longueur du degré. *La multiplicité des éléments* de cette supputation, et le *long circuit qu'il falloit faire* pour atteindre le but, ne me rebutèrent point: je fis le calcul tout au long; et après un travail opiniâtre je trouvai la distance de l'observatoire de l'Isle de l'Inca au sommet d'Iliniça, la hauteur de cette montagne et celle de Pitchincha les mêmes, à 2 o 3 toises (!) près, que M. Bouguer" (La Condamine, *Journal du voyage à l'équateur*, pp. 94 and 111). It is hinted, in the *Mesure des trois premiers degrés du méridien dans l'hémisphère austral* (p. 52), that the height of Inca Island, above the level of the South Sea or the mouth of the Río de las Esmeraldas, has been determined only by estimating the incline and the distance, and that La Condamine and Bouguer differ in the respective estimates by 12 toises height. How much easier is direct geodetic measuring, using one or two elevation angles from point locations of a well-measured base line, whether pointed toward the summit or in the direction of known deviation! The barometric formulas that we now have adjust the base line to sea level with great reliability, in order to translate relative into absolute elevation. Bouguer himself seemed to sense the unreliability of his complicated elevation [169] calculations; when he complains about the effect of refraction on the many depression angles, he adds that elevation could not have been calculated with the same precision as the distance of the signals (*Figure de la terre*, pp. 119–22 and 167). Even if the two-month work in the forest plains of the Isla del Inca did not yield particularly reliable hypsometric results, Bouguer still has the great satisfaction that, after Pascal Mariotte and Halley, he was the first to develop a true and convenient barometric formula, even if it was imperfect. Many years had to pass until the barometric coefficient for the temperature of mercury and the air also included geographic latitude and the decrease of gravity in a formula like Laplace and Ramond's!

The doubts that I have seeded here about Bouguer and La Condamine's measurements of Chimborazo's elevation are solely the result of the observation of the entirety of the process, not of an overly great confidence in my own outcome. For half a century, I have expressed, in the liveliest of terms, the wish that Chimborazo be remeasured geodetically by an experienced observer with precise instruments and by using a carefully determined base line. As Oltmanns has already noted, my measurements would assume that a difference of 100 toises in the final result was due to an error of 10′ 54″ in the angle between the endpoints of the base line and 21′ 58″ in the elevation angle. If the reason were refraction, then the difference would instead have had to have been increased to −1.39 of the arc between one station and the summit, rather than being −0.042. Will anyone ever carry a barometer up to this summit, as their bold spirit of adventure has inspired physicists to do during the past decades in the cases of the Finsteraarhorn, Jungfrau, and Schreckhorn?

5. (P. 136) The highest elevation for a phanerogamic plant which Colonel Hall found on the slope of Chimborazo was for *Saxifraga Boussingaulti*, at 2466 toises (14,796 feet); but this was at a time when the eternal snow line had been lower (see my *Asie centrale*, vol. 3, p. 262). We collected the following plants between 14,000 and 15,000 feet: cryptogams: *Stereoczulon botryosum* (very different from *S. paschale*); *Lecidea atrovirens*; *Gyrophora rugosa*; *Bryum argenteuml*; *Polytrichum juniperinum*; *Grimmia longirostris* at an elevation of 2380 toises; *Jungermannia setacea* (Hooker); and *Gynostomum jucaleum*; of phanerogams: *Gentiana rupicola* and *G. cernua*; *Culcitium rufescens*; *C. nivale* (substituting for the thick wooly [170] espeletia of the Páramos and Cordilleras of New Granada); *Lysopomia reniformis*; *Ranunculus Gusmanni*; three Calceolaria (*C. saxatilis*, *C. rosmarinifolia*, and *C. hysopifolia*); the crucifers *Draba Bonplandiana*, *Eudema nubigena*, and *Arabis andicola*, which are very rare in the tropics; in lower areas only between 10,000 and 11,000 feet: *Arenaria serpens*; *Andromachia nubigena* (a new species closely related to *Senecio*); *Dumerilia paniculata*. Among the many above-mentioned compositae (family of the Synantheria), one stands out on Chimborazo: the beautiful *Bacharis gnidiifolia*, one of 54 new types of Bacharis that we found and described. See *Synopsis plantarum quas (quas in itinere ad plagam aequinoctialem orbis novi) collegerunt Al. de Humboldt et Am. Bonpland*, by C.S. Kunth (in octavo), 1823, vol. 2, pp. 376–88, and our *Nova genera et species plantarum* (folio), vol. 4, pp. 48–68. Immediately after our return from Mexico, Sir William Hooker described some of the mosses, to which we paid particular attention, in *Muscis exoticis*. Contrary to long-standing opinion, there were among them many true European species, for example, *Brynum argenteum*, *Sphagnum acutifolium*, *Polytrichum juniperinum*, *Trichestomum polyphyllum*, *Neckera crispa*, *Funaria hygrometrica*, etc. I also believe that I must repeat here a fact that is important for the geography of plants and the dissemination of forms, namely, that in the colder regions of the tropics, *Musci frondosi* occurs by no

means just as an alpine plant. We found moss beds in some very shaded places in the hot region, a few hundred feet above sea level, beds of such a fresh, abundant growth that it was just like in my Nordic fatherland. "Est enimen incredibilis numerus muscorum, lichenum et fungorum, non solum in cacumine Andium, aëre frigido circumfuso, sed etiam in calidis et opacissimis sylvis, ubi, sub luco viridente, plantae agamiae irriguam obtegunt terram. Exempla praebent regiones ferventissimae ad ripam fluminis Magdalenae, Hondam inter et Aegyptiaeam, sylvae Orinocenses propter Esmeraldam et Manldaracam, littora maris Antillarum prope ostia fluminis Sinu, ubi fere totum per annum aëris temperies inter 23° et 25° Reaum. consistit" (Humboldt, *De distributione geografica plantarum*, p. 29). I have depicted Chimborazo's vegetation and that of the nearby snow-capped mountains in a large image (*Atlas géographique et physique de la relation historique*, Plate IX) that encompasses the climates one stacked above the other, from sea level [171] to 15,000 feet elevation, and shows around 400 plants in their own characteristic regions (hypsometric positions).

6. (P. 137) My barometric measurement showed 2890, Boussingault's 2870 meters. My friend determined the mean temperature of the high plains of Tapia according to the heat of the earth at 16.4 °C.

7. (P. 139) I recall the Mexica (Aztec) legend that is linked with the flattened pyramid of Cholula (Cholollan) slightly to the west of *La Puebla de los Angeles*. In the important manuscript by the Dominican monk Pedro de los Ríos, who copied hieroglyphic paintings in New Spain in 1566, I discovered the following passage in the Vatican Library (I translate from the Spanish text): "Before the great flood (*apachihuiliztli*), ..., the land of Anahuac was inhabited by giants (*Tzocuillixeque*). All those who did not perish were turned into fish, with the exception of seven, who took refuge in caves. When the waters subsided (in the fourth age of the world), one of these giants, Xelhua, known as the architect, went to Cholollan, where, in (monumental) memory of *Tlaloc* Mountain, which had served as a shelter for him and six of his brothers, he built an artificial hill in the shape of a pyramid. He had bricks made in the province of Tlalmanalco, at the foot of the Sierra de Cocotl, and, in order to transport them to Cholula, he placed a line of men (many miles long) who passed them along by hand. The gods were incensed by the sight of this structure, whose top was meant to reach the clouds; enraged by Xelhua's audacity, they cast fire upon the pyramid (the god-dwelling, *teocalli*). Many workers perished, the work was discontinued, and it was afterwards consecrated to the god of the air, Quetzalcoatl." At the time of Cortés's expedition, the Cholulans preserved a stone that had fallen, shrouded in a globe of fire, from the heavens onto the top of the pyramid; this aerolite resembled a toad. (See my *Vues des Cordillères* [octavo edition], vol. 1, p. 114, Plate III, and *Essai politique sur la Nouvelle-Espagne*, vol. 2 [second ed. from 1827], p. 151; also Prescott, *Conquest of Mexico*, vol. 3, p. 380.)

8. (P. 146) The sand flea, called *la chique* by the French colonists of the Antilles, burrows into the human skin and causes infections, because the egg sack of the fertilized female swells up considerably. What is physiologically remarkable is that only newly arrived whites and blacks are afflicted by this insect, from which I had so often suffered; Indians (indigenous Americans) and almost all American-born Spanish Creoles are not.

9. (P. 150) *Mechanik der menschlichen Gehwerkzeuge*, [172] 1836, para. 64, pp. 147-60. More recent experiments by the brothers Weber in Berlin have reliably confirmed that the leg is held in the pan of the pelvis by the pressure of the atmospheric air.

10. (P. 156) My own observations, partly geodetic, partly barometric measurements (the former are starred), show that the height of the lower edge of the eternal snow line in the cordilleras of Quito (between 0° and 1 1/2° southern latitude) is at 2472 toises, or 4816 meters. This number is the arithmetic average of measurements carried out between February and June 1802, but which include small fluctuations caused, in such proximity to the equator, by the season itself.

On	Antisana*	2493	toises
"	Cotopaxi*	2490	"
"	Chimborazo*	2471	"
"	Huahua-Pichincha	2460	"

```
"    Rucu-Pichincha......    2455      "
"    Corazón.................   2458      "
```
Boussingault found in 1831:

```
On   Antisana..........   4871 meters = 2499   toises
 "    Chimborazo.....    4868 meters = 2455     "
 "    Cotopaxi..........   4804 meters = 2464     "
```

The mean is 2453 toises (4720 meters); the difference from my own results is only 19 toises. The small oscillation of the lower edge of the snow line, and the few changes in the temperature of layered air masses in the tropics, makes the snow line on the slopes of the cordilleras, seen at such great altitude, appear in perfect horizontality – a remarkable view for the European traveler. In the Swiss Alps, a number of irregularities in the surface of the ground (clefts and slight unevenness in the valley) disturb this impression of horizontality. In the temperate zone, especially in very northern latitudes, the line appears not cleanly cut but as if it were broken up, marred by the phenomenon of glaciers, which depends on the temperature. Wherever, in the tropics, several snow-capped mountains (*Nevados*) can be seen together in groupings, the horizontality gives the uneducated peasants among the indigenous peoples a very good idea about the relative height of neighboring peaks. They recognize as highest those mountains whose eternally snow-covered masses rise the most above the lower edge of the snow line. Long before any measurements were made in the cordilleras, the natives (*los Indios* [173] *del país*) knew that Capac-Urcu and Chimborazo were the tallest mountains in the region. Temporary snowfall, which produces the same regularity for miles downward and the impression of a similar horizontality, also leads to a correct judgment of elevations where mountains are lower than the normal height of the perpetual snow line (14,830 feet).

According to my research, the first snow-capped mountains seen on the New Continent were the *Sierra de Citarma* (now called *Sierra de Santa Marta*) east of Cartagena de Indias, at 11° northern latitude. The expedition of Colmenares from 1510 first spread this news in Spain, along with the idea of "how close to the equator colossal mountains had to be in order still to show eternal snow." One already recognized then the rising of the snow line from the pole to the tropics. Actual measurements of the height of the snow line were carried out by Bouguer and La Condamine between 1736 and 1742; that is, earlier than such similarly precise measurements were made in the Alps and the Pyrenees. Bouguer, who had incomplete but quite correct notions about the origins of the mountain cold and the effect of elevation on decreases in temperature (*Figure de la terre*, pp. xlvi–lii), set out to "déterminer la hauteur de la surface courbe qui passe par le bas de la neige sur toutes les montagnes du Globe." He reports for the equator 2434 toises, for 28 1/4° at most 1950 toises, below 43° latitude (in France and Chile) 1500 to 1600 toises. These figures are less imprecise for the northern hemisphere than one should have thought. On the marble tablet that is preserved in the university building in Quito, and which I found there fully intact, one also reads: "Altitudo acutioris ac lapidei cacuminis nive plerumque operli 2432 hexap. Paris., ut et nivis infernae permanentis in montibus nivosis." If, because of the error, one adds 32 toises to the elevation of the city of Quito, one gets 2462 toises and, through a great number of accidental combinations up to +9 toises (54 feet), the height that both Boussingault and I found (see my *Asie centrale*, vol. 3, pp. 251–6).

11. (P. 156) Arago in *Annuaire du Bureau des Longitudes pour 1830*, p. 331, and *Asie centrale*, vol. 3, pp. 273–81.

12. (P. 156) About the difference in the height of the snow line on the northern and southern slopes of the Himalayas, which I have proven since 1820, see *Ansichten der Natur*, 1840 ed., vol. 1, p. 126; *Asie centrale*, vol. 3, pp. 293–326; Joseph Hooker, *On the Elevation of the Great Table Land of Thibet*, 1850, p. 6 [174]; [R.A.] Strachan, "On the Snow-Line in the Himalaya," *Journal of the Asiatic Society of Bengal* (April 1849, no. 29). More recent observations have irrefutably confirmed the difference between the Indian and the Tibetan slopes; but the extent of the difference in these latitudes from 30° to 31° in the temperate zone appears not to be the same for different seasons. It is difficult to distinguish the edges of sporadic snowfall from the eternal snow line; and such sporadic snowfall does not characteristically occur at

the same time on the southern and the northern slopes. My earliest data were 12,180 pieds de Paris for the south and 15,600 for the north; the difference is 3420 feet; Hodgson and Joseph Hooker: 14,073 in the south, 18,764 in the north, a difference of 4691 feet; Strachey: 14,543 in the south, 17,358 in the north, a difference of 2815 feet. My own result lies between the latter two. In a letter that my friend Dr Joseph Hooker wrote to me, this time no longer from Darjeeling but from Tangu, one could read: south 14,073 feet, north 15,006 feet; difference 933 feet. The small elevation of the southern, Indian, slope which is mentioned here likely points either to the great effect of sporadic snowfall or to the local situation of the pass itself through which the journey led.

13. (P. 159) On the trigonometric measurement of Chimborazo, see above, pp. 166–9.

14. (P. 160) On Capac-Urcu and the legend of its collapse, see my *Géographie des plantes*, p. 119, and the essay in this volume [*Kleinere Schriften*] that follows "Boussingault's Besteigung des Chimborazo."

15. (P. 160) The following analysis of summit rock from Chimborazo, which I had hacked off at an elevation of 2530 toises (15,180 feet), was sent to me by a superb geognost, Mr Hermann Abich, to whom we owe a thorough knowledge of the Caucasus:

Silica........................	3136 grams =	65.09%
Clay..........................	0.770 grams =	15.98%
Iron oxide.................	0.278 grams =	5.77%
Limestone................	0.126 grams =	2.61%
Talc..........................	0.198 grams =	4.10%
Potassium.................	0.096 grams =	1.99%
Sodium.....................	0.215 grams =	4.46%
Volatile substances and chloride..............	0.019 grams =	0.41%
	4.8381 grams =	100%

Index